The Perfe

Tennessee Delivers Woman Suffrage

Carol Lynn Yellin & Janann Sherman, Ph.D.

Edited by Ilene Jones-Cornwell

GOAL!

First Edition 1998
ISBN 1-882595-14-9
Printed by Wilson Graphics,
Memphis, Tennessee, USA

The Perfect 36: Tennessee Delivers Woman Suffrage staff:
Authors: Carol Lynn Yellin & Dr. Janann Sherman
Editor: Ilene Jones-Cornwell
Editorial Coordinator: Paula F. Casey
Production Coordinator: Patrick Dugan
Graphic Design: Tom Foster & Patrick Dugan
Exhibit Photographer: Lynette Dalton
*A special thanks to "Doctor" (Pat) Dugan who doggedly
dodged a donnybrook to develop our dream document.*

This book available from:

Serviceberry Press
P.O. Box 241963
Memphis, TN 38124-1963
Make checks payable to Serviceberry Press
$24.95 plus $4.50 shipping
(TN residents add $2.43 sales tax)

e-mail: serviceberrypress@juno.com
website: www.serviceberrypress.com

2

For

Paula Casey

without whose valiant perseverance,

equaling that of our

suffragist foremothers,

this book

would never have become

a reality.

Carol Lynn Yellin   Janann Sherman

STILL TRYING TO BUTTON IT UP

TABLE OF CONTENTS

FOREWORDS

When the 75th anniversary of woman suffrage was celebrated across the nation in 1995, we were fortunate in Tennessee to have several individuals who made our celebration as "The Perfect 36" particularly meaningful.

First, we had premiere woman suffrage historian, Carol Lynn Yellin of Memphis, who wrote the definitive article — "Countdown in Tennessee" — that appeared in *American Heritage* in December, 1978. No one else in Tennessee had her knowledge and research on this important subject.

Then, we were fortunate to have Dr. Janann Sherman, historian and biographer of the late Senator Margaret Chase Smith, who joined the faculty at the University of Memphis in 1994. Dr. Sherman agreed to undertake another massive project — mounting an exhibit at the university's Art Gallery unlike any that had ever been done before. For the first time, original artifacts, papers, photographs and memorabilia about the struggle for woman suffrage were gathered under one roof.

This outstanding exhibit, which traveled across the state, featured materials that had never been seen before by the general public. Photographs of that exhibit are seen throughout this book, and they help tell the story of how American women won the right to vote after a 72-year struggle.

This celebration of Tennessee's pivotal role in the passage of the 19th Amendment coincided with another important celebration — Tennessee's Bicentennial. It has been our great privilege to be in the Executive Residence as these celebrations unfolded throughout 1995 and 1996. We have learned so much about what Tennessee has contributed to our great nation. It has also reminded us of how our democracy works and the role that all citizens can play.

The struggle for American women to win the vote is one of the greatest in our nation's history. They achieved their goal against enormous odds. Generations of women and the men who supported them are recounted in this magnificent story. It is a story of dedication, courage, persistence, patriotism, bipartisanship and undaunting faith.

We are proud of the Tennessee General Assembly in 1920 — both Republicans and Democrats — who worked together to secure our state's place in this great history. It was Harry Burn, a Republican and the youngest member of the Legislature, who cast the deciding vote. Susan B. Anthony, the great suffrage leader, was a Republican as was suffragist Alice Paul, whose grandfather founded the Republican Party in New Jersey.

It was Governor Al Roberts, a Democrat, who called the Legislature into special session to vote on the 19th Amendment. We are proud of the members of the Shelby County legislative delegation who led the way, and especially Representative Joe Hanover of Memphis, the second-youngest member who kept the pro-suffrage forces together as floor leader. A Polish immigrant, he believed so strongly that everyone should have the right to vote in a democracy that he ran for the General Assembly just to cast his vote for the 19th Amendment.

That it happened in Tennessee — when no other state was close — is a source of immense pride. We hope that, after reading this inspiring story of the difficult struggle the suffragists endured, you will cherish your right to vote.

Don Sundquist
Governor of Tennessee

Martha Sundquist
First Lady of Tennessee

Shelby County Tennessee

This volume chronicles one of Tennessee's proudest moments, the ratification of woman suffrage and how a bastion of male dominance — the Tennessee Legislature — became the unlikely vehicle that changed the course of American history.

I have been proud to serve as honorary chair for this book because of the importance of accurately recording this historic event for all future generations of Tennesseans.

The story of "The Perfect 36" provides all of us with valuable lessons, such as the inexorable force of basic human rights, the ability of ordinary citizens to shape their own destiny, and, ultimately, the role that a single individual, armed with a vision and a sense of morality, can mold a courageous future.

I commend the many people who made this volume possible, but particularly Paula Casey, because it is a testament to her commitment and her leadership to ensure that future generations understand the significance of this historic event.

Jim Rout

Mayor of Shelby County

Photos by Morgan Murrell

Shelby County Mayor Jim Rout presents the keys to the city of Memphis to Jane Cox, portraying Carrie Chapman Catt, at a ceremony the final evening of The Perfect 36 *exhibit, August 18, 1995. Seventy-nine years earlier, in 1916, Memphis Mayor Ashcroft presented the real Mrs. Catt with the keys to the city. Jane Cox starred in a one-woman play,* The Yellow Rose of Suffrage, *depicting significant portions of Catt's life, performed at the University of Memphis Theater.*

7

Senate Chamber
State of Tennessee
NASHVILLE

It has been my pleasure to help preserve the story about this important event in Tennessee's history. As a state senator, I am proud that the state Senate voted overwhelmingly in favor of the 19th Amendment in 1920. The ratification of the 19th Amendment on August 18, 1920, with the House following the Senate in concurrence, was Tennessee's greatest gift to this country.

I was proud to be the sponsor of the legislation, with my House colleague, Rep. Brenda Turner (D-Chattanooga), creating the suffrage sculpture which was placed in the State Capitol in 1998. No monument to the suffragists of Tennessee or to this momentous occasion when 27 million American women became enfranchised has existed in our Capitol. We have rectified this lack of awareness with the publication of this book and the sculpture.

Future generations will be able to read about this 72-year struggle which is among the most compelling in American history. They can tour the State Capitol in Nashville and see the powerful bas-relief created by sculptor Alan LeQuire commemorating the suffragists' victory.

All Americans can take great pride that generations of suffragists achieved their goal of obtaining equal suffrage through dedication and nonviolence. They proved democracy and our U.S. Constitution work. It is a story well worth preserving.

Steve Cohen

State Senator (D-Memphis)

It Happened in Nashville...

...in August, 1920, when Tennessee's all-male, all-white, mostly good-ol'-boy legislature met for three weeks in special session to defend, denounce, cuss, discuss, and finally to ratify — with a majority of but a single vote — the so-called Susan B. Anthony Amendment.

This action, in effect, marked the moment of enfranchisement for one-half the adult population of the United States, because Tennessee (which was immediately proclaimed "The Perfect 36" by commentators and cartoonists of the day) thereby became the pivotal 36th state needed to complete ratification by three-quarters of the then 48 states.

It also marked the climax of 72 years of ceaseless campaigning by four generations of American women activists. Seasoned veterans of the suffragist struggle said this last battle — Armageddon in Nashville — was the toughest ever. Such it may well have been, since among the things the suffragists and their supporters had to contend with en route to victory were threats, bribes, lawsuits, cajolery, dirty tricks, injunctions, tapped telephones, rumors of kidnappings and double-crossings, fugitive quorums and other parliamentary shenanigans, not to mention overwrought propaganda leaflets distributed by flag-waving, rose-bedecked, anti-suffrage Southern ladies, and free-flowing, Tennessee-brewed Jack Daniel's whiskey dispensed 24 hours a day from the liquor lobby's "Hospitality Suite" on the eighth floor of Nashville's Hermitage Hotel. Yet, with all of that, the decisive drama that unfolded during those hectic days in Tennessee that summer must be counted as one of democracy's finer triumphs. Which is, as a matter of fact, pretty much the way the suffragists themselves saw it.

The most undeviating of American idealists, these persevering right-to-vote crusaders at both the national and the home-grown Tennessee level, had become, by 1920, as skilled at the art of the possible as any politicians this nation has ever produced. Even though they themselves did not yet have the vote to use as leverage to reward legislators who supported their cause or to punish those who did not, they triumphed. The suffragists won with luck, pluck, and the help of their true-blue menfolk, because they knew, by long experience, that the American system could be made to work.

How they made it work in Nashville, for themselves and for generations of women to come, was the story recreated by "The Perfect 36" exhibit at the University of Memphis, mounted in celebration of the 75th anniversary of the enactment of woman suffrage in the summer of 1995.

It is also the story documented here.

Visitors to The Perfect 36 exhibit were met by this suffragist at the wheel of her suffrage-yellow Model-T Ford Depot Hack Express. (Car loaned by Ernest Sutherland; Exhibit photos by Lynette Dalton)

"The Perfect 36" exhibit

was mounted at the University of Memphis Art Museum in the summer of 1995 – July 6 through August 18 – to celebrate the 75th anniversary of woman suffrage.

Tracing the story of the women's rights movement that culminated in the passage of the 19th Amendment to the U.S. Constitution granting American women the right to vote, the exhibit focused particular attention on Tennessee's pivotal role in its passage. After a 72-year struggle for women's right to vote, in the summer of 1920 and by a single vote, Tennessee became "The Perfect 36," the final state needed to ratify the amendment.

"The Perfect 36" exhibit was developed with the enthusiastic support of Art Museum Director Leslie Luebbers and the Museum Registrar Lisa Francisco, a handful of impassioned volunteers, and the able assistance of graduate students in Luebbers' University of Memphis Museums course, who adopted the exhibit as a class project. The exhibit subsequently traveled to The East Tennessee Historical Society in Knoxville, East Tennessee State University in Johnson City, and Fisk University in Nashville.

Numerous people made this exhibit possible. I wish to extend my heartfelt gratitude to Leslie Luebbers and Lisa Francisco, volunteers: Paula F. Casey, Karen B. Shea, Stephanie Gilmore, Paula Barnes, Martha Feldmann, Patricia Vieira, Carol Lynn Yellin, Theresa Mauer and U of M students: Cathy Gillaspey, Laura Hudson, CarrLee Rasberry, Janette C. Russell, Arlene Weinrich and Nicole Williford. Financial support for the exhibit was provided by Mertie Buckman, Jim and Ellida Fri, Jim and Lucia Gilliland, Happy Jones, Maybelline, Inc., U of M Student Activity Fee through SAC Special Events Committee, and Wang's Inc. Lenders to the exhibit were: Gloria Andereck, Brian Bright, Corinne Byers, Alberta Church, Edith Dixon, Marcy Hale, Jim Jacobs, Wanda Mathis, Karen B. Shea, Memphis Pink Palace Museum, UT-Knoxville Special Collections Library, Ernest Sutherland, Annie Taylor, and Marilyn VanEynde from the Woodruff-Fontaine House.

— *Dr. Janann Sherman, Curator*

Left: Even W. K. Kellogg and Company joined the parade to support the suffrage cause and incidentally to sell corn flakes. (Carroll-Mathis Collection)

Above: Millions of buttons like these adorned turn-of-the-century women - and men. (Carroll-Mathis Collection).
Below: Poster for Jane Cox's one-woman show, The Yellow Rose of Suffrage *(designed by Peri Motamedi)*

The War
of the Roses

VOTES
FOR
WOMEN

The Des Moines Register

SUFF AMENDMENT IS WINNING

This seven-ton white marble sculpture, the "Portrait Monument," was sculpted by Adelaide Johnson to pay tribute to the initial founders of the woman suffrage movement, (l-r) Elizabeth Cady Stanton, Susan B. Anthony, and Lucretia Mott. It was presented to Congress in a dedication ceremony in 1921 (the year after the 19th Amendment's passage) on February 15, Anthony's birthday. Stanton and Mott were the co-conveners of the first Women's Rights Convention in Seneca Falls, New York, in 1848. Anthony founded the first woman suffrage organization in the country, the National Woman Suffrage Association, in 1869. The monument, which sat in the crypt of the U.S. Capitol for many years, was moved to the Rotunda in 1997.

The Long Road to Nashville

by Janann Sherman, Ph.D.

> We hold these truths to be self-evident, that all men and women are created equal, that they are endowed by their creator with certain inalienable rights, that among these are life, liberty, and the pursuit of happiness.

he 72-year quest for women's voting rights in America is one of the great stories of American democracy. It is an ultimately triumphant tale of a long tenacious struggle by several generations of suffragists. To fight the long battle, as suffrage leader Carrie Chapman Catt wrote,

> Hundreds of women gave the accumulated possibilities of an entire lifetime, thousands gave years of their lives, hundreds of thousands gave constant interest and such aid as they could. It was a continuous, seemingly endless, chain of activity. Young suffragists who helped forge the last links of that chain were not born when

it began. Old suffragists who forged the first links were dead when it ended. It is doubtful if any man, even among suffrage men, ever realized what the suffrage struggle came to mean to women before the end was allowed in America.

The first episode of that campaign happened in 1848, when Elizabeth Cady Stanton, Lucretia Mott, and about 300 others (40 of them men) met in Seneca Falls, New York, and drew up the first public protest in America against the political, economic, and social inequality of women. The delegates based their program directly on the Declaration of Independence, a document that 72 years earlier, in 1776, had failed to include them. Their new version, dubbed the Declaration of Sentiments, proclaimed that the signers held "these truths to be self-evident, that all men *and women* are created equal."

Indeed, it might just as easily be argued that the struggle for women's rights in America really began with the Revolution itself. Certainly, women were fired by the revolutionary rhetoric of human rights and political liberties. And the war profoundly affected women's lives, changing forever their sense of themselves as citizens of the republic. A review of women's status in the new world, and the changes wrought and hopes unrealized by the Revolution, render the expressed frustration of the women at Seneca Falls understandable.

Early American culture prescribed specific tasks and subordinate status to women. Women managed the domestic sphere of rearing the children and laboring on the family farm, duties which included cooking, cleaning, washing, spinning, weaving, gardening, raising poultry, tending cattle, and trading in the local market. Under English common law a married woman was "covered" by her husband. The name given to her legal status was *femme covert*, which meant that she had virtually no rights at all. Everything she owned and everything she earned belonged to her husband. She did not even have legal claim to her own children.

For more than 200 years, women complained about their lot — about their exclusion from participation in public affairs, about being denied education, about religious rules that oppressed them, about their subordinate status in the community, and their dependence upon undependable men. Such protests, though, were likely to be infrequent, private, and voiced only when some particular humiliation compelled a woman to violate the stricture that she remain silent and subservient.

Within the confines of their circumscribed lives, women often found solace in religion, particularly that which arrived on a great wave of religious enthusiasm in the mid-18th century, known as the Great Awakening. This new religion exalted the individual's ability to "choose God" and take control of his or her spiritual destiny. Evangelicals' emphasis on the inner experience of God's grace and the rejection of established religious authority particularly appealed to women who found in it divine sanction for their spirituality and validation of their own religious experiences. Some women seized this liberating potential, claiming they had been called by God to pray for others, to preach, to lead. Many more found a rationale for public activity.

A great moment of opportunity for women's equality seemed to arrive with the determination to break with Great Britain. The American Revolution transformed the lives of many women, through the experience of wartime itself and the movement's expressed ideals of liberty and equality. Women assumed control of farms and businesses while husbands, fathers and sons fought at the front. They were called upon to make crucial decisions about matters from which they had been excluded. After some initial trepidation about their abilities, many women experienced growing pride and self-confidence as they learned to act autonomously as "deputy husbands." And, in acting with other women in support of the war, they gained a new appreciation for the capacity of their sex to handle the demands of public life. As the war developed, women participated in crowd actions, signed pledges, raised funds, joined and, in some cases, led boycotts of British goods, fed and clothed armies. Their humble household tasks and home manufactures became imbued with patriotic spirit and assumed political importance. In the process, women acquired organizational skills, self-respect, and an interest in political developments previously considered of consequence only to men. What's more, revolutionary ideals of equality and liberty fired women's imaginations. "All power is derived from the people," said one federalist. "Liberty is everyone's birthright."

The distinction between the public sphere of men and the private sphere of women collapsed during the war, as women increasingly participated in public events. When the Townshend Acts of 1767 imposed duties on many British imports, including tea, women organized themselves with the express purpose of boycotting these products and substituting home-manufactured ones. Three hundred "Mistresses of Families" of Boston signed a petition agreeing "totally to abstain from the Use of Tea," a move they made in support of "the true Friends of Liberty in all Measures they have taken to save this abused Country from Ruin and Slavery." Others agreed to substitute homespun for imported brocades and not to consider any suitors who wore British apparel.

Eventually whole communities became involved in the women's activities; hundreds of spectators came to watch spinning bees. Ministers who supported them and newspaper editors who described them recognized their vital symbolic importance.

Cartoon of "a society of patriotic ladies" signing a petition not to buy tea or use British cloth.

The Reverend John Cleaveland of Ipswich speculated that with such efforts "the women might recover to this country the full and free enjoyment of all our rights, properties and privileges (which is more than the men have been able to do)." In reporting on a spinning bee in Long Island, the *Boston Evening Post* expressed that hope that "the ladies, while they vie with each other in skill and industry in their profitable employment, may vie with the men in contributing to the preservation and prosperity of their country and equally share in the honor of it."

Unfortunately, women were not to "equally share in the honor of it." They experienced few gains in terms of status, work, and public roles. As men returned to take control again of family business, women, despite demonstrations of competence, were ejected. One notable example was that of Mary Katherine Goddard, who had so successfully managed the family newspaper and printing business that the Continental Congress made her the official printer of the Declaration of Independence. But when the war was over and the paper running well, her brother returned and assumed control.

Another was Abigail Adams, married to a prominent member of the Continental Congress, who ran the family farm and produced the entire family income while her husband, John, engaged in politics. Yet when she wrote to him in Philadelphia and expressed her desire that he "Remember the Ladies, and be more generous and favourable to them than [his] ancestors" in constructing the new nation's laws, he treated her request as a joke. "As to your extraordinary Code of Laws, I cannot but laugh," he replied, chiding her for being "so saucy." "Depend upon it," he continued, "We know better than to repeal our Masculine systems…[and submit to] the Despotism of the Peticoat [*sic*]." Refusing to concede the justice in her request, he facetiously blamed the clergy for "stirring up Tories, Landjobbers, Trimmers, Bigots, Canadians, Indians, Negroes, Hanoverisans, Hessians, Russians, Irish Roman Catholicks [*sic*], Scotch Renegadoes, at last they have stimulated the ladies to demand new Priviledges [*sic*] and threaten to rebell."

The equality and natural rights extolled in the Declaration of Independence and the Constitution did not apply to women. The founding fathers believed the dependence of women, like that of slaves and propertyless men, disqualified them from a voice in the polity. Moreover, the common law tradition of *femme covert* stood in the new nation. Power and authority rested in the public realm of men, and women resumed their well-established roles as wives and mothers, but with an interesting new twist.

Although the Revolution did not change women's legal status, it did encourage people of both sexes to re-evaluate the contributions of women to the family and society. The problem of female citizenship was solved by giving motherhood a political purpose. Mothers had the particularly important task of instructing their children in the virtues that a republican citizenry needed, so "Republican motherhood" assumed a patriotic mission.

Such moral and civic responsibilities in turn stimulated a debate about how mothers could raise their children to be enlightened if the mothers themselves were uneducated. Before the Revolution, little thought had been paid to women's education. Such instruction as was available was limited to the daughters of the well-to-do and, at best, provided a rudimentary literacy with more ornamental accomplishments like music and embroidery.

To properly rear virtuous sons and future citizens, women needed suitable training, argued Benjamin Rush, a trustee of the Young Ladies' Academy in

Philadelphia: "The equal share that every citizen has in liberty and the possible share he may have in the government of our country make it necessary that our ladies should be qualified to a certain degree by a peculiar and suitable education, to concur in instructing their sons in the principles of liberty and government." Despite abundant arguments that "unnatural stimulation" of the female brain would render her unwomanly and would "damp that vivacity and destroy that disengaged ease and softness, which are the very essence of [her] graces," the needs of future male citizens of the republic took precedence. Such concerns encouraged the creation of female academies and, eventually, public schools to include girls.

Little did those who advocated women's education anticipate the consequences. Schools produced a new generation of literate women with self-esteem, strong identification with other women, and a sense of themselves as having a special mission to go beyond the assigned role of wife and mother. Many of the graduates became self-supporting teachers, and these early female academies produced the first generation of women's rights leaders, including Elizabeth Cady Stanton, a graduate of Emma Willard's Troy Female Seminary; Lucy Stone, a student of Oberlin College, founded by abolitionists and the only college in the nation to admit women and blacks; and Susan B. Anthony, a product of Deborah Moulson's Female Seminary, a private Quaker boarding school outside Philadelphia.

Women's particular sense of mission was further shaped by another wave of religious revivals around the turn of the century and the increasing importance of women in traditional churches. The withdrawal of state support in the 1780s left churches dependent upon the active involvement of their members, and those active members, by and large, were predominantly women.

As the new century developed, increasingly centralized commerce and industrial growth encouraged a greater separation between the public and private worlds, between the workplace and the home. Men engaged in commerce and political affairs, women in domesticity and the church. During the early 1800s, countless women organized charitable and reform societies at the same time that Victorian ideals of "true womanhood" elevated women's special virtues of piety and purity. These very distinctions, in turn, justified expanding women's domain within church-sanctioned ladies'

Library of Congress

Lucretia Mott

societies. As women extended their distinctly feminine qualities of tenderness, benevolence and succor to the dependent and needy in the community, they quite literally moved out of the home and into avenues of social responsibility. One concern inevitably led to others: prayer groups, missionary societies, mothers' clubs, relief of poor widows and children, the rescue of "fallen women," orphan asylums, hospitals, moral reform, and temperance.

With the impetus of the Second Great Awakening, a movement that stressed the moral imperative to end sinful practices and emphasized each person's responsibility to uphold God's will in society, many women who had served apprenticeships in church societies began challenging that great national sin: slavery. And before long, abolitionism became intertwined with attacks against the traditional subordination of women.

Women were central to antislavery agitation, acknowledged African-American abolitionist Frederick Douglass:

When the true history of the antislavery cause shall be written, women will occupy a large space in its pages, for the cause of the slave has been peculiarly woman's cause. Her heart and her conscience have supplied in large measure its motive and mainspring. Her skill, industry, patience and perseverance have been wonderfully manifest in every trial hour…her deep moral convictions, and her tender human sensibilities found convincing and persuasive expression in her pen and her voice.

Those very same skills would later be used by women in their fight for their own rights. In abolition, they learned to lecture and petition, how to organize and raise funds. They also gained valuable experience in resisting male objections and attacks. This was perfectly illustrated by the experiences of Lucretia Mott, founder of the Philadelphia Female Antislavery Society in 1833. When she assumed such a heady assignment, she said,

> I had no idea of the meaning of preambles and resolutions and votings. Women had never been in any assemblies of the kind…that was the first time in my life I had ever heard a vote taken…. There was not a woman capable of taking the chair, and organizing that meeting in due order, and we had to call on James McCrummell, a colored man, to give us aid in the work….

Four years later, when Mott stood before The Anti-Slavery Convention of American Women, she exuded a self-confidence born of hard experience and a critique of woman's restricted sphere. "The time has come," she said, "for woman to move in that sphere which Providence has assigned her, and no longer remain satisfied in the circumscribed limits which corrupt custom and a perverted application of Scripture have encircled her." On the contrary, she told the assembled women, "it is the duty of women, and the province of women, to plead the cause of the oppressed in our land, and to do all that she can by her voice, and her pen, and her purse, and the influence of her example, to overthrow the horrible system of American slavery."

The first woman in America to speak in public to a large audience of both men and women did so to oppose slavery and to argue that women were men's equals. In 1828, Scotswoman Frances Wright broke all rules of decorum by violating the rigid sexual boundary that separated woman from the public podium. Dressed in white and carrying the Declaration of Independence, Wright spoke for abolition, women's rights, sexual emancipation, and "mental independence." Her message was a radical one, and one not necessarily intended to mobilize women as a group to join her crusade, except those who were willing to eschew traditional society for her utopian community in the wilds of western Tennessee. Three

years earlier, on 320 swampy acres some 15 miles from the trading post of Memphis, Wright used part of her inheritance to establish a commune called Nashoba for the express purpose of training slaves for freedom. Wright's ambitious plan for gradual emancipation involved the purchase of slaves who would earn their freedom with five years work, learn a trade to support themselves, and then be freed and colonized in Haiti.

Nashoba also became a place for experimentation with sexual emancipation. Wright embraced the benefits of free love, denounced "the tyranny of matrimonial law," and favored racial amalgamation as the solution to racism. Although she was repeatedly denounced as a dangerous infidel, "a bold blasphemer and a voluptuous preacher of licentiousness," ultimately it was Wright's financial difficulties, as much as her unnerving ideas, that doomed Nashoba.

It was a clergyman's call that inspired large numbers of women to take up the cause of antislavery. When William Lloyd Garrison launched his radical crusade for immediate emancipation in the 1830s and organized the American Anti-Slavery Association, he called upon women to join him, on the assumption that "the cause of bleeding humanity is always legitimately the cause of women. Without her powerful assistance, its progress must be slow, difficult,

Cartoon ridicules bold lecturer Frances Wright.

Sojourner Truth

of those present at The Anti-Slavery Convention of American Women in 1837. Still, many abolition societies remained all white.

Relationships between black and white women took strength and perseverance to sustain; the battle against racism called for moral, and sometimes physical, courage. Yet many women believed true Christianity required it. African-American Sarah L. Forten's poem speaks to the effort:

> We are thy sisters. God has truly said,
> That of one blood the nations he has made.
> O, Christian woman! in a Christian land,
> Canst thou unblushing read this great command?
> Suffer the wrongs which wring our inmost heart,
> To draw one throb of pity on thy part!
> Our skins may differ, but from thee we claim
> A sister's privilege and a sister's name.

One of the most remarkable black women abolitionists was a former slave named Isabella Baumfree who addressed antislavery gatherings as Sojourner Truth. She described her name and her mission this way:

> …when I left the house of bondage, I left everything behind…. I went to the Lord an' asked him to give me a new name. And the Lord gave me Sojourner, because I was to travel up an' down the land, showin' the people their sins, an' bein' a sign unto them…and the Lord gave me Truth, because I was to declare truth to the people.

Supported by the Reverend Garrison, who made women's equality in the movement a priority, women moved into the public arena in increasing numbers to lecture and petition against the evils of slavery. Although they were moved by the same moral indignation against slavery as men, their public activism violated gender conventions and provoked sometimes violent reactions. In city after city, women abolitionists were harassed and sometimes physically attacked for speaking before "promiscuous" or mixed-sex audiences and for traveling in racially mixed company. In the face of such reactions, abolitionist women inevitably began to see similarities between their own confined status and that of slaves. "We have good cause to be grateful to the slave," said abolitionist Abby Kelley. "In striving to strike his irons off, we found most surely that we were manacled ourselves."

There were three fundamental convictions of abolitionists regarding slavery, all with important consequences for women's equality as well: 1) that men

imperfect." In attempting to arouse women to sympathy for the cause, Garrison did so with reference to members of their sex in bondage who were "held as property — or used for the gratification of the lust or avarice or convenience of unprincipled speculators…."

The sexual tyranny of slavery and the plight of the slave woman was a consistent trope in some of the most powerful abolitionist writings, used by white women and men, and the handful of free black women abolitionists active in the movement. Black women were present in the abolition movement from its beginning, working alongside whites wherever they were welcomed. In Philadelphia, Boston, Rochester, New York, and Salem and Lynn, Massachusetts, female antislavery societies were integrated. Of the 18 women who signed the constitution of the Philadelphia Female Anti-Slavery Society in 1833, at least seven were black, as were nearly one in ten and women had an ability to do what was right and therefore were morally accountable for their actions; 2) that the intolerable social evils were those that degraded the image of God in human beings, corrupting people's capacities for self-control and self-respect; 3) the goal of all reform was to free individuals from being manipulated like physical objects. These beliefs, in combination with the obstacles women faced in their efforts for the cause, animated a new feminist consciousness that would result in the women's rights movement.

The pivotal moment came in 1840 when the American delegates to the World's Anti-Slavery Convention arrived in London to find that the women delegates among them were excluded from participation. The women were forced to sit in a curtained balcony while the men debated. Elizabeth Cady Stanton, whose new husband Henry B. Stanton was a prominent abolitionist, was furious at how effortlessly her male associates could undertake "the crucifixion [of woman's] pride and self-respect, the humiliation of [her] spirit." With Mott, she decided that it was time to fight back. Said Stanton, "As Mrs. Mott and I walked home, arm in arm, commenting on the incidents of the day, we resolved to hold a convention as soon as we returned home, and form a society to advance the rights of women."

Eight years were to pass, however, before Stanton and Mott were able to call the convention into session. Despite their resolve, both women hesitated on the brink of such bold public activity. No woman was willing to chair the meeting, so they recruited Lucretia Mott's husband, James. Faced with the task of delineating their grievances, Stanton confessed that they felt "as helpless and hopeless as if [we] had been suddenly asked to construct a steam engine."

Nonetheless, The Declaration of Sentiments issued by this first national gathering of feminists was a remarkable document. Besides claiming their inalienable rights, women held men responsible for a host of grievances. They complained that men monopolized law-making, taxed women without representation, denied them an education, barred them from most "profitable employments," and excluded them from "all avenues to wealth and distinction." Indeed,

> The history of mankind is a history of repeated injuries and usurpations on the part of man toward woman, having in direct object the establishment of an absolute tyranny over her.... He has usurped the prerogative of Jehovah himself, claiming it as his right to assign for her a sphere of action, when that belongs to her conscience and her God. He has endeavored, in every way that he could, to destroy her confidence in her own powers, to lessen her self-respect, and to make her willing to lead a dependent and abject life.

The meeting in Seneca Falls passed a dozen resolutions demanding equal rights for women in marriage, education, religion, and employment. Stanton shocked the convention with one additional resolution — that women "secure for themselves their sacred right to the elective franchise." She was particularly incensed by the fact that not only men of quality but *all men* had the vote. Had it been reserved for men of stature like Webster, Clay, or Van Buren, she indicated, women might not complain,

> But to have drunkards, idiots, horse-racing, rumselling rowdies, ignorant foreigners, and silly boys fully recognized, while we ourselves are thrust out from all the rights that belong to citizens, it is too grossly insulting to the dignity of woman to be longer quietly submitted to. The right is ours. Have it we must. Use it we will.

The right of suffrage was acknowledged to be "the cornerstone of this enterprise, since we do not seek to protect woman, but to place her in a position to protect herself."

The women had few illusions about the difficult road ahead. Elizabeth Cady Stanton told the assembly:

> We do not expect our path will be strewn with the flowers of popular applause, but over the thorns of bigotry and prejudice will be our way, and on our banners will beat the dark storm-clouds of opposition from those who have entrenched themselves behind the stormy bulwarks of custom and authority, and who have fortified their position by every means, holy and unholy. But we will steadfastly abide the result. Unmoved we will bear it aloft. Undaunted we will unfurl it to the gale, for we know that the storm cannot rend from it a shred, that the electric flash will but more clearly show to us the glorious words inscribed upon it, "Equality of Rights."

Throughout the 1850s, national women's rights conventions were held annually, as were numerous local and regional meetings. By the 1860s, efforts for women's rights had become a movement.

Three women played vital leadership roles in the women's rights movement for more than half a century. Stanton was an inventive thinker and a forceful writer, Lucy Stone was the movement's greatest orator, and Susan B. Anthony was the consummate organizer.

With oratorical skills honed in the cause of abolition, Lucy Stone moved listeners with her eloquence and passion for women's liberty. An independent spirit, she held out for a promise of matrimonial equality before she consented to marry abolitionist and feminist Henry Blackwell. The word "obey" was omitted from their marriage vows, and Stone kept her own last name after the marriage.

Susan B. Anthony joined the cause in 1851. A member of a Massachusetts Quaker family, Anthony participated in moral reform and abolition. She had resigned a teaching position in a bitter protest over discrimination against women and joined the temperance movement, an experience that taught her "the great evil of woman's utter dependence on man for the necessary means to aid reform movements." Anthony forged an enduring friendship with Stanton and the two leaders had a remarkable working relationship, each supplying abilities the other lacked. Henry Stanton once described it this way to his wife: "You stir up Susan, and she stirs the world."

In many ways, the two women were polar opposites. Anthony never married, while Stanton was the mother of seven. While she was tied down with domestic duties, she counted on her friend to represent her in meetings she could not attend. The press of household obligations and the endless pressures of child rearing did not rest lightly. Stanton asked Anthony to "Imagine me, day in and day out, watching, bathing, dressing, nursing…. I pace up and down these two chambers of mine like a caged lioness, longing to bring to a close nursing and housekeeping cares." Stanton also railed against the opposition of men, particularly her father and husband, upon whom she was dependent. To her friend, Susan, she wrote:

> I wish that I were as free as you and I would stump the state in a twinkling. But I am not, and what is more, I passed through a terrible scourging when last at my father's. I cannot tell you how deep the iron entered my soul. I never felt more keenly the degradation of my sex. To think

Elizabeth Cady Stanton and Susan B. Anthony

that all in me of which my father would have felt a proper pride had I been a man, is deeply mortifying to him because I am a woman. That thought has stung me to a fierce decision —☐to speak as soon as I can do myself credit. But the pressure on me just now is too great. Henry [her husband] sides with my friends, who oppose me in all that is dearest to my heart. They are not willing that I should write even on the woman question. But I will both write and speak.

For Stanton, silence was never an option. At one point she wrote, "If I do not find some day the use of my tongue on this question, I shall die of an intellectual repression, a woman's rights convulsion!"

It took a long time for women's rights to win any popular support, even among women. Most people, male and female, approved separate spheres for men and women. Susan B. Anthony was convinced that women did not support suffrage because they did not realize what its absence cost them. In frustration, she wrote,

I do pray, and that most earnestly and constantly, for some terrific shock to startle the women of the nation into a self-respect which will compel them to see the absolute degradation of their present position; which will compel them to break their yoke of bondage and give them faith in themselves; which will make them proclaim their allegiance to women first…. The fact is, women are in chains, and their servitude is all the more debasing because they do not realize it. Oh to compel them to see and feel and to give them courage and the conscience to speak and act for their own freedom, though they face the scorn and contempt of all the world for doing it!

Still, to its critics, suffrage was a very radical demand, threatening the very foundations of society. Ministers, journalists, and social commentators of every stripe dismissed women's rights advocates as "old maids whose personal charms were never very attractive" and "women who have been badly married." Through their organizations, newspapers, and political crusades, anti-suffragists associated suffrage with divorce, promiscuity, and neglect of children:

> Women's participation in political life…would involve the domestic calamity of a deserted home and the loss of the woman's qualities for which refined men adore women and marry them…. Doctors tell us, too, that thousands of children would be harmed or killed before birth by the injurious effect of the untimely political excitement of their mothers.

One of the most prominent churchmen of the time, the Reverend Horace Bushnell of Hartford, Connecticut, was horrified at the idea of women voting. His tract, *Woman Suffrage: The Reform Against Nature*, is a tour de force of the anti's argument: a woman's power lay in her beauty and her dependence. Any attempt to assert authority violates her nature so it must inevitably fail. Engaging in the rough and tumble world of politics, Bushnell warned, would damage "the delicate organization, and the fearfully excitable susceptibilities of women." She would be risking the very source of her "honor and power [in her] subject state…which she can little afford to lose by a sally to gain the noisier, coarser kind that does not belong to her — which also she will as certainly fail of, as the gov-

erning of men she is after, is both against their nature and her own." More to the point, she would lose her looks: "…the very look and temperament of women will be altered…and we shall have…a race of forward, selfish, politician-women coming out in their resulting type, thin, hungry-looking…touched with blight and fallen out of luster."

With the outbreak of the Civil War in 1861, women suspended their activities on their own behalf to devote all their energies to the "noble purpose" of freeing the slaves. Stanton and Anthony formed the Women's Loyal League in May, 1863, launching a massive petition drive that delivered some 400,000 signatures to the Congress the following year in support of the Thirteenth Amendment to the U.S. Constitution prohibiting slavery. Once its ratification in 1865 was accomplished, Stanton, Anthony, Stone, Mott, and others formed the American Equal Rights Association (AERA) to press for universal adult suffrage, combining demands for black and woman suffrage into a single campaign. From the beginning of the movement, abolitionists encouraged the equality of women, but they did not think

Library of Congress

Lucy Stone

NAWSA gets organized.

the public was ready for the idea and that the association of the two could doom the franchise for blacks. As abolitionist Wendell Phillips told the feminists, "One question at a time. This hour belongs to the Negro."

The Fourteenth Amendment, introduced to the Congress in the summer of 1866 and ratified in 1868, represented a serious setback to the cause of women's rights. The amendment included the first use of the word "male" in the Constitution, thereby explicitly repudiating woman suffrage. Stanton and Anthony felt intense betrayal, renounced their male collaborators, and argued for the development of an independent political position. The issue split the AERA apart. One group, determined to press for the Fifteenth Amendment (prohibiting federal and state governments from denying the vote to anyone "on account of race, color, or previous condition of servitude"), believed the cause of the newly freed blacks came first and that the women could wait. Lucy Stone, Henry Blackwell, Julia Ward Howe, and others formed the American Woman Suffrage Association (AWSA) to continue that work. While Stone expressed her disappointment with the Fourteenth Amendment, she added wearily, "I will be thankful in my soul if any body can get out of this terrible pit." Stanton and Anthony disagreed, believing the cause of women's rights was paramount. Anthony

threatened to "cut off this right arm of mine before I will ever work for or demand the ballot for Negroes and not the women." Their group, the National Woman Suffrage Association (NWSA), committed itself to a platform of sweeping social change in women's status and a constitutional amendment on their own behalf. Their motto: "Men their rights and nothing more; women their rights and nothing less."

The two groups competed for leadership of the women's movement for 21 years. Both engaged in organizing and educational efforts, traveled and lectured, distributed leaflets and pamphlets, petitioned state legislatures to support suffrage referenda, secured thousands of signatures on petitions, and lobbied the Congress. Despite all their efforts, congressional hearings were rarely held; the question of suffrage was sent to the floor only once and failed. In the states, they faced defeat after defeat. After the first state referendum in Kansas in 1867, which failed, 55 more such popular votes on state woman suffrage amendments took place over the next 50 years.

Success came first in Wyoming territory, where the tiny legislature enfranchised women in hopes of improving the territory's rowdy reputation by attracting females, then outnumbered six to one. When Wyoming applied for statehood in 1890, they faced objections to their enfranchised women in the U.S. House of Representatives. In response, the Wyoming legislature sent a message to Congress stating, "We may stay out of the Union for 100 years, but we will come in with our women." Wyoming became the first woman suffrage state. Colorado joined it in 1893, then Utah and Idaho became states with enfranchised women in 1896.

By the 1890s, the fierce animosity between the two suffrage groups had abated, a new generation had joined the ranks, and the AWSA and NWSA combined into the NAWSA — The National American Woman Suffrage Association — and became a truly national organization. Before long, Susan B. Anthony's protégé, Carrie Chapman Catt, took the helm and molded the organization into a tightly controlled lobbying machine. Other changes at the turn of the century, outside the suffrage movement, also were aiding the cause.

The 1890s up to the beginning of the first world war witnessed the first modern American reform movement called Progressivism. What prompted the progressive era was, simply put, a combination of severe social problems and a growing and concerned middle-class that wanted to solve them. Most importantly, they thought they *could* do something to solve these problems. Progressives were mostly urban and highly educated, many of them women. They tried to restore (what they saw as) the proper balance among Protestant moral values, capitalistic competition, and democratic processes to an increasingly disorderly society wracked with poverty, social violence, and corruption. Progressive reform seemed a natural to women. In the newly industrialized society, women found that in order to protect their traditional women's sphere of home, household, and children, they needed to move out of that sphere into the public world and extend their women's concerns and women's points of view to become involved in community service.

Central to the Progressive movement were college-educated women. By the turn of the century, women made up more than one-third of the total college student population. When they emerged with a diploma and a commitment to independence and self-sufficiency, they found they had graduated into a society that had no use for them. Some, like Jane Addams, invented their own professions. When she founded Hull House, a settlement house located in the slums of Chicago, with Ellen Gates Starr in 1889, Addams trained women much like herself, offered them an alternative to marriage, and they in turn provided crucial services to slum dwellers.

Many married middle-class women, bored with unchallenging domestic routines and concerned about a disordered society's impact on their homes and families, joined the new female white-collar workers and college grads in progressive reform. Their vehicles for activism were the women's clubs. Clubs that had begun largely as cultural outlets, by the turn of the century had shifted to more socially responsible work. Women's clubs were tremendously important in establishing libraries, funding hospitals, supporting schools and settlement houses, visiting nurse services, lobbying for child labor laws — extending, in other words, their traditional roles into the public world. As Jane Addams observed, "Politics is housekeeping on a grand scale." Similarly, journalist Rheta Childe Dorr defined an expansive women's sphere in 1910: "Woman's place is Home…. But Home is not contained within the four walls of an individual house. Home is the community. The city full of people is the Family. The public school is the real Nursery. And badly do the Home and Family need their Mother."

American women had long been regarded as the guardians of virtue and morality, and now, in the Progressive era, they began exercising their influence to clean up the messes men made in society. As the social justice movement expanded, club women supported such measures as workmen's compensation, pure food and drug legislation, prison reform, welfare work, prohibition, labor arbitration, public health, tenement reform, occupational safety, child labor reform, sweatshop regulation, day nurseries, adult education, and, ultimately, woman suffrage.

Women furnished the agenda of humanitarian social welfare programs. But women worked outside political institutions, at least in part, because they could not vote. As they confronted the scope of the problems and the inadequacies of private solutions, they began to advocate a larger role for government to balance contending interests and ameliorate social distress. And they realized that the social policies they supported could only be realized if women had the vote. In the context of all this reform, the idea of woman suffrage no longer seemed outlandish or bizarre, but a perfectly logical step. Or so it would seem.

About this time, huge national organizations like the Young Women's Christian Association and the Women's Christian Temperance Union also became politicized. The WCTU, for example, concentrated on anti-liquor laws and municipal reform. Under the leadership of suffragist Frances Willard, the WCTU emphasized the necessity for political action to achieve their goals. That meant the vote. Adding the moral weight of women to the electorate would, the argument went, ensure prohibition, purify politics, and make war a thing of the past.

Also in the early 1900s, hundreds of small local women's groups consolidated into large federations like the General Federation of Women's Clubs, the National Council of Jewish Women, the National Association of Colored Women, and so forth, providing yet another base of support for the enfranchisement of women.

Black women occasionally joined clubs dominated by whites, but by and large most were unwelcome. Besides, as victims of both racial and gender prejudice, their reform agendas were different; they included a strong emphasis on racial uplift, as well as gender equality. Black women started clubs around the country to address their communities' most pressing needs — establishing settlement houses for blacks migrating to urban areas, funding libraries and schools, pushing legislation against lynching, protesting aspects of Jim Crow segregation, strengthening black women's moral reputation, and working to win the vote. Soon they became aware, as white women had, of the importance of a national network. To this end, they organized themselves into the National Association of Colored Women (NACW), a coalition of affiliated clubs that would eventually record over 50,000 members.

Among the leadership in the black women's suffrage movement were three with Tennessee connections: Ida B. Wells-Barnett, Mary Church Terrell, and Margaret Murray Washington. Wells-Barnett, a native of Mississippi, launched her journalism career in Memphis by attacking lynching and was exiled. After settling in Chicago, she continued to campaign for federal legislation against lynching, was a founding member of the National Association for the Advancement of Colored People (NAACP), and a prominent suffragist. Wells-Barnett founded the interracial Alpha Suffrage Club in Chicago and worked closely with Susan B. Anthony.

Mary Church Terrell was from a prominent Memphis family, attended Oberlin College, and married attorney Robert Terrell, one of the first blacks to be graduated from Harvard and the first black federal judge. Terrell, like Ida B. Wells-Barnett, was a charter member of the NAACP (she and Wells-Barnett were the only two women invited to its organiza-

tional meeting), and the first president of the NACW. Margaret Murray Washington attended Fisk University in Nashville, then took a job as an administrator at Tuskegee Institute in Alabama, eventually marrying its founder and arguably the nation's most influential black man, Booker T. Washington.

Black women as well as white recognized the vote as essential to improving their lives and communities. Terrell, like her foremother Sojourner Truth, reminded white women of black women's double oppression by sex and race. Truth had arrested an 1851 women's rights meeting with her retort to a clergyman who asserted woman's weakness disqualified her from equal rights. Truth asked,

A'n't I a woman? I could work as much and eat as much as a man — when I could get it — and bear de lash as well! And a'n't I a woman? I have borne thirteen chilern and seen 'em mos' all sold off to slavery, and when I cried out with my mother's grief, not but Jesus heard me! And a'n't I a woman?

Terrell asked white suffragists nearly 50 years later to recognize that "not only are colored women handicapped on account of their sex, but they are everywhere mocked on account of their race. We are asking that our sisters of the dominant race do all in their power to find solutions to the injustices to which colored people are victims."

The suffrage message was gaining momentum as the century turned, partly because supporters were better organized and more politically sophisticated, but also because suffrage leaders had narrowed their goals and found ways to justify the enfranchisement of women in less threatening ways. Gone were the radical messages of Elizabeth Stanton and Susan Anthony, who had called for a major overhaul of gender roles and full equality for women. Women's rights had become submerged in the ballot. Additionally, suffrage would not challenge the separate sphere in which women resided. Instead, it would allow women to bring their special and distinct virtues, developed and nurtured in that sphere, to bear upon society. It was precisely because women possessed these virtues, they claimed, that woman suffrage could make such important and positive contributions to politics.

Despite this apparent logical and reassuring message, powerful forces were mobilizing against the cause. Their arguments echoed those used a half century before: women's weak minds and delicate tem-

Susan B. Anthony at her desk. A photograph of Frances Wright, who founded the Nashoba Community in Shelby County, is directly above her right hand. Her lifelong friend, Elizabeth Cady Stanton, is pictured on the frontispiece of the book propped before her.

peraments could not survive the hurly-burly of public life; the complexity of politics and the rough election-day crowds would either frighten women into simpering fools or transform them into unnatural amazons; gone would be the charm and serenity of the tender sex and with it woman's capacity to create havens of domestic tranquility in a tumultuous world. Voting would overtax women's inferior intellects; women would be exposed to the corrupt influences of dissolute men. Worse, by choosing their own political candidate, they might become independent of their husbands and lose their traditional feelings of subservience. In short, the pillars of civilization would come crashing down.

In 1911, Josephine Dodge, widow of one of New York's richest capitalists, formed the National Association Opposed to Woman Suffrage based in her Fifth Avenue apartment. Women already had vast behind-the-scenes influence, Dodge argued, and to invade the male realm of politics could only tarnish their moral and spiritual role. Her associate, Mrs. A.J. George, told Congress: "The woman suffrage movement is an imitation-of-man movement and, as such, merits the condemnation of every normal man and woman." The vote, she warned, would condemn women to jury duty and, quite possibly, military service.

More sinister forces also strenuously opposed woman suffrage. Political machines that ran many state and local governments were reluctant to introduce a new set of voters into the electoral system; women were an unknown force that might threaten their power. Businessmen feared the influence of women's votes on working conditions in their factories. Liquor interests felt threatened because the prohibition crusade drew so much of its strength from women. Anti-suffrage in the South included the additional arguments that a federal amendment would usurp state sovereignty and bring suffrage to black women. The struggle was far from over.

Susan B. Anthony, who had fought the hard fight for over 50 years, retired from the presidency of NAWSA in 1901, passing the mantle to Carrie Chapman Catt. Sadly, none of the original suffrage mothers lived to see their dream fulfilled. Lucy Stone died in 1893; Stanton died in 1902 at age 87; Anthony died four years later at age 86. At her last public appearance, Anthony supplied the movement with its rallying cry: "Failure is impossible!"

Catt assumed command of a disorganized and discouraged association. With the support of her second husband, a wealthy mining engineer who signed

Alice Paul leaves National Woman's Party headquarters on her way to the White House.

a prenuptial agreement allowing her to spend two months in the spring and two months in the fall devoted entirely to the suffrage movement, Catt set about rebuilding and reorienting NAWSA. Only four years after she began, Catt left the post to care for her dying husband, turning it over to Anna Howard Shaw. A veteran suffragist, medical doctor, and Methodist minister, Shaw embodied the essence of emancipated woman. While her compelling oratory championed suffrage in every state in the Union, Shaw lacked Catt's vision and organizational skills, and she struggled to steer NAWSA for eleven years until Catt resumed the presidency in 1914.

Two years later, Catt unveiled her "Winning Plan" for suffrage: a tightly centralized, coordinated state-by-state effort aimed at the ultimate achievement of a constitutional amendment. Suffrage groups in the states were organized to mirror political boundaries and legislative districts, in order to concentrate efforts on legislative momentum. Catt was certain that as states passed woman suffrage and the number of suffrage supporters in the House and Senate increased, the passage of a constitutional amendment would follow.

Another significant suffrage leader, Harriot Stanton Blatch, daughter of Elizabeth Stanton, re-

turned to New York after many years in London, where she had witnessed the radical and innovative British suffrage movement. Blatch organized working women, believing they needed the vote to improve their economic status and the suffrage movement needed working-class support. She excelled at pulling together political alliances between middle-class reformers and working-class women to rally for suffrage, infusing the campaign with new life and broadening its constituency.

Under the NAWSA umbrella, a small band of women, led by Alice Paul and including Tennessean Sue Shelton White, organized a delegation, known as the Congressional Union, to directly lobby Congress for a woman-suffrage amendment. Paul had participated in Britain's woman's suffrage campaign, and she adopted their aggressive, confrontational techniques. Britain suffragists stormed the Houses of Parliament, planted bombs, destroyed mail, burned men's clubs and social pavilions, damaged golf courses, and even attempted to take the crown jewels from the Tower of London. It was necessary, Paul believed, to get people's attention — and she did that very well.

Since Alice Paul believed that women had to hold the party in power accountable for its stand on suffrage, she chose a dramatic public action to make her point. She organized some 8000 women to march in protest at Woodrow Wilson's inauguration in 1913, a not inconsiderable achievement. Among them were several black women's suffrage clubs, including Ida Wells-Barnett's Alpha Suffrage Club and Mary Church Terrell's contingent from Washington. In deference to Southern suffragists, Paul asked the black women to march at the end of the parade. Terrell's group agreed to do so, but Wells-Barnett angrily refused. She insisted she would march with the club she had established or not at all. She disappeared as the parade began; then, as the Chicago delegation rounded a corner, she slipped into line between two white women and completed the parade. The incident was indicative of black women's position in the suffrage movement. A close alliance with black women came at too high a price for most white suffragists, many of whom shared the racism and nativism of turn-of-the-century America. Moreover, passage of suffrage in Congress depended upon Southern Democrats, and ratification would also require Southern cooperation. Hence two principal arguments involving race characterized the movement: that white women ought not be the political

inferiors of black men and that woman suffrage would not threaten white supremacy.

The massive suffrage parade was led by a tall stunning young woman in flowing white robes on horseback. Thousands of women assembled in costumed marching units — each with its own colorful banners — marched toward the White House, accompanied by bands and suffrage floats. Suffrage yellow glittered in the sunlight. First used in the Kansas state campaign where it was adapted from the state flower, the sunflower, splashes of yellow, coupled with depictions of the sun's rays, symbolized the "dawn of a new day" for women. Also prominent were the British colors of purple, representing loyalty, and white, for purity. Washington had never seen anything like it. One Baltimore newspaper described the scene:

> Eight thousand women, marching in the woman suffrage pageant today, practically fought their way foot by foot up Pennsylvania Avenue, through a surging throng that completely defied Washington police, swamped the marchers, and broke their procession into little companies. The women, trudging stoutly along under

National Woman's Party suffragists demonstrating in front of the White House.

Dr. Anna Howard Shaw

woman suffrage and that his task was to see that the Congress concentrated on the issues of currency and tariff reform. Paul responded: "But Mr. President, do you not understand that the Administration has no right to legislate for currency, tariff, and any other reforms without first getting the consent of women to these reforms?" Somewhat taken aback, Wilson promised to give the subject his "most careful consideration." Paul sent a second deputation, and a third. Wilson flatly stated that he had no time to consider suffrage for women, despite Paul's insistence that this involved the liberty of half the American people.

The Congressional Union staged a second mass demonstration on April 7, the opening day of the Congress. Women delegates representing every one of the 435 congressional districts in the country carried petitions signed by the people back home asking for passage of the Susan B. Anthony Amendment. She had drafted it in 1875. It read:

Section 1. The right of citizens of the United States to vote shall not be denied or abridged by any State on account of sex.

Section 2. Congress shall have the power, by appropriate legislation, to enforce the provisions of this article.

All spring, suffragists held large gatherings throughout the country. The publicity and pressure resulted in a favorable report by the Senate Committee on Suffrage for the first time in 21 years. The measure was on the calendar for action in July. Suffragists from around the country converged on Washington, parading through the streets in gaily decorated automobiles and bearing "a monster petition" signed by hundreds of thousands of citizens. Many took their seats in the Senate gallery, where the day was given over to suffrage discussion. In the first Senate vote on the matter since 1887, the tally was 36 - 34, eleven short of the two-thirds majority needed. In the House, the Rules Committee split 4 - 4 over creating a suffrage committee, and no action was taken. The Democratic Party caucus voted on the issue and decided 123 - 57 that suffrage was a state matter.

At the end of 1913, Paul and her Congressional Union left NAWSA to become an independent body. She wanted her Union to concentrate all suffrage work on pressuring Congress and the president for a federal amendment. She also wanted to follow a more vigorously militant policy than the more conservative leaders of NAWSA would tolerate.

great difficulties, were able to complete their march only when troops of cavalry from Fort Myers were rushed into Washington to take charge of Pennsylvania Avenue. No inauguration has ever produced such scenes, which in many instances amounted to nothing less than riots.

The mistreatment of many socially prominent women in the parade was embarrassing to the new Wilson administration. The Congress held hearings into police failure to protect them, and the police chief was fired. Alice Paul got exactly what she wanted: the issue of suffrage squarely on the front pages.

On March 3, 1913, four days after the parade, Paul organized the first deputation of women ever to appear before a president. They had come to enlist his support for the passage of a national suffrage amendment. President Wilson told Paul and her four companions that he had no opinion on the subject of

PRESIDENT WILSON IS DECEIVING THE WORLD
WHEN HE APPEARS AS THE PROPHET OF DEMOCRACY
PRESIDENT WILSON HAS OPPOSED THOSE WHO
DEMAND DEMOCRACY FOR THIS COUNTRY
HE IS RESPONSIBLE FOR THE DISFRANCHISEMENT
OF MILLIONS OF AMERICANS
WE IN AMERICA KNOW THIS
THE WORLD WILL FIND HIM OUT.

When their country went to war to fight for democracy abroad, members of the National Woman's Party, determined to fight for democracy at home, stationed a "perpetual delegation" in front of the White House to remind President Wilson with his own words to support the enfranchisement of the female half of American citizens.

In the meantime, a few more states had moved into the fold. In 1910, Washington became the first state in 14 years to extend suffrage. California followed a year later, and in 1912, Oregon, Kansas, and Arizona joined them. In 1913, Illinois became the first state east of the Mississippi to grant women the right to vote. By the end of the year, when NAWSA held its national convention in Washington, fortuitously timed for the reconvening of the Congress, woman suffrage states elected one-fifth of senators, one-seventh of representatives and one-sixth of presidential electors.

Just before President Wilson's address to the Congress on December 2, a delegation of 73 women from his home state of New Jersey urged Wilson to include a suffrage resolution in his message. Perhaps they reminded him that New Jersey had once been the only state that allowed women to vote — and then rescinded it. It happened in the period right after the Revolutionary War. The Provincial Congress prepared an ordinance extending the vote to "every person worth fifty pounds," which New Jersey incorporated into its state constitution. For over 30 years (1776-1807), New Jersey women could vote.

Then, in an act passed in November of 1807, the state ensured the exclusion of women by limiting the franchise to "free white male citizens, twenty-one years of age, and worth fifty pounds." Perhaps they told the president they had come to reclaim the franchise.

At any rate, they were disappointed. Wilson made no mention of women. Yet another deputation, composed of representatives from each state and led by NAWSA President Anna Howard Shaw, confronted Wilson. Shaw boldly asked, "Mr. President, if *you* cannot speak for us and your party will not, who then, pray, is there to speak for us?" When Wilson jokingly replied, "You seem very well able to speak for yourselves," she snapped back. "We mean, Mr. President, who will speak for us with *authority!*" He reportedly made no reply.

Over the next four years, Paul and her organization, now called the National Woman's Party (NWP), as well as countless other groups of suffragist women, led numerous delegations to plead with the president to support woman suffrage, but to little avail. NAWSA affiliates, now led by Catt, continued pressing on the local level with similar results. Nonetheless, the tide seemed to be turning in 1916 when, under heavy pressure from women's groups, both major parties adopted woman suffrage planks in their national platforms. And even President Wilson, in his election campaign, promised support. But that endorsement was hedged by advocating state-by-state decisions rather than backing a federal suffrage amendment.

By this time, the nation's attention was overtaken by the war in Europe, which the United States earnestly hoped to avoid. Wilson won re-election on the slogan, "He Kept Us Out of War." On January 7, 1917, he received a delegation of the Woman's Party again pressing for a federal amendment, but Wilson was adamant. The following day, the NWP stationed a "perpetual delegation"—10 a.m. to 5:30 p.m., 6 days a week — in front of the White House so that, as Alice Paul said, "he wouldn't forget." They were the first group in American history to employ this form of protest. These "Silent Sentinels" remained outside the White House gates, rain or shine, day after day. As President Wilson went out for his afternoon drive, banners would ask him, "MR. PRESIDENT! HOW LONG MUST WOMEN WAIT FOR LIBERTY?" On his inauguration day, a thousand women walked slowly around and around the executive mansion.

On April 4, 1917, President Wilson asked the Congress for a declaration of war on Germany. The mood of the country shifted radically, and Carrie Chapman Catt, a prominent pacifist, faced a dilemma. Just two years earlier, she had chaired the opening meeting of the Woman's Peace Party in Washington, attended by 86 delegates from all the major women's groups, including the National Council of Women, the National Federation of Women's Clubs, and the WCTU, with such prominent female leaders as Jane Addams, Charlotte Perkins Gilman, Emily Greene Balch, Rose Pastor Stokes, and Crystal Eastman. Together they had drafted a pacifist manifesto presenting the views of "the mother half of humanity." This noble effort collapsed when the United States entered the war. Almost overnight, pacifism had become treasonous. Catt was also a realist. NAWSA would choose patriotism over peace. Most of the nation supported the war, including the vast majority of NAWSA members. She determined that the best course for her and for her organization was to back away from the peace movement and capitalize on women's contributions to the war effort. NAWSA would suspend suffrage activities until the end of the war.

The NWP disagreed, recalling that the same logic had severely damaged the woman's movement dur-

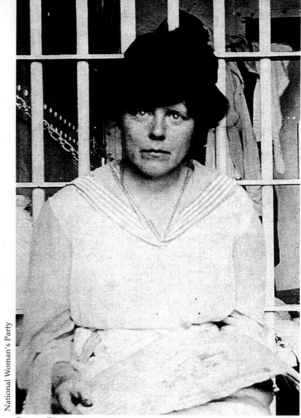

National Woman's Party

Lucy Burns

ing the Civil War. NWP spokesperson, Katharine Fisher asserted: "We must not let our voice be drowned by war trumpets or cannon. If we do, we shall find ourselves, when the war is over, with a peace that will only prolong our struggle, a democracy that will belie its name by leaving out half the people." They would maintain their daily vigil at the White House.

Wilson's patriotic rationale for entering the war provided some of the most powerful rhetorical arguments for woman suffrage. One sign at the White House gate mocked his war message, in which he said, "We shall fight for the things which we have always held nearest to our hearts — for democracy, for the right of those who submit to authority to have a voice in their own government." The women added that half the American population had no such voice. Another large sign read:

PRESIDENT WILSON IS DECEIVING THE WORLD WHEN HE APPEARS AS THE PROPHET OF DEMOCRACY.... HE IS RESPONSIBLE FOR THE DISENFRAN-CHISEMENT OF MILLIONS OF AMERI-CANS. WE IN AMERICA KNOW THIS. THE WORLD WILL FIND HIM OUT.

By that summer, the suffragists became more restive, and the placards became more provocative. The

President Wilson walks past pickets at the gates of the White House.

president was called "Kaiser Wilson," he was burned in effigy, and signs stated that there was no real democracy in the United States. Onlookers heckled the women, snatched and broke their signs, pushed and shoved them, called them traitors. The president, too, was becoming impatient.

The suffragists were hauled to jail on charges of obstructing the sidewalk or refusing to cooperate with police. They were convicted and sentenced to prison terms of up to six months in the District of Columbia Jail and the Occoquan Workhouse in Virginia. Alice Paul told reporters as she was led from the courtroom to begin her sentence: "We are being imprisoned, not because we obstructed traffic, but because we pointed out to the President the fact that he was obstructing the cause of democracy at home, while Americans were fighting for it abroad." In all, 218 women from 26 states were arrested, 97 of whom went to prison.

Many of the women were roughly handled by guards; several were clubbed and beaten and hung by their handcuffs high on cell doors. Mrs. Mary Nolan, age 73, describes the group's arrival at Occoquan: "I saw Dorothy Day brought in. She is a frail girl. The two men handling her were twisting her arms above her head. Then suddenly they lifted her up and banged her down over the arm of an iron bench — twice...."

Some of the women were held in solitary confinement on bread and water — one slice of moldy bread and one cup of water per day. Paul was sent to the psychiatric ward where doctors attempted to find symptoms of "persecution mania," to prove she "had an obsession on the subject of President Wilson." Paul wrote,

> ...all through the day once every hour, the nurse came to "observe" me. All through the night, once every hour she came in, turned on an electric light sharp in my face and "observed" me. This ordeal was the most terrible torture, as it prevented my sleeping for more than a few minutes at a time. And if I did finally get to sleep it was only to be shocked immediately into wide-awakeness with the pitiless light.

Insisting that they be regarded as political prisoners, several of the women, including Alice Paul, went on hunger strikes. Authorities responded with a harsh and cruel procedure of "forcible feedings," done with tubing forced down the mouth or nos-

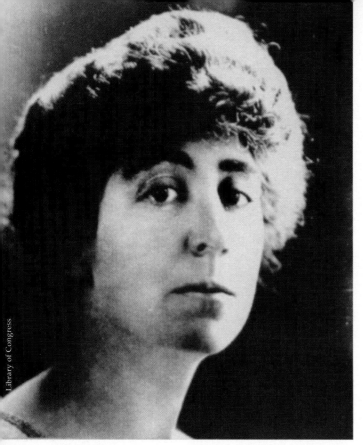

Jeannette Rankin

trils, three times a day. One woman, Rose Winslow, smuggled out notes to her husband on tiny scraps of paper describing her torture this way:

> I had a nervous time of it, gasping a long time afterward, and my stomach rejecting during the process…. I was vomiting continually…. The tube has developed an irritation somewhere that is painful…. I heard myself making the most hideous sounds…. The same doctor feeds both Alice Paul and me. Don't let them tell you we take this well…. One feels so forsaken when one lies prone and people shove a pipe down one's stomach…. We think of the coming feeding all day. It is horrible.

Lucy Burns' description, also smuggled out on tiny scraps of paper:

> I was held down by five people at legs, arms, and head. I refused to open mouth. [Dr.] Gannon pushed tube up left nostril. I turned and twisted my head all I could, but he managed to push it up. It hurts nose and throat very much and makes nose bleed freely. Tube drawn out covered with blood. Operation leaves one very sick. Food dumped directly into stomach feels

like a ball of lead. Left nostril, throat and muscles of neck very sore all night.

Mrs. Lawrence Lewis later also wrote of her ordeal:

> I was seized and laid on my back, where five people held me, a young colored woman leaping upon my knees, which seemed to break under the weight. Dr. Gannon then forced the tube through my lips and down my throat, I gasping and suffocating with the agony of it. I didn't know where to breathe from and everything turned black when the fluid began pouring in. I was moaning and making the most awful sounds quite against my will….

Undaunted in the face of such brutal treatment, in spite of physical injury and deeply felt disillusion and anger, most suffrage prisoners came out of jail renewed in purpose. Pickets of the White House persisted, others burned copies of the president's speeches about democracy and self-government with the words, "The torch which I hold symbolizes the burning indignation of the women who for years have been given words without action." Some suffragists, dressed in prison garb and riding a train they called "The Prison Special," made a national speaking tour and collected signatures on suffrage petitions. Katharine Fisher spoke:

> Five of us who are with you tonight have recently come out from the workhouse into the world. A great change? Not so much of a change for women, disenfranchised women. In prison or out, American women are not free…. Disenfranchisement is the prison of women's power and spirit…. Prison life epitomizes all life under undemocratic rule.

Jeannette Rankin, herself a suffragist and the only female member of Congress, introduced a resolution calling for a congressional investigation of the workhouse. The stories of the arrests and harsh treatment of the suffragists embarrassed the Wilson administration, attracted a great deal of national attention, and probably won some converts. At the same time, they also attracted the anger and condemnation of more temperate women who considered militant suffragists unladylike and provocative. Chief among them was Carrie Chapman Catt.

Although united in an unflagging pursuit of votes for women, the two leaders and their organizations, their tactics, and their philosophies could hardly have been more different. And both of them thought the other wrong-headed. NAWSA aimed at, and was attractive to, mainstream women. Transforming domestic roles into political qualifications, they emphasized the role of women defined in service to family, community, and state and what the nurturing and redemptive qualities motherhood and family could bring to the political arena. For their part, the National Woman's Party seemed to embody the worst predictions of women's emancipation. They held that men and women were essentially equal except for differences in biology; that equality, freedom and personal empowerment were theirs by right, and that they meant to use any means necessary to achieve equal rights.

Still, in many ways the two groups' tactics were complementary. The radicalism of the NWP created a situation in which something had to be done. They made the president and the Congress nervous about what they might do next. In comparison, Catt's suffragists looked much more reasonable. The combination of militant agitation by the NWP and the persistent pressure by NAWSA gradually moved government leaders toward their goal.

Meanwhile, countless American women were demonstrating their loyalty to the nation at war. Hundreds of thousands of women moved to fill "men's jobs" while they fought at the front. They worked in offices, hospitals, and munitions factories. Women served as farm and factory laborers, medical volunteers, municipal workers, elevator operators and streetcar conductors. Clubwomen plunged into war work — selling bonds, saving food, providing support for the troops.

While Alice Paul and war news were capturing national headlines, NAWSA suffragists continued to quietly win support state by state, city by city. Since 1913, Montana and Nevada had voted for suffrage. Then in 1917 and 1918, New York and Michigan, two of the most populous states in the Union, moved into the suffrage column. By 1919, 29 states had granted women the right to vote in at least some elections; 15 allowed full participation. In Washington, where NAWSA had established its own lobbying organization to counter the militancy of the NWP, Catt approached the president to support the suffrage amendment as a "war measure," a reward for the loyal support of his nation's women.

On January 9, 1918, President Wilson came out in favor of a federal amendment. The next day, the

Carrie Chapman Catt

House passed the Anthony amendment by a vote of 274 - 136, a two-thirds majority with one vote to spare. Passage in the Senate seemed unlikely; tallies indicated the measure would fall at least two votes short. The suffragists increased the pressure. A special deputation of women munitions workers, under the auspices of the NWP, waited a week to see the president, then finally put their message in writing:

> We are only a few of the thousands of American women who are forming a growing part of the army at home. The work we are doing is hard and dangerous to life and health, making detonators, handling TNT, the highest of all explosives. We want to be recognized by our country, as much her citizens as our soldiers are.

The president said he was doing all that he could.

Carrie Catt, as president of the International Woman Suffrage Alliance, submitted a memorial to the president, endorsed by woman suffrage groups of Italy, Belgium, Portugal, and Great Britain (which, along with Russia, had enfranchised its women), on behalf of the French Union for Woman Suffrage urging Wilson to promote their efforts and thereby assert his "powerful influence for woman suffrage in

The GREATEST MOTHER in the WORLD

Women's contributions to The Great War won them support for suffrage.

the entire world." Wilson rose to the occasion to profess:

> The democratic reconstruction of the world will not have been completely or adequately obtained until women are admitted to the suffrage. As for America, it is my earnest hope that the Senate of the United States will give an unmistakable answer by passing the federal amendment before the end of this session.

Still two votes short in September, the president pulled out all the stops. He told the recalcitrant Senate that he regarded "the concurrence of the Senate in the constitutional amendment proposing the extension of the suffrage to women as vitally essential to the successful prosecution of the great war of humanity in which we are engaged." The world is watching us, he said,

> looking to the great, powerful, famous democracy of the West to lead them to the new day...and they think, in their logical simplicity, that democracy means that women shall play their part in affairs alongside men and upon equal footing

with them. If we reject measures like this, in ignorance or defiance of what a new age has brought forth, they will cease to follow or to trust us…. We have made partners of the women in this war; shall we admit them only to a partnership of sacrifice and suffering and toil and not to a partnership of privilege and of right? This war could not have been fought, either by the other nations engaged or by America, if it had not been for the services of the women…. We shall not only be distrusted but shall deserve to be distrusted if we do not enfranchise them with the fullest possible enfranchisement, as it is now certain that the other great free nations will enfranchise them.

Not only were women vital to the war effort, Wilson contended that they also would be vital to the peace: "We shall need their moral sense to preserve what is right and fine and worthy in our system of life as well as to discover just what it is that ought to be purified and reformed. Without their counselings we shall be only half wise." After this eloquent and historic appeal, the vote taken on October 1 was 62 - 34, or two votes short. The issue was dead.

Democrats lost the majority in the mid-term elections that fall. Two days after the 66th Congress convened, suffrage was born again. On May 21, 1919, the Republican-controlled House passed the Susan B. Anthony amendment 304 - 89, 42 votes more than needed. Two weeks later, the Senate passed it 66 - 30, two more votes than necessary, and submitted it to the states for ratification on June 4, 1919.

The measure, most believed, would likely have tough going. The Deep South so strongly opposed equal suffrage that it would be necessary to sweep the rest of the country to win the necessary three-fourths of the states — 36 of them — to make it law. Fortunately, nearly every state in the union had groups of highly organized and motivated women poised for the final showdown.

References

Barry, Kathleen. *Susan B. Anthony: A Biography of a Singular Feminist.* New York: Ballantine Books, 1988.

Buechler, Steven M. *Women's Movements in the United States.* New Brunswick, N.J.: Rutgers University Press, 1990.

Catt, Carrie Chapman, and Nettie Rogers Shuler. *Woman Suffrage and Politics.* New York: Charles Scribner's Sons, 1923.

Cott, Nancy, ed. *Root of Bitterness: Documents of the Social History of American Women.* Boston: Northeastern University Press, 1986.

DuBois, Ellen Carol. *Feminism and Suffrage: The Emergence of an Independent Women's Movement in America, 1848-1869.* Ithaca, New York: Cornell University Press, 1978.

DuBois, Ellen Carol, ed. *Elizabeth Cady Stanton, Susan B. Anthony: Correspondence, Writings, Speeches.* New York: Schocken Books, 1981.

Evans, Sara M. *Born for Liberty: A History of Women in America.* New York: The Free Press, 1989.

Giddings, Paula. *When and Where I Enter: The Impact of Black Women on Race and Sex in America.* New York: Bantam Books, 1984.

Hewitt, Nancy A. and Suzanne Lebsock, eds. *Visible Women: New Essays on American Activism.* Urbana: University of Illinois Press, 1993.

Kerber, Linda K. *Women of the Republic: Intellect and Ideology in Revolutionary America.* New York: W.W. Norton and Company, 1986.

Kraditor, Aileen S. *The Ideas of the Woman Suffrage Movement, 1890-1920.* New York: W.W. Norton and Company, 1981.

Lerner, Gerda, ed. *The Female Experience: An American Documentary.* New York: Oxford University Press, 1992.

Morris, Celia. *Fanny Wright: Rebel in America.* Urbana: University of Illinois Press, 1992.

Moynihan, Ruth Barnes, Cynthia Russett, and Laurie Crumpacker, eds. *Second to None: A Documentary History of American Women.* Lincoln: University of Nebraska Press, 1993.

Norton, Mary Beth. *Liberty's Daughters: The Revolutionary Experience of American Women, 1750-1800.* Boston: Little, Brown and Company, 1980.

Riley, Glenda. *Inventing the American Woman: An Inclusive History.* Wheeling, Ill.: Harlan Davidson, Inc., 1995.

Scott, Ann Firor. *Natural Allies: Women's Associations in American History.* Urbana: University of Illinois Press, 1991.

Scott, Ann Firor, and Andrew M. Scott. *Half the People: The Fight for Woman Suffrage.* New York: J.P. Lippincott Company, 1975.

Sherr, Lynn. *Failure is Impossible: Susan B. Anthony in Her Own Words.* New York: Times Books, 1995.

Sklar, Kathryn Kish, and Thomas Dublin. *Women and Power in American History: A Reader.* Englewood Cliffs, N.J.: Prentice-Hall, Inc., 1991.

Stanton, Elizabeth Cady, Susan B. Anthony, and Matilda Joslyn Gage, eds. *History of Woman Suffrage.* Rochester, New York: Charles Mann, Publisher, 1887.

Stanton, Elizabeth Cady. *Eighty Years and More: Reminiscences, 1815-1897.* New York: Schocken Books, 1971.

Stanton, Theodore, and Harriot Stanton Blatch. *Elizabeth Cady Stanton as Revealed in Her Letters, Diary and Reminiscences.* New York: Harper and Brothers, 1922.

Sterling, Dorothy, ed. *We Are Your Sisters: Black Women in the Nineteenth Century.* New York: W.W. Norton and Company, 1984.

Stevens, Doris. Edited by Carol O'Hare. *Jailed for Freedom: American Women Win the Vote.* Troutdale, Oregon: NewSage Press, 1995.

Ware, Susan. *Modern American Women: A Documentary History.* Chicago: The Dorsey Press, 1989.

Wheeler, Marjorie Spruill, ed. *One Woman, One Vote.* Troutdale, Oregon: NewSage Press, 1995.

Wheeler, Marjorie Spruill, ed. *Votes for Women! The Woman Suffrage Movement in Tennessee, the South, and the Nation.* Knoxville: The University of Tennessee Press, 1995.

Woloch, Nancy. *Women and the American Experience.* 2nd Ed. New York: McGraw-Hill, Inc., 1994.

Yee, Shirley J. *Black Women Abolitionists: A Study in Activism, 1828-1860.* Knoxville: The University of Tennessee Press, 1992.

TENNESSEE EQUAL SUFFRAGE CAMPAIGN COMMITTEE

Quote .... Unquote

Some memorable comments and writings about woman suffrage made in the years, months, weeks, and days preceding and immediately following the Extraordinary Session of the Tennessee legislature in Nashville in 1920.

A Rebuttal to Arguments Against Woman Suffrage

1. "A woman who takes proper care of her household has no time to know anything about politics." Why not say, "A man who properly supports his household has no time to know anything about politics"?

2. "The polls are not decent places for women at present." Then she is certainly needed there to make them decent.

3. "I should not wish to hear my wife speak in town meeting." I should think not, unless she spoke more to the point than the average of men.

4. "Politics are necessarily corrupting." Then why not advise good men, as well as good women, to quit voting?

5. "Women are entirely distinct from men, altogether unlike, quite a different order of beings." Indeed? Then how can men represent them, make laws for them, administer their rights, judge them in court, spend their tax-money?

6. "Women, after all, are silly creatures." No doubt they are, often enough. God Almighty made some of them foolish, to match the men. But it is the theory of democracy that every man has a right to express his own folly at the ballot-box, and in time, perhaps, learn more sense by so doing. Why not every woman, too?

—From a pamphlet published by suffragists in 1865.

It is contempt, not reverence, that has kept men from allowing women to be free, and it is self-contempt that has kept women from daring to desire freedom.... The less women want their freedom, the more they need it.

—From a letter to the editor by suffragist pioneer Elizabeth Lisle Saxon of Memphis, president of the Tennessee division of National Woman Suffrage Association, 1885.

It would be better for all concerned if more women discussed "domestic economy" and left "political economy" to the fellows who wear breeches, and don't wear bustles.

—Editorial in Memphis Daily Avalanche, *October 10, 1888.*

We have a few women suffragists in the South, but the blessed creatures do not mean it.... The idea of attending ward meetings will never be a pleasing subject of contemplation to the Southern woman.

—The Commercial Appeal, *Memphis, April 26, 1903.*

American Woman and Her Political Peers. Center: Frances Willard, National president, WCTU. Clockwise from upper left: Idiot, Convict, Insane, Indian.

Since I discovered I possessed a thinker, I have preferred to be recognized as a citizen, instead of being classed with the "unpardoned" criminals, lunatics and idiots. The highest law says, "Taxation without representation is tyranny," and this was the outgrowth of that little tea party many years ago. So I ask, are the daughters of men made of different material from the sons of women?

—Bettie M. Donelson, longtime suffrage leader in Nashville and president of Davidson County Women's Christian Temperance Union, quoted in the Nashville Tennessean, *January 30, 1910.*

We, The Undersigned Women of Tennessee, Do and Should Want The Ballot Because:

1. Being twenty-one years old, we object to being classed with minors.

2. Born in America and loyal to her institutions, we protest against being made perpetual aliens.

3. Costing the treasuries of our counties nothing, we protest against acknowledging the male pauper as our political superior.

4. Being obedient to the law, we protest against the statute which classes us with the convict and makes the pardoned criminal our political superior.

5. Being sane, we object to being classed with the lunatics.

6. Possessing an average amount of intelligence, we protest against legal classification with the idiot.

7. We taxpayers claim the right to representation.

8. We married women want to own our clothes.

9. We married breadwinners want to own our earnings.

10. We mothers want an equal partnership in our children.

—Petition circulated by Lide Meriwether, president of the newly-organized Memphis Equal Suffrage League, and signed by more than 500 Tennessee women, 1895.

We have a vision of a time when a woman's home will be the whole wide world, her children all those whose feet are bare, and her sisters all who need a helping hand; a vision of a new knighthood, a new chivalry, when men will not only fight for women but for the rights of women.

—Anne Dallas Dudley of Nashville, a vice president of the National American Woman Suffrage Association, in a speech made in 1916.

… There is no doubt that one of the main causes of this sinister feminism of which we read so much and see quite enough, is what would appear to be a growing weakness on the part of the manhood of the Nation. The very fact that women are so often clamoring to take all power and authority into their hands is certainly no compliment to the manhood of the Nation…. After all, women, the wife and the children, expect a father to have and to exercise the rightful authority due to his position. But if he abdicates that position…well, no one can be surprised if, little by little, women learn to do without the authority of man and to usurp a great deal of it themselves. That leads to a false feminism which certainly, unless it is curbed in time, will have disastrous results for humanity, because it is unnatural….

—Bishop O'Connell of Boston, in an address on the mission for men, reprinted in the New York World, *March 9, 1920, and circulated by the Antis during ratification struggle in Nashville in August, 1920.*

SECOND SECTION—12 PAGES   NEW YORK, SUNDAY, MAY 4, 1913   PRICE FIVE CENTS.

TEN THOUSAND WOMEN MARCH FOR SUFFRAGE CAUSE IN FIFTH AVENUE
WITH BANNERS FLYING, GAY IN COLORS, SINGING THEIR BATTLE HYMN

Some Signs Carried In Early Suffrage Parades

WOMEN BRING ALL VOTERS INTO THE WORLD.
LET WOMEN VOTE!

HOW LONG MUST WOMEN WAIT FOR JUSTICE?

NO NATION CAN RISE ABOVE THE LEVEL
OF ITS WOMANHOOD

ARE POLITICS DIRTY?
THEN CALL IN THE CLEANING WOMAN

You say we should not mingle with these horrid men in voting booths, but these are the same horrid men we live with the rest of the year.

—*Dr. Anna Howard Shaw, physician, ordained Methodist minister, and president of National American Woman Suffrage Association, 1905-1914.*

In taking the ballot, we women will only be selling our birthright…tearing down the Chinese wall of reverence our fathers built around our mothers, making of them queens and rulers supreme in the home where the influence of the wife and mother can be so great as to control every voter in the household. If woman sends forth well-trained manly sons whose love and respect for "Mother" will make them vote thinkingly and judiciously, she need not step down from her throne to wear the cap and bells of the fool.

— *Mrs. Edward W. Foster, past president of Nashville United Daughters of the Confederacy, Chapter No. 1, quoted in* Nashville Tennessean, *January 30, 1920.*

Why We Don't Want Men To Vote

1. Because man's place is in the army.
2. Because no really manly man wants to settle any question otherwise than by fighting about it.
3. Because if men should adopt peaceable methods women will no longer look up to them.
4. Because men will lose their charm if they step out of their natural sphere and interest themselves in other matters than feats of arms, uniforms and drums.
5. Because men are too emotional to vote. Their conduct at baseball games and political conventions shows this, while their innate tendency to appeal to force renders them unfit for government.

—*Nationally prominent suffragist and poet, Alice Duer Miller, 1915.*

The review in Monday's *Tennessean* of Rev. T. H. Harrison's sermon called "Sin in High Places Woman Suffrage" impels me to make public the opinion of a suffragist…. In begging that the woman not be given the ballot, he puts himself in the class with the men of a century and a half ago who felt that education for women would ruin them as homemakers and mothers and "unlock the gates of Hell." The women have survived education. They are today, thank God, better mothers and citizens than ever before.

—*From a letter to the editor by Caroline Kimbrough of Nashville, treasurer of the Tennessee Equal Suffrage Association, 1915.*

From a cartoon by "Ding"

It is far better for society and for woman herself that woman have her privileges rather than her supposed rights.

—A member of the Board of Trustees of Vanderbilt University, in a letter to the editor, Nashville Tennessean, *on August 11, 1920.*

Like most Southern women, I was born and bred in the briar patch of politics. From childhood, we women of the South breathe an atmosphere of political interest…. No shirkers or slackers among the suffragists of Tennessee! When we asked 100 women to the Capitol, 200 came, then more and more….

—Fanny Moran Ezzell of Newsom Station, district chairman, Tennessee Equal Suffrage Association, Inc., in 1914, describing Tennessee's persevering suffragists — herself included.

Insofar as women are like men, they ought to have the same rights; insofar as they are different, they must represent themselves.

—Harriet Burton Laidlaw, national auditor for NAWSA, from a speech, "Twenty-five Answers to Antis," delivered March 11, 1912.

I favor the enfranchisement of women, both by our state and nation, not only as an act of simple justice to our women but because I am firmly convinced that it will result in better laws, better officials, better government, marked improvement in social and civic conditions, and the advancement of a higher type of civilization.

—Guston T. Fitzhugh, Memphis attorney who drafted legislation granting women the vote which was introduced (and defeated) in 1917 in the Tennessee legislature, quoted in Nashville Tennessean, *Feb. 25, 1917.*

A vote for Federal Suffrage is a vote for Organized Female Nagging forever.

—From an anti-suffrage leaflet circulated in 1920.

Our fathers and our brothers love us, our husbands are our choice, and our sons are what we make them. We are content that they represent us in the cornfield, on the battlefield, and at the ballot box, as we represent them in the school room, at the fireside, and at the cradle.

—A petition circulated among Tennessee women by Antis in 1920.

Slowly but surely suffrage is coming. There are men who are generous and broad-minded enough not to be deceived by the sentimentality of a threadbare chivalry, who see that the ballot given to women will benefit her and the community. After all, it is simply a matter of justice. The woman who thinks it will injure her womanliness to vote can resort to the remedy of staying away from the polls.

—Mrs. Alex Caldwell, Chairman of Civics, Nashville Housekeepers Club, quoted in Nashville Tennessean, *January 30, 1920.*

We are determined to prevent women from descending to the political level of men, which, if accomplished, will cheapen women and draw them into the mire of politics. The Tennessee legislators should have the moral courage to refuse to subordinate womanhood to political expediency.

—Charlotte Rowe, Field Secretary for National Association Opposed to Woman Suffrage, as quoted in The Chattanooga Times, *July, 1920.*

Let the women pray and the men vote.

— Malcolm R. Patterson, Governor of Tennessee, 1908.

Representative Southern women resent the very word "emancipation." They were born queens of homes, be it a mansion or a cabin.

—Josephine Pearson, Tennessee President of the Southern Women's Rejection League, as quoted in various newspapers during 1920 ratification struggle, along with her references to suffrage supporters as "strong-minded women and weak-minded men" or, on other occasions, as "long-haired men and short-haired women."

I believe in woman suffrage, whether all women vote or no women vote, whether all women vote right or all women vote wrong, whether women will love their husbands after they vote or forsake them, whether they will neglect their children or never have any children.

—Dr. Anna Howard Shaw, past president of National American Woman Suffrage Association. This statement, quoted in The Dark and Dangerous Side of Woman Suffrage, *a pamphlet circulated by the Antis in Nashville in 1920, omits Dr. Shaw's main point: "As a matter of principle, no nation calling itself a democracy can disenfranchise one-half its citizens."*

The Battle of Nashville in 1864 was a five-o'clock tea in comparison to this one.

—A participant in the ratification battle in Nashville in 1920.

Warnings from California for the South: Southern men should refuse to heed the fatal song of "the suffrage sirens".... There is no lack of testimony that the wrong-minded, the women of low character, do vote.... The day after a California election, the *San Francisco Examiner* stated: "Political bosses had several automobiles busy all day long hauling Barbary Coast dance hall girls and the inmates of houses on Commercial Street to the different booths, and always the women were supplied with a marked sample ballot."

—Josephine Pearson, Tennessee President, Southern Women's Rejection League, in a letter to the editor, Nashville Banner, August 8, 1920.

Woman suffrage would carry us back to the worst kind of savagery; the home would become a memory. Tennessee legislators should kill this thing on the first ballot.

—A prominent attorney from Camden, Tennessee, in a letter to the editor, Nashville Tennessean, *on August 7, 1920.*

We feel that if you men are good enough to work for us, die for us, live for us, you are good enough to vote for us. To give woman the ballot will be the beginning of socialism in America.

—Charlotte Rowe, Field Secretary for National Association Opposed to Woman Suffrage, addressing joint committee hearing of Tennessee General Assembly, August 12, 1920.

The bitterest, bare-fisted, name-calling, back-biting session in the state's history.

—Nashville newspaperman Joe Hatcher, remembering the ratification battle in the Tennessee legislature in 1920.

Never in the history of politics has there been such a nefarious lobby as labored to block the ratification in Nashville. In the short time I spent in the capital I was more maligned, more lied about, than in the thirty previous years I worked for suffrage. I was flooded with anonymous letters, vulgar, ignorant, insane. Strange men and groups of men sprang up, men we had never met before in the battle.... They appropriated our telegrams, tapped our telephones, listened outside our windows. They attacked our private and public lives. I had heard of the "invisible government." Well, I have seen it at work, and I have seen it sent into oblivion.

—Carrie Chapman Catt, in a statement issued from National American Woman Suffrage Association headquarters, upon her return to New York following Tennessee's ratification in August, 1920.

Elizabeth Avery Meriwether

Pioneers, O Pioneers!

All during the last two decades of the Nineteenth Century and throughout the first two decades of the Twentieth, a few dedicated Tennessee women were campaigning relentlessly for the cause of woman suffrage. Remembered here are the stories of some of these trailblazers whose perseverance in bringing the message of Votes for Women to the people of their state paved the way for the suffragists' victory in Nashville in 1920.

Lide Smith Meriwether

The Crusading Sisters-In-Law

At a national suffragists' convention in 1879, the two delegates from Memphis were Elizabeth Avery Meriwether, the first woman in Tennessee to champion voting privileges for women, and her ever-supportive husband Minor L. Meriwether, an attorney. A source of great pride to Elizabeth was the fact that among their earliest converts to the suffragist cause had been Minor's brother Niles, the Memphis city engineer, and his wife, Lide Smith Meriwether. By 1880, the two Meriwether families lived in a single home on Peabody Avenue while Elizabeth and Lide went forth together to work for temperance and women's rights.

Elizabeth Avery Meriwether had started advocating full equality for women long before such an idea was acceptable. Before their wedding on January 1, 1850, she and Minor had signed a marriage contract agreeing to share and invest equally. Soon Elizabeth could be seen driving around Memphis collecting rents, maintaining property, banking her own money — in every way an accomplished businesswoman. (In another unusual demonstration of the Meriwethers' moral convictions and belief in justice, they had agreed shortly before their wedding that Minor Meriwether would free all the slaves inherited from his parents, and pay for their voyages to the African state of Liberia to join other freed American slaves.)

In 1872, when Elizabeth Meriwether read that Susan B. Anthony attempting to vote in Rochester, New York, was arrested, tried and fined, she announced that she intended to vote in Memphis at the next election. "If I am arrested for that crime," she said, "I shall be glad to share Miss Anthony's cell." But when Elizabeth walked into the Fifth Ward polling place, she was handed a ballot, filled it out, and dropped it in the ballot box. Afterward she was never certain why she was not opposed, but concluded the poll workers were overawed by her status as "Southern Aristocracy."

That same year, she founded her own newspaper, *The Tablet*, using every issue to promote votes for women. She also used her own money to rent The Memphis Theater, largest in town, and on May 5, 1876, flouting all rules of "ladylike" decorum, delivered a public address on women's rights. More than 500 women attended. Next day, *The Memphis Appeal* reported that "Mrs. Meriwether has proven a worthy advocate of her sex. She was interrupted frequently with bursts of applause." Not long after that, she led a delegation of women appearing before the Memphis School Board to demand that, in the name of justice, women and men teachers be paid the same salaries. They were unsuccessful, but the seeds of the idea that women should have equal economic opportunities had been planted in the city.

During the 1880s, Elizabeth Avery Meriwether's scope widened to cover most of the nation. She traveled with Susan B. Anthony from Connecticut to Texas, advocating votes for women in public speeches with telling impact. For this, she was denounced variously as "that heathen woman with infidel ways," "a lewd woman of the streets," and "a towering virago" — this last despite her petite stature of five feet, two inches. In 1883, Elizabeth and Minor Meriwether and their children moved to St. Louis, driven from Memphis by the threat of a yellow fever epidemic. She continued her campaigning and pleading the cause before three national presidential nominating conventions.

Meanwhile, in Tennessee, her sister-in-law had assumed the leadership role in the suffrage crusade, becoming an activist of the first rank. Originally the editor of a literary journal for "genteel females," Lide Smith Meriwether had championed the "rescue of fallen women" by taking prostitutes into her home and training them for other occupations.

A vigorous advocate for the temperance cause, her efforts as a member of the Women's Christian Temperance Union to organize Southern black women on behalf of temperance had resulted in the formation of black WCTU groups in several Tennessee communities. Lide and other progressive women found the temperance issue provided a wedge by which they could promote the idea of suffrage without seeming to engage in inappropriate behavior. Defending home and family seemed to require such public action.

In 1886, the National Woman Suffrage Association employed Lide to lecture and organize groups in the state of Tennessee. She mounted an intensive campaign and in two weeks visited most sizable towns in Tennessee and helped organize fledgling Equal Rights clubs in Nashville, Knoxville, Jackson, Greeneville, and Murfreesboro.

When Lide left for Nashville to attend a Prohibition Party national convention in 1888, her husband Niles urged her to win a woman suffrage plank in the party's platform. "We can't win equal wages for equal work, or any other just legislation for women," he said, "until women themselves can legislate." Back in Memphis, it was Lide and her group who influenced J. M. Keating, editor of *The Memphis Appeal*, to publish its first pro-suffrage editorial on July 29, 1888, proclaiming that "intelligent people realize the injustice of withholding the ballot from women."

On May 21, 1889, a Woman Suffrage League was organized in Memphis (the first group in Tennessee to adopt so forthright a name), and Lide Meriwether was elected president. Later, in the 1890s, she was elected to several terms as president of the Tennessee Equal Suffrage Association and became their "Honorary President for Life" in 1900. Her specialty was petitions — she gathered thousands of signatures on scores of petitions.

Lide Meriwether, representing Tennessee, joined Iowa's Carrie Chapman Catt and women from 26 other states in Washington in 1892 to testify before a U.S. House of Representatives committee hearing on woman suffrage. A friend once said of Lide that "her wit could have convulsed a tombstone," and she evidently offered her testimony with her usual engaging liveliness. According to observers, hers were the only remarks to which committee members, mostly Southerners, seemed to pay much heed.

Though they never stopped working and writing, and kept pleading all of their days for women's enfranchisement, neither Lide Smith Meriwether, who died in 1913 at the age of 84, nor Elizabeth Avery Meriwether, who was 92 when she died in 1917, lived to see their dreams fulfilled. But the great victory won by a later generation of suffragists in Nashville in 1920 was built, in no small part, on a strong foundation created by the ground-breaking efforts of Tennessee's crusading Meriwether sisters-in-law.

—Adapted from the research and writings of Elinor B. Bridges in Tennessee Women, Past and Present *and* The Wheel, *a newsletter published in the 1970s by Women's Resource Center of Memphis, Inc.*

McClung Historical Collection, Knoxville

Lizzie Crozier French

Peerless Pathfinder, Fearless Feminist, Superb Suffragist

The subjects of religion and politics, often considered unladylike for discussion, did not deter Lizzie Crozier French, as she demonstrated in a speech given in February, 1895, before a new Unitarian society in the small city of Knoxville, Tennessee. Today, Mrs. French is generally recognized as the most remarkable woman in the history of Knoxville.

It was not due to any lack of energy or devotion on her part that the tiny, nonconformist congregation was unable, at that time, to survive more than a year or two. As a local historian wrote, "The city was not ready for Unitarian doctrine." However, Lizzie Crozier French was more successful in her other innovative organizational attempts in the fields of education, community affairs, and woman suffrage.

She was born in 1851 into one of Knoxville's most prominent families, the daughter of John H. Crozier, a lawyer and U.S. Congressman before the Civil War, who was known as a brilliant orator and conversationalist. When Lizzie, at age 21, married W. B. French, also a member of a blueblood Knoxville family, she seemed destined for the life of a society matron. Instead, when her husband died eighteen months later, she became a single parent, left alone to rear and educate their infant son.

Lizzie bore her grief with stoicism, but her desire for an active life of service was too great for her to allow herself to be confined to her home by widowhood. Fortunately, her excellent education gave her the necessary background to found a local Female Institute in 1885. Under her direction for the next five years, the school challenged traditional educational practices for young girls, encouraging them to develop their bodies as well as their minds, and to study "elocution" in order to be effective speakers.

Meanwhile, she continued to educate herself and other women. In the 1880s, the cause of women's rights was considered so subversive, particularly in the South, that the women's groups formed to discuss such issues posed as literary societies or disguised their purpose with innocuous-sounding names. (A study group in New Orleans, for example, called itself the New Era Club — the E-R-A standing for Equal Rights Association.) Lizzie founded her own "literary society," the Ossoli Circle, in Knoxville in 1885. It was the first women's club in Tennessee and is still active today. The group's esoteric name was chosen to honor New England's Margaret Fuller, the brilliant, free-thinking, nineteenth-century Transcendentalist whose "literary conversations" had inspired the whole idea of women's clubs and whose marriage to an Italian count had made her the Countess Ossoli. Since some of the founders feared their husbands or fathers would oppose their joining a "club," they called themselves a "circle" — church circles for ladies being highly approved of by Southern society.

But Lizzie French was not the kind of person to be satisfied by a mere discussion group. In 1890, she founded and was the first president of the Woman's Educational and Industrial Union, created to promote social measures to assist working-class women and women offenders. In its first year, the Union persuaded the city of Knoxville to appoint a police matron to supervise female prisoners. Mrs. French, having made the suggestion, was appointed temporarily, thus becoming the first police matron in the South.

While still a young woman, Lizzie had become convinced that women should have the right to vote. However, she realized that her conservative community was no more ready to listen to radical suffrage arguments than to unorthodox religious doctrines. It was not until 1910 that she became a founder and the first president of the Knoxville Equal Suffrage League.

At last she had found a cause that used all her abilities as a speaker, writer, and organizer, not just in Knoxville, but all over the state. Readers of local newspapers became accustomed to seeing her "open letters," defending suffrage and attacking arguments of its opponents. The pastor of Knoxville's First Baptist Church had declared, "God shows clearly man should work for, plan for, think for woman." In a letter to the local newspaper, she replied, "Drudgery and all tasks that carry no pleasure, riches, power, nor glory have always been freely allowed to women as carrying out God's intentions as to the work proper to her sex." To arguments that only those who can back their vote with arms (meaning military service) should vote, Mrs. French responded, "Woman has no greater claim to the rights of the ballot than that she is a producer, not a destroyer, of life." As for those who claimed that women should be satisfied with the "security and protection" afforded them by men, Lizzie stated, "Nobody can revere and respect people who have no power. Reverence and respect are given to those who have power, and by power I do not mean force, but I mean there must be some way to compel."

Members of the Tennessee Bar Association must have been startled when Lizzie Crozier French arose at their state meeting in Knoxville in 1912 to speak on state laws affecting women. Tennessee women, she said, are made "non-persons" upon marriage, by laws requiring wives to turn over their property, their wages, even rights to guardianship of their children to their husbands. "A prominent lawyer of our city," she reported, "has put it this way: 'The laws of Tennessee declare husband and wife are one and that one is the husband.'" In her final salvo she declared that Tennessee could not become a progressive state by simply altering one law concerning women, but must "take the whole bunch and burn them up and begin over again."

Lizzie lived to see Tennessee become the final state to ratify the 19th Amendment in August, 1920. She proudly wrote "suffragist" as her occupation on the application form when she cast her first ballot in November of that year. In 1923, when no other qualified woman was prepared to make the race for a seat on the Knoxville city council, she decided to run as an independent candidate. This 72-year-old woman carried on an active campaign, traveling all over the city in stifling summer heat. Though she did not win, her candidacy broke ground for other women to run, and to win, in later elections.

Lizzie Crozier French's death came suddenly in May, 1926, while she was in Washington to lobby for the rights of working women. Back in her native city, hundreds of people viewed her body as it lay in state and attended her funeral service, where her achievements received this tribute from one of her close associates: "She believed in women and in their power to develop individually and collectively. The woman's movement has not lost her. She lives in the organization she helped to build, in the thought she helped to direct, in the faith and purpose she inspired."

— Adapted from research and articles written by Jean K. Lacey.

Mrs. Dudley with her children: Trevania, left, and Guilford, Jr.

The Lady Who Made Suffrage Fashionable

Anne Dallas Dudley was beautiful, articulate, and privileged; a wife and the mother of two children, she gave more than ten years of her life to the campaign for woman suffrage. How and why did a society matron become a political activist and an outspoken suffragist? Dudley's career, particularly in the crucial years between 1911 and 1920, gives us some clues and tells us much about the history of the women's movement. For generations, feminists had been a tiny unheard and unheeded minority, and nowhere were they more isolated than in the South. Nevertheless, Anne Dudley spoke for and to the women of her time and helped make possible the freedoms women enjoy in our time.

Her father, Trevanion B. Dallas, was one of the bustling entrepreneurs of the New South. A newcomer to Nashville in 1869, he brought both social and financial assets with him. His father was Commodore Alexander J. Dallas, once the commander of the U.S. Pacific squadron; his uncle, George Mifflin Dallas, had been Vice President in Polk's administration. The family was committed to the Union, but Trevanion broke ranks and served with the Confederate army, which undoubtedly made him more welcome in postwar Nashville. He joined a leading mercantile firm and began to build and buy cotton mills in Nashville and later in Huntsville, Alabama.

Anne Dallas was brought up as a belle of the New South. She was educated at Nashville's fashionable Ward Seminary. After her social debut, she was chosen the first president of Nashville's exclusive Cotillion Club and her gowns, her parties, and her beaus were material for the gossip columns. In 1902, she married widower Guilford Dudley, a banker and insurance broker, and together they occupied a prominent place in Nashville "society." Proper notions of a woman's circumscribed role had been part of her implicit, unspoken education. She reported at one point that of course she had once been an "anti" — *i.e.*, an anti-suffragist. "But reading and studying showed me that it was the only way that women could come into their own…. Not only does the world need women's votes, but woman needs the ballot for her own development." In a way, this idea, too, was an outgrowth of her Southern heritage.

The terrible demands of the Civil War and the upheaval of the postwar period had added new virtues such as strength and endurance to those that Southern women had traditionally been expected to embody. Courage, independence, and self-reliance had been absolutely essential for wartime survival. And in the new and revitalized towns and cities of the 1880s and 1890s, middle- and upper-class women built a very substantial women's culture. Groups that met initially for self-improvement, for discussions of books and music and drama, began to talk also about the problems of urban living; to concern themselves with the schooling of children, the purity of milk and water, and the working conditions of women not as comfortable as themselves. Inevitably, as they enlarged the sphere of women's concern, they came up against the need for political power to enact laws, appropriate money, and initiate programs. They needed the VOTE!

But just getting a hearing for the idea of women voting was a major problem. Almost all men and a great majority of women were initially horrified by the picture of women actually participating in the political process, casting a ballot in a public polling place, choosing candidates who might possibly differ from those chosen by their husbands and fathers. Changing public opinion became the immediate task of suffragists. And so Anne Dudley's work was mapped out.

Maria Daviess, a close friend, has left a delightful picture of herself and Anne as they discovered writers whose insights on the need for emancipation of women inspired them to act. She remembered them, their hands resting on the books by two leading proponents of women's rights, the English philosopher John Stuart Mill and the South African novelist Olive Schreiner, and vowing to "do something." Another Nashville friend, Ida Clyde Clark, brought word from the president of the National American Woman Suffrage Association: "Organize!"

In September of 1911, these three gathered together a handful of other Nashville women to form the Nashville Equal Suffrage League, with Anne Dudley as president. They linked up with a network of committed women throughout Tennessee, including the indomitable Lizzie Crozier French, who had been founding and nurturing women's circles, societies, and associations in Knoxville since 1885; Sarah Barnwell Elliott of Sewanee, a well-known novelist soon to head the Tennessee suffrage forces; and the established and ever-persevering suffrage crusaders of Memphis.

These newly-activated suffragists spoke, wrote, argued, and organized. They instituted giant May Day parades from downtown Nashville to Centennial Park, usually led by Anne Dallas Dudley and her children. Making use of their social connections, they moved from town to town like itinerant preachers, finding sponsors (often the local WCTU chapter), calling women's groups together, persuading editors to carry their appeals, creating a sense of excitement that would rally a crowd, and always leaving behind an equal suffrage society that could consolidate support for the vote. Between 1912 and 1919, they helped found suffrage organizations in 78 towns in Tennessee.

And always, Anne Dudley brought the movement her particular presence: eloquent, elegant, sure of her ground. This helped her deal with the ugly names, the catcalls and heckling she met during the campaign. She was enthusiastic, full of the fun of the movement as well as its purpose. When

Anne arrived for a weekend in Memphis that was to include a suffrage parade, her chauffeur unloaded a steamer trunk full of hats, dresses, and scarves to make the weekend a fashionable success.

But Anne Dudley had much more to offer than her presence. In a period when women who made speeches were considered dangerous to the morality and stability of the country, she insisted on being heard. If women were not allowed to speak in halls and assemblies, they must take to the streets. Open-air speeches became one of the shocking new tactics of the suffragists. And Anne, whether she was speaking to groups gathered on the square of a county seat or to the Tennessee House of Representatives, addressed the issues over and over again with patience, humor, and verve. She ridiculed the notion that women would be corrupted by becoming involved with politics: women read the papers, they knew of the corruption, their participation would cleanse the political arena. Against those who argued that politics would distract women from their duties in their homes, she pointed out with some sharpness that more women might be distracted by bridge parties than by voting and that "no woman can intelligently supervise her home without the ballot."

She also rejected the notion that upper-class Southern women were too timid or too genteel to approach the ballot box. Addressing a woman's club in Nashville, she put the question directly: "Do you think a lady would hesitate to walk up to the ballot box to vote for some measure to protect her own home and children, or for the protection of some little laborer or other less fortunate woman? Do you think she would hesitate even if her cook should be standing in front of her?"

By 1915, Anne Dallas Dudley's political acumen was widely recognized. She was elected president of the Tennessee Equal Suffrage Association and helped introduce a suffrage amendment to the state constitution. It failed, so she pushed an alternative measure which would give women the right to vote in presidential and municipal elections. When the state Senate refused to enact this alternative, she proclaimed, "We are not cry-babies," and reassembled her workers. In fact, presidential and municipal suffrage did win in the state legislature in 1919, but by this time Anne was working in the movement at the national level, having been elected a vice president of NAWSA in 1917 and given charge of their Congressional

Steering Committee, which was engaged in a fierce push to enact a federal suffrage amendment.

Anne Dallas Dudley was especially important on the national level as a representative of the South, the region most reluctant to enact woman suffrage. She rejected out of hand the states' rights argument against a federal amendment, noting its arbitrary use by suffrage opponents. As for Southern anti-suffragists' "hysterical anxieties" that enfranchisement of women would bring on Negro domination of the region, she countered their virulently racist rhetoric by sometimes resorting to a pro-suffrage argument, itself patently racist, which was then in vogue — *i.e.*, that there were more white women than black women. But there was more realism than cynicism in her observation that restrictions on black male voters then current in the South would apply equally to black women.

More revealing to those studying the movement today, however, was the way in which she and other white suffragists crossed racial barricades their contemporaries accepted without question and encouraged black women to join them, despite the taboos of segregation. In Nashville, for example, once municipal suffrage was won, an all-out effort was made by black and white suffrage leaders to register black women. And the registration and voting record of these black women proved, as one of Anne Dudley's co-workers in Nashville proudly pointed out, that "a little patience, trust, vision, and the universal ties of motherhood and sisterhood could overcome the prejudice against them as voters."

Anne Dallas Dudley's decade of commitment to the cause of suffrage came to a spectacular climax when the fate of the 19th Amendment to the federal constitution came to rest on the 36th and decisive vote for ratification by the Tennessee state legislature assembled in her own Nashville. During the course of the long battle, she had developed her own talent and power and left far behind the old idea of woman's proper circumscribed sphere. In the larger view, she had been part of an essential battle to widen the meaning of American democracy.

— *Adapted from "Anne Dallas Dudley, 1876-1955" by Anita Shafer Goodstein,* Franklin County Historical Review, *Vol. XXIII, No. 1, 1992.*

Nashville Tennessean

Sue Shelton White

A Tribute To Miss Sue, The Practical Idealist

There is one word that to her many friends always best described Sue Shelton White. The word is "unwavering." Even in the last weeks before her far too early death on May 6, 1943, those who saw her found stimulus in her persistent courage and humor — always a part of her clear thinking — which never faltered. Appreciation of the meaning of a person's life often waits for death, perhaps because, as in the case of Sue White, it is only when a life ends that a full picture of its place in the pattern of the future can be seen.

"Miss Sue" — for that is how she always was known throughout her own state of Tennessee and in her own Democratic Party — was typical of that middle generation of feminists, who took over directly from the hands of the early pioneers the struggle for the equality of women and advanced it with a vision of the day of final victory. Through her own career, she justified women's claims to full public responsibility and helped solidify positions gained in earlier years.

In Jackson, Tennessee, in 1907, when she became one of the first women court reporters in her state, Sue braved prejudice and criticism to help open a profession that in itself broke down barriers in the legal field. She was one of the organizers of the Jackson Equal Suffrage League in 1911 and went on to further strengthen the voice and influence of women in public affairs by taking an active part in Business and Professional Women's Clubs, Federated Women's Clubs, and Parent-Teacher Associations, and by steadily making her way in the Democratic Party. The National Woman's Party enlisted her help in its suffrage campaign in Tennessee in 1917, first as state secretary and later as state chairman. Her work and her position in that party proved of crucial importance when the 19th Amendment came before the states; it was the ratification by Tennessee which, at the last moment, when there was no hope of action by any other legislature, enabled women to vote in the 1920 presidential election. Political leaders, both nationally and in her home state of Tennessee, gave a major share of credit for this historic success to the invaluable contributions made by Miss Sue.

Earlier, Sue White had played a highly courageous and important part in the battle for suffrage in Washington, D.C., by repeatedly picketing the White House. One of the most dramatic moments in the Washington demonstrations had come when Miss Sue, ardent Democrat and staunch party worker, burned in front of the White House the words of an unfulfilled pledge of President Wilson to extend voting rights to women. Defending her action, she said, "We are in a war for democracy. To rout a foe in a fight for principle is one thing. To save the principle is the main thing." For this act, she served a sentence of five days in the workhouse. And in February and March of 1919, when the suffragists' "Prison Special" train toured the country, Sue White was on board wearing her prison garb.

Sue's complete sincerity and political acumen

Sue Shelton White

were so clearly recognized that her attacks on the Democratic administration advanced her, if anything, in the Party's councils. In 1920, after the ratification victory, she returned to Washington as secretary to U.S. Senator Kenneth McKellar of Tennessee. While serving in that capacity, she studied law at the Washington College of Law and was admitted to the bar in 1923. Still a trailblazer, she returned to Tennessee in 1926 to establish a law practice in Jackson — becoming the city's first female attorney. She remained active in the state Democratic Party and, four years later, was back in Washington as executive secretary of the women's division of the Democratic National Committee. After Franklin D. Roosevelt's election, she became assistant to the chairman of the Consumers Advisory Board of the National Recovery Administration. In 1936, she became the first attorney for the Social Security Board and was named, in 1938, the principal attorney and assistant to the general counsel of the Federal Security Agency.

Miss Sue once defined her fundamental attitude toward the struggle for women's rights during a memorable speech in her hometown in Tennessee. Addressing members of the Jackson Business and Professional Women's Club after her election as their president in 1929, she said:

> We must remember the past, hold fast to the present, and build for the future. If you stand in your accepted place today, it is because some woman had to fight yesterday. We should be ashamed to stand on ground won by women in the past without making an effort to honor them by winning a higher and wider field for the future. It is a debt we owe.

Remembering Sue Shelton White today, we can see that this creed was expressed even more eloquently by her life itself.

—Adapted from a tribute to Sue Shelton White by Florence Brewer Boeckel, in an obituary published in the National Woman's Party publication, Equal Rights, *July-August, 1943.*

THE MAKING OF SUFFRAGETTE ORATORS

With the Growth of the Feminist Movement Mrs. Grace Gunn's Public Speaking Club Has Instilled Eloquence and Magnetism Into Scores of Fair Advocates of the Ballot.

The Stump Speaker—
A Common but Wrong Position.

A Dignified Gesture of Disapproval.

Never Scold Your Audience.

Forcible but Not Graceful.

An Earnest Appeal—Correct Position of Feet.

Driving It Home.

Overcoming Their Diffidence.

The Art of Gesticulation.

Success of Miss Hill.

All Encouraged to Speak.

Suffragette Leaders in a Model Republic of Indians

Girl Members of the Government. Left to Right—Nan Saunooke, Clara Mellor, Cora Buarte, Anna Houser and Agnes Ware.

School Supreme Court. Left to Right—William Garlow, Nan Saunooke, Cora Buarte and Edson Mt. Pleasant.

The Debate Heats Up: Suffs and Antis

Beginning around 1900, the question of woman suffrage was debated nationally and locally in hundreds of publications. Here, condensed from articles in national magazines, are the pro-suffrage arguments made by two well-known women, one a Tennessean, the other not. Following their testimony, abridged versions of the locally-published writings of two prominent Tennessee Antis of the day, both men, present counter-arguments which confront the issue with a Southern accent.

Ladies Home Journal

Jane Addams

In 1910, Ladies Home Journal *published the comments of social worker Jane Addams, founder of Chicago's famous Hull House, on the much-discussed issue of granting the municipal ballot to women, which was regarded by many as a first step toward full enfranchisement of women nationwide. Jane Addams' plea for votes for women is based on her experience doing settlement house work with residents of Chicago's tenements. The ballot, she believed, would enable all women not only to better preserve the safety of their homes and the well-being of their families, but also to help improve the quality of civic life.*

Why Women Should Vote
by Jane Addams

For many generations it has been believed that woman's place is within the walls of her home, and it is indeed impossible to imagine the time when her duty there shall be ended, or to forecast any social change which shall release her from that paramount obligation.... [Yet] many women today are failing to discharge their duties to their own households properly, simply because they do not perceive that, as society grows more complicated, it is necessary that woman shall extend her sense of responsibility to many things outside of her own home if she would continue to preserve the home in its entirety….

A woman's simplest duty, one would say, is to keep her house clean and wholesome and to feed her children properly. Yet if she lives in a tenement house, as so many of my neighbors do, she cannot fulfill these simple obligations by her own efforts because she is utterly dependent upon the city administration for the conditions which render decent living possible. Her basement will not be dry, her stairways will not be fireproof, her house will not be provided with sufficient windows to give light and air, nor will it be equipped with sanitary plumbing, unless the Public Works Department sends inspectors who constantly insist that these elementary decencies be provided….

In a crowded city quarter, if the street is not cleaned by the city authorities no amount of private sweeping will keep the tenement free from grime; if the garbage is not properly collected and destroyed a tenement-house mother may see her children sicken and die of diseases from which she alone is powerless to shield them, although her tenderness and devotion are unbounded. She cannot even secure untainted meat for her household, she cannot provide fresh fruit, unless the meat has been inspected by city officials, and the decayed fruit, which is so often placed upon sale in the tenement districts, has been destroyed in the interest of public health. In short, if woman would keep on her old business of caring for her house and rearing her children, she will have to have some conscience in regard to public affairs lying quite outside her immediate household. The individual conscience and devotion are no longer effective.

Chicago one spring had a spreading contagion of scarlet fever just at the time the school nurses had been discontinued because business men had pronounced them too expensive. If the women who sent their children to the schools had been sufficiently public-spirited and had been provided with an implement through which to express that public spirit they would have insisted that the schools be supplied with nurses in order that their own children might be protected from contagion. In other words, if women would effectively continue their old avocations they must take part in the slow upbuilding of that code of legislation which is alone sufficient to protect the home from the dangers incident to modern life….

Who shall say that women are not concerned in the enactment and enforcement of legislation if they would protect their homes?…. One of the interesting experiences in the Chicago campaign [to enact the municipal franchise for women] was the unexpected enthusiasm of large groups of foreign-born women who took the prospect of the municipal ballot as a simple device — which it is — to aid them in their daily struggle with adverse city conditions. The duty of a woman toward the schools which her children attend is so obvious that it is not necessary to dwell upon it…. But women are also beginning to realize that children need attention outside of school hours….

To turn the administration of our civic affairs wholly over to men may mean that the American city will continue to push forward in its commercial and industrial development, and continue to lag behind in those things which make a city healthful and beautiful. After all, woman's traditional function has been to make her dwelling-place both clean and fair. Is the present dreariness in city life due to a withdrawal of one of the naturally cooperating forces? Women have long taken responsibility for the gentler side of life which softens and blurs some of its harsher conditions. May they not now have a duty to perform in our American cities?….

If woman would fulfill her traditional responsibility to her own children; if she would educate and protect from danger the factory children who must find their recreation on the street; if she would bring the cultural forces to bear upon our materialistic civilization; and if she would do it all with the dignity and directness fitting one who carries on her immemorial duties, then she must bring herself to the use of the ballot — that last best implement for self-government. May we not fairly say that American women need it to preserve the home?

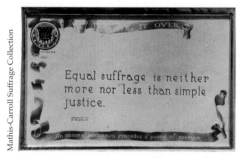

Mary Church Terrell

Memphis-born Mary Church Terrell, who had won national prominence as a founding member of the National Association for the Advancement of Colored People and as the first president of the National Association of Colored Women, had her say on the suffrage question in 1912 in the following article, appearing in the NAACP's magazine, The Crisis. *A longtime critic of any denial of the rights of American citizenship because of race or gender, Mary Church Terrell urged all people of color, both men and women, to support woman suffrage as a matter of simple logic — and justice.*

The Justice of Woman Suffrage
by Mary Church Terrell

It is difficult to believe that any individual in the United States with one drop of African blood in his veins can oppose woman suffrage. It is queer and curious enough to hear an intelligent colored woman argue against granting suffrage to her sex, but for an intelligent colored man to oppose woman suffrage is the most preposterous and ridiculous thing in the world. What could be more absurd than to see one group of human beings who are denied rights which they are trying to secure for themselves working to prevent another group from obtaining the same rights? For the very arguments which are advanced against granting the right of suffrage to women are offered by those who have disfranchised colored men.

If I were a colored man, and were unfortunate enough not to grasp the absurdity of opposing suffrage because of the sex of a human being, I should at least be consistent enough never to raise my voice against those who have disfranchised my brothers and myself on account of race. However, the intelligent colored man who opposes woman suffrage is very rare, indeed. While on a lecture tour recently I frequently discussed woman suffrage with the leading citizens in the communities in which I spoke. It was very gratifying, indeed, to see that in the majority of instances these men stood right on the question of woman suffrage.

Frederick Douglass did many things of which I am proud, but there is nothing he ever did in his long and brilliant career in which I take greater pride than I do in his ardent advocacy of equal political rights for women, and the effective service he rendered the cause of woman suffrage sixty years ago. When the resolution demanding equal political rights for women was introduced in the meeting held at Seneca Falls, N.Y., in 1848, Frederick Douglass was the only man in the convention courageous and broad-minded enough to second the motion. It was largely due to Douglass's masterful arguments and matchless eloquence that the motion was carried, in spite of the opposition of its very distinguished and powerful foes....

To assign reasons in this day and time to prove that it is unjust to withhold from one-half of the human race rights and privileges freely accorded the other half, which is neither more deserving nor more capable of exercising them, seems almost like a reflection upon the intelligence of those to who they are presented. To argue the inalienability and the equality of human rights in the twentieth century in a country whose government was founded upon the eternal principles that all men are created free and equal, that governments get their just powers from the consent of the governed, seems like laying one's self open to the charge of anachronism. For 2,000 years mankind has been breaking down the various barriers which interposed themselves between human beings and their perfect freedom to exercise all the faculties with which they have been divinely endowed. Even in monarchies old fetters, which formerly restricted freedom, dwarfed the intellect and doomed certain individuals to narrow, circumscribed spheres because of the mere accident of birth, are being loosed and broken one by one.

What a reproach it is to a government which owes its very existence to the love of freedom in the human heart that it should deprive any of its citizens of their sacred and cherished right. The founders of this republic called heaven and earth to witness that it should be called a government of the people, for the people and by the people; and yet the elective franchise is withheld from one-half of its citizens, many of who are intelligent, virtuous and cultured, and unstintingly bestowed upon the other half, many of who are illiterate, degraded and vicious, because by an unparalleled exhibition of lexicographical acrobatics the word "people" has been turned and twisted to mean all who were shrewd and wise enough to have themselves born boys instead of girls, and white instead of black.

But why grant women the suffrage when the majority do not want it, the remonstrants sometimes ask with innocent engaging seriousness. Simply because there are many people, men as well as women, who are so constructed as to be unable to ascertain by any process of reason what is the best thing for them to have or to do. Until the path is blazed by the pioneer, even some people who have superior intellects and moral courage dare not forge ahead. On the same principle and for just exactly the same reason that American women would reject suffrage, Chinese women, if they dared to express any opinion at all, would object to having the feet of their baby girls removed from the bandages which stunt their growth. East Indian women would scorn the proffered freedom of their American sisters as unnatural and vulgar and would die rather than have their harems abolished. Slaves sometimes prefer to bear the ills of bondage rather than accept the blessings of freedom, because their poor beclouded brains have been stunted and dwarfed by oppression so long that they cannot comprehend what liberty means and have no desire to enjoy it.

When the author, a prominent physician, recorded his reactions to the convention of the National American Woman Suffrage Association held in Nashville in 1914, he intended it for publication in a local newspaper. Instead, Dr. Lyon published his comments in pamphlet form at his own expense the following year. A great favorite with Tennessee Antis, the pamphlet was distributed widely during the battle for ratification of the 19th Amendment in Nashville in 1920.

Suffragettes And Suffragettism
by A. A. Lyon, A.M., M.D.

I trust no one will construe what is written here as an attack upon the aspiring suffragists, among whom I reckon some of my most delightful acquaintances and valued friends. Nevertheless! Ladies, I sincerely believe that your persistence in this agitation will bring evil in the end, rather than good, whether you win or lose…I am not fighting you, I am only trying to save you from yourselves…. It was in October last that "The National Woman's Rights Association" convened in this city…in the State House, into which my business office directly opens…I necessarily saw and heard much that was going on, and I have often been asked what my impressions were. The leaders were women of unmistakable intellect, forcefulness and culture, yet I could not stifle the feeling that much of their zeal was due to love of the limelight, rather than a heart-felt religious desire to work a great reform in behalf of their downtrodden sisters.

There seemed to be a large contingent of the Connecticut spinster type — prim, nice and exact, thoroughly at home in any presence…. Next, came a rugged brand, strong and aggressive, from the West and Northwest, the region whence sprang this latter-day abomination of split-skirts, breeches, top-boots, cross-saddles and straddle riders. Then followed a host of young women representing the so-called "working girls," chasing after Votes for Women under the impression that when this goal was reached, their monthly wage would equal that of men, but apparently forgetting that the question of wages was a matter purely commercial, and overlooking also their inferiority in physical strength and powers of endurance, and the periodical uncertainty of health that is peculiar to the sex.

Finally, there was a small contingent of typical

Southern women that I will liken to a bevy of white doves — symbolic of peace, gentleness and love — lamely and feebly attempting to follow and to imitate the eagles and other kindred birds in their magnificent aerial sweeps and predatory swoops. They were, of course, highly decorative, but seemingly they were "of it," not "in it," especially when it came to the distribution of the coveted offices. No man holds true womanhood in higher esteem than I do, or…would more strenuously demand that justice and fairness be meted out to them under all circumstances. I am their friend in this contention, but I cannot approve their methods or endorse their modes of procedure….

Woman's influence over man, when exercised in the woman's way, is well nigh irresistible…. In fact, as I see it, woman by indirection rules all christendom, but she has done it in the home and in the true woman's way: as mother, the bearer and trainer of her children; and as wife, the faithful and ever-continuing source of inspiration, comfort and encouragement to her husband. Without the benign and uplifting co-operation of woman in this sinful world, we men, long ago, would have degenerated into semi-barbarism and savagery….

I was led into a reflective train of thought as I looked upon the strong aggregation of strong women, busy as bees, energetic as beavers, persistent as flies. I mentally asked myself the question: Suppose Susan B. Anthony, Lucy Stone and Company had initially organized themselves, *not* into a "Woman's Rights Association," but instead, into a "Woman's Protective Association," with the avowed purpose, systematically to look into the statute books of all the states, and bring to bear their united influence upon the respective legislatures in the woman's way, to purge the codes of the entire nation of everything invasive of the natural rights of woman? Is it not fair to conclude, with the hearty co-operation of all chivalrous and fairminded men, that they would long ago have achieved all their normal rights, and would today be in happy possession of them?

Instead, however, they began with Madam Bloomers, knee skirts and baggy breeches…. From year to year, the clamorous agitation has been carried on. Bolder and still more bold, have these women grown until of late they have stormed the Halls of Congress and directly faced the law-makers, and even the President himself. They thrust out their breasts like pouter pigeons, swish their scanty skirts, stamp the floor with their dainty feet (I reckon some of them are dainty), and with militant bearing exclaim, "We come not to ask you for our rights, but to *demand* them." We hear of sensational street parades in the big cities, and so-called

Supreme Law of Tennessee Prohibits the Ratification

THE Constitution of the State of Tennessee, adopted by the people of Tennessee, March 26, 1870, by a vote of 98,128 to 33,872 (nearly three to one) provides as follows:

Article II—Section 32—Amendments to Constitution of United States. No convention or General Assembly of this State shall act upon any amendment of the Constitution of the United States, proposed by Congress to the several States, unless such convention or general assembly shall have been elected after such amendment is submitted.

Oath of the Legislator that Prohibits Ratification

ARTICLE X, Section 2 of the Constitution of the State of Tennessee provides for the following oath or affirmation for each member of the senate and house of the General Assembly of Tennessee:

Section 2. Each member of the Senate and House of Representatives, shall before they proceed to business, take an oath, or affirmation, to support the Constitution of this State, and of the United States, and also the following oath: "I,_____, do solemnly swear (or affirm) that, as a member of the General Assembly * * * * * I will not propose or assent to any bill, vote or resolution, which shall appear to me injurious to the people, or consent to any act or thing whatever that shall have a tendency to lessen or abridge their rights and privileges, as declared by the Constitution of the State."

The people of Tennessee, under their Constitution, have a right to elect a new legislature before action on the Nineteenth amendment. Every legislator has solemnly sworn to safeguard that right.

—Chattanooga Times, July 25, 1920.

ISSUED BY
**Tennessee Division
Southern Woman's League for Rejection of the
Susan B. Anthony Amendment**

"hikes" across the country, mid wind and rain, mud and slush, alike ridiculous, ludicrous, and intensely vulgar, all in the name of Woman's Emancipation!

To my mind, they are rapidly breaking down the social barriers between men and women. The instinctive gallantry of chivalrous men is vanishing into thin air, and the trend today is in the direction of the ultimate animalization of the sexes…. It is, therefore, tragic to note in this great country of high civilization and enlightenment, the sexes at war with one another in a great civic conflict.

The proposition to inject into the Constitution of the United States, a universal suffrage amendment is altogether chimerical…the thirteen former slave-holding states will never agree to enfranchise four or five million negresses [sic] under any circumstances. The Southern states would defeat the amendment…. For this reason, I believe the ambitions of our lady agitators will never be realized.

I love my native Southland, and…appeal, therefore, to my sisters and my daughters — especially of Tennessee — to stand by the traditions of their mothers, and continue to bear aloft the spotless white banner symbolizing the purity, chastity and modesty that has ever been so luminously exemplified by the women of the South.

In 1916, when John J. Vertrees, a well-known Nashville attorney, privately published this pamphlet, he addressed it to the only Tennesseans who were qualified at that time to vote — the men. Since Mr. Vertrees was married to the then-president of the Tennessee chapter of the National Association Opposed to Woman Suffrage, it can be safely assumed that his lengthy arguments, presented below in abridged form, were offered in gallant support of his wife's favorite cause.

An Address to the Men of Tennessee on Female Suffrage
by John J. Vertrees

I cannot believe that the men of this Republic and of Tennessee really approve of female suffrage…. I do not believe the women of Tennessee *want* the ballot, but even if they do, it is not a question of what women *want,* but what they *ought* to have, and as men only now vote, it is a question for men alone to determine. Because it is also a question relating to those who are dearest to men, and for whom they labor and live, the decision should be made with an eye to what is *best* — not for women, not for men, but for all, for the men, women and children of Tennessee.

A great deal has been written and said for female suffrage since this modern Woman's Movement began…. The suffragists of the United States speak in an impressive way of "equality" and of "rights." They contend that all persons are "created equal;" that for the same work, men and women should receive the same wage; that "taxation without representation is unjust;" that woman is man's "equal," and therefore should have equal rights. But catchy as this phrasing may be, there is something else which they studiously leave out of consideration — something undeniable, controlling, and determinative. That "something else" is the human reproductive system.

In all the past, political institutions have been framed with regard to the differences and the inequalities of males and females, so that the race shall not perish from the earth. Political institutions assumed that the stronger males should defend, and work, and the weaker females should be mothers and perpetuate the race; that the males should discharge the duties in the field, and females the duties of the home. The modern Woman's Movement proposes to reverse all this….

This brings us to the proposition that *the inher-*

ent nature of government requires the elective franchise be confined to males. Government can be maintained only by force. Vicious persons will not respect the right of others. Rebellions arise. Civil wars break out. Foreign foes attack and invade. The honor of the nation must be maintained. The only *guaranties* of good government and peace are "the ballot-box, the jury-box, the sentry-box, and the cartridge-box" — the soldier, the sheriff, the policeman and the gun. This is a *fact,* and on it rests this impregnable proposition: Only those who can bear arms should have a voice in deciding questions which may lead to war, or in enacting laws which may require soldiers, sheriffs, posses and policemen for their enforcement. This alone puts female suffrage altogether out of consideration…. The woman's ballot is a "blank-cartridge" ballot.

Our political institutions should continue to recognize the differences and inequalities of sex…. If the race is to survive, women must bear children. In the nature of things motherhood must be her supreme function, if civilization is to be preserved, much less advanced…. One Nashville suffragette has said that "woman is something higher than merely a mother. She is an individual, with power to work out her own salvation." Upon the contrary, I would say that no woman can be higher than when she is a mother, and that her rights and duties should be such as motherhood requires….

Up to about forty-five years of age, a woman's life is one of frequent and regular periods marked by mental and nervous irritability, when oftentimes even her mental equilibrium is disturbed…. Then there is pregnancy with its profound effects. And infancy — years of constant nursing and attention. Undeniably, individual women can vote and can labor — can engage in politics and business; but the effect on the race forbids it….

Of course, the mere act of going to the polls and voting once a year is of little moment — a thing of minutes, or maybe an hour, but the right of suffrage would put women in politics…. The refining influence of woman, within her sphere, has long been acknowledged. The suffragettes seize on this to justify the claim that female suffrage will "purify" politics.

"Wherever woman has gone, in whatever walk of life," says Mrs. Leslie Warner, president of the Nashville Equal Suffrage League, "she has always improved conditions, purified the atmosphere, and elevated morals. The time has come when we must step into the arena where we can give a helping hand." I venture to think that woman has purified the atmosphere and elevated morals when she has stayed, not when she has gone into the arena. The result of such a "step" will be, not that men have been made better, but women worse….

Mr. Brooks Adams, in an address in Quincy, Massachusetts, admirably expressed what a real man feels and knows: "From the remotest antiquity women have formed the cement or core of society, and represented the constant in human relations…. But to perform her office the woman has to divest herself of outside interests and live at home, for all obedience, all discipline, and all moral influence is rooted in unremitting personal supervision. Most unhappily, I have seen during my lifetime, a growing tendency among women to sneer at this supremest of human functions, as though maternity, with its restraints and sacrifices, were a task below their genius. To me, the spectacle is repellent, I may say shocking, for it is casting from the world its purest ideal and highest source of happiness."

Does not Mr. Adams express the sentiment of Tennesseans, whether they be Republicans or Democrats? If so, they should be vigilant to preserve their existing political institutions.

America When Feminized

SUFFRAGIST—FEMINIST IDEAL FAMILY LIFE.

The More a Politician Allows Himself to be Henpecked
The More Henpecking We Will Have in Politics.

A Vote for Federal Suffrage is a Vote for Organized Female
Nagging Forever.

Women of Color, Women of Courage, Women of Vision

The full significance of equal suffrage was never more clearly manifested than it was in the lives of three remarkable Tennessee women — Ida B. Wells-Barnett, Mary Church Terrell, and J. Frankie Pierce. And few women were more eloquent than they in advocating the suffrage cause and relating it to the larger issue of human rights. All three were born during the Civil War to parents not yet emancipated from slavery. All three fought for and lived to see the end of their country's legal denial of a citizen's right to vote on the basis of gender as well as race. Their words and deeds still inspire admiration today.

ary Church Terrell, born in Memphis in 1863, was the first-born child of Robert R. Church (a mulatto slave born in 1839 in Holly Springs, Mississippi) and Louisa Church. After slavery was abolished in Tennessee on February 22, 1865, Robert Church soon established himself in Memphis as an astute businessman and political leader in the black community. When many white citizens were fleeing a city decimated by yellow fever epidemics in 1878-1879, he wisely chose to invest in Memphis real estate — a move that in due course made him a wealthy man — and, when Memphis was reduced to a "taxing district," Church was the first citizen to purchase a bond to restore the city's charter.

Robert Church also invested in the education of his intelligent and independent-minded young daughter. He sent her to school in Yellow Springs, Ohio, then enrolled her in Oberlin College, Ohio, which had been founded by abolitionists prior to the Civil War and, in 1869, had become the first institution of higher learning in the United States to admit women. There, Mary Church thrived from the start, choosing as the topic for one of her first freshman essays, "Resolved: There Should Be A Sixteenth Amendment To The Constitution Granting Suffrage To Women." As she later explained, "I cannot recall a time since I first heard the subject discussed, that I did not believe in woman suffrage with all my heart."

After earning her degree in the "Classical Course" in 1884, Mary Church decided to use her education for the benefit of her people. Forswearing the life of ease and privilege she could have enjoyed, she took a position teaching languages and science at Wilburforce University in Ohio. Then, in 1888, she moved to Washington, D.C., to join the faculty at a new high school, where she was assistant to the Latin teacher, Robert H. Terrell, the first black man to be graduated *magna cum laude* from Harvard in 1884.

These two accomplished young persons soon fell in love, but they postponed marriage until 1891, after Robert Terrell had earned a law degree at Howard University in 1889. While Mary Church spent two years abroad studying languages and touring Europe, Robert Terrell began work on a master's degree in law — which he would complete in 1893. When she returned, they were wed and began a durable and compatible union of shared common interests and similar views. (In her 1940 autobiography, Mary Church Terrell noted that her husband "believed ardently in woman suffrage when few men took that stand.")

Mrs. Terrell became deeply involved in public affairs and service to her people. In 1895, she was appointed to the District of Columbia Board of Education, the first black woman to hold such a post. She founded the Colored Woman's League in 1892 and, as founding president of the National Association of Colored Women in 1896, she led the group's efforts to establish day-care centers for children of black working mothers. The group also encouraged local affiliates to work with juvenile delinquents and assist sharecroppers.

Mary Church Terrell

All the while, her interest in woman suffrage remained constant. Forthright as always, she attended a National American Woman Suffrage Association convention in Washington, D.C., in 1890 and spoke out from the floor:

> As a colored woman, I hope this Association will include a resolution on the injustices of various kinds of which colored people are the victims.... My sisters of the dominant race, stand up not only for the oppressed sex but also for the oppressed race!

In 1902, her husband, Robert Terrell, was appointed to a federal judgeship by President Theodore Roosevelt,

becoming the first member of his race to serve on the federal bench. That same year, her father, who had gained even greater political power as he became ever more prosperous, invited the President to be guest of honor at a reception in Robert Church's Park and Auditorium in Memphis. Mary Church Terrell and her husband were among the 10,000 persons present for the occasion.

During the next few years, her effectiveness grew as a leading champion of human rights. In 1904, she represented American Negro women abroad at the International Congress of Women in Berlin. Speaking fluently in both German and French, she was the only American delegate who addressed the assemblage in a language other than her own. In 1909, Mary Church Terrell was one of two black women (the other being Ida B. Wells-Barnett) who became charter members of the National Association for the Advancement of Colored People.

A few years earlier, her scathing article, "What It Means To Be Colored In the Capital of the United States," had been published in Washington's *The Independent*, drawing wide attention to early efforts to desegregate public accommodations in the nation's capital. As she gained support within the women's groups, she implemented her words with action, first using the tried and true method of picketing (in her hat and white gloves, she lent dignity to picket lines demanding equal treatment of Negroes by local businesses). She also popularized the earlier strategies of anti-segregation protests, such as the nonviolent sit-in demonstration. Especially effective was her tactic of "buying out the house." She would purchase all tickets for a single performance at the one legitimate downtown theater and distribute them among blacks. Five minutes before curtain time the ticketholders would show up *en masse*, forcing the management to make hard choices: cancel the performance, or let the cast play to empty seats, or welcome an entire audience whose ethnic identity would normally be cause for denial of admission.

During World War I, she demanded equal facilities for black soldiers. In the months leading up to passage of the 19th Amendment by the Congress in 1919, she and her daughter Phillis (named for the early American poet Phillis Wheatley) marched together in suffrage parades and joined suffragists in vigils at the White House.

For more than 66 years, Mary Church Terrell kept up her fight on all fronts for first-class citizenship for all, without regard to race or gender. Becoming increasingly the militant activist in her senior years, she was 85 years old when she broke the color bar in the American Association of University Women. Then, at age 89, she marched at the head of a picket line and led a three-year struggle in court that ended discrimination in public eating places and other public facilities in Washington. The case of *District of Columbia v. John Thompson* became "a national symbol against segregation in the United States." Before she died in 1954, she had the satisfaction of knowing, two months earlier, that the U.S. Supreme Court had handed down its landmark decision for school desegregation in the *Brown v. Board of Education of Topeka, Kansas* case.

In October of the previous year, Mary Church Terrell's service to humanity had been recognized on her 90th birthday at a dinner given in her honor at the Statler Hotel in Washington. There, hundreds of admirers, black and white, stood up and took a solemn vow to continue fighting to end discrimination in America until victory was won. They had been inspired by words from one of Mary Church Terrell's most famous speeches, which were quoted that night: "Keep on going, keep on insisting, keep on fighting injustice."

—Compiled from research and writings by Linda T. Wynn, Roberta Church, Beverly Washington Jones, Ilene Jones-Cornwell, and Carol Lynn Yellin.

University of Chicago Library

Ida B. Wells

Ida B. Wells-Barnett was born in 1862 in Holly Springs, Mississippi, the oldest of eight children whose parents, Jim Wells and Lizzie Warrenton Wells, once freed from slavery, instilled in their offspring a love of liberty and a thirst for education. While she was attending Shaw University (later Rust College) in Holly Springs, where her father, a carpenter and community activist, served on the first board of trustees, the 1878 yellow fever epidemic swept through northern Mississippi and claimed the lives of her mother, father, and youngest brother (another brother had died several years earlier). At age 16, an orphaned Ida Bell Wells assumed responsibility for rearing her five siblings. She spent the next year teaching in a one-room school for black children in rural Mississippi, then moved to Memphis with her two younger sisters in 1879. She secured a teaching position in the rural Shelby County town of Woodstock.

In May of 1884, Ida B. Wells took a brave stand against injustice that foreshadowed by almost three-quarters of a century a similar history-changing act of defiance by a black woman named Rosa Parks in Montgomery, Alabama, in 1955. Having purchased a first-class ticket on a local Memphis-to-Woodstock railway line, owned by the Chesapeake and Ohio Railroad, she took a seat in the white ladies' coach.

When the conductor grabbed her arm and tried to remove her forcibly to the segregated "smoker" car reserved for colored passengers, she resisted forcefully. (She bit his hand!) Ejected from the train, she subsequently sued the railroad for failing to provide the "equal" in their supposedly "separate-but-equal" accommodations. She prevailed in a local court and was awarded $500 in damages, but the railroad appealed the case, and in 1887, the Tennessee Supreme Court reversed the decision, charging the costs to a bitterly disappointed but not dispirited Ida B. Wells. The incident set her feet on the path of her lifelong public crusade for human rights.

That same year, she discovered her journalistic abilities. Using the pseudonym "Iola," she wrote an article about her lawsuit against the railroad and its outcome, which caused a stir when it was published by a religious weekly, *Living Way*. Soon she was contributing to other black publications — so many that she became known as the "Princess of the Press." In 1889, the ever self-reliant Ida B. Wells invested her savings to become part-owner and part-time editor of the *Free Speech and Headlight*, a small but militant Memphis journal that served as the voice of the black community. Within two years, her outspoken editorials criticizing the Memphis school board for its inferior segregated Negro schools led to her dismissal from her teaching job. Undeterred, she continued publishing accounts of unfair treatment of Negroes.

On March 9, 1892, three young black businessmen, whose Memphis grocery store had won customers away from a white-owned store, were falsely accused of attacking a white woman. After their arrest, they were dragged from the jail by a white mob, shot, and then hanged. Voicing the outrage of the city's black citizens, Ida B. Wells wrote that, unless the murderers were brought to justice as "decency and the equality of law" demanded, Negroes should boycott the street railway or, better yet, leave the city. Many, taking her advice, became known as "Exodusters" as they headed west to Kansas.

For three months, the young editor continued her bitter attacks on the racial hypocrisy of the city's white citizens who allowed, even condoned, lynching atrocities. Her newspaper was blamed for paralyzing downtown business. One evening an angry mob broke into her office, wrecked her press, made a bonfire of her papers, and would have lynched her, had she not been in Philadelphia covering a convention for her paper.

The 23-year-old Ida B. Wells relocated in New York and never returned to Memphis. She joined the staff of the *New York Age* and continued her writings on lynching. In 1892, her research resulted in a feature story, "Southern Horrors: Lynch Law in All Its Phases" (later reprinted as a brochure), which brought her national attention. She spent the next several years writing and lecturing in the cities of the North and throughout England, Scotland, and Wales. Recognized as the originator and leader of an international anti-lynching campaign, she won support and praise for her "passion for justice" from such other crusaders as Susan B. Anthony and the great abolitionist and suffragist, Frederick Douglass.

In 1895, Ida B. Wells married attorney Ferdinand Barnett, founder and editor of the *Chicago Conservator*, a kindred soul who was her ardent supporter and whose devotion to the cause of equal rights matched her own. In time, they became parents of two sons and two daughters. In Chicago, Ida B. Wells-Barnett was instrumental in forming numerous reform organizations. Two of the groups were the Ida B. Wells Women's Club and the Negro Fellowship League. She enlarged the scope of her involvement, becoming one of two black women (the other being Mary Church Terrell) to become founding members in 1909 of the National Association for the Advancement of Colored People. Having always perceived the Votes-for-Women cause as an inherent part of the struggle for human equality, in 1913 she founded Chicago's Alpha Suffrage Club, the first organization for black women suffragists in Illinois.

University of Chicago Library

Ida B. Wells-Barnett

From its inception, members of the Alpha Suffrage Club, including the founder's daughters, Ida and Alfreda, marched side by side with white suffragists in local Chicago parades, wearing the movement's symbolic white dresses with purple sashes. But when Ida Wells-Barnett traveled to Washington, D.C., in 1913 to join in a national parade, she was asked by Alice Paul, redoubtable leader of the National Woman's Party which was organizing the demonstration and was wary of offending the South, not to march alongside Chicago's white suffragists but to join the delegation of black suffragists at the rear of the formation. Free spirit that she was, Ida B. Wells-Barnett would have none of it. She later reported:

> I was told I could bring up the rear…. But when the marched started, I appeared out of the crowd of onlookers as the Chicago delegation made its way past me. I joined them, and marched as I pleased.

Ida B. Wells-Barnett would continue her unrelenting battle against injustice in newspapers and on lecture platforms across the nation until her death in 1931 at age 68. It was her bold heroism in the fight against the atrocities of lynching that made her unique, but her equally enduring dedication to the cause of women's rights was no less remarkable. As early as 1894, a young Ida B. Wells had first stated her strong pro-suffrage sentiments in a speech that, typically, was both incisive and pragmatic. The advice she gave then still resonates today:

> To give women of this country an equal share in all the privileges of citizenship is right, she declared, but will the millennium [sic] come when women get the ballot? Will that change human nature or change the political situation? Remember — the gods help those who help themselves.

—Compiled from research and writings by Wanda Hendricks, Linda T. Wynn, Ilene Jones-Cornwell, and Carol Lynn Yellin.

Courtesy of Virginia Edmondson

J. Frankie Pierce

J. Frankie Seay Pierce was born c.1864 in Nashville to Frank Seay, a freedman, and Nellie Seay (1814-1931), a native of Carthage, Tennessee. Her mother was a house slave of Smith County's Colonel Robert Allen, who represented Tennessee in the U.S. House of Representatives. It probably was his son, Dixon T. Allen (member of the Tennessee House of Representatives during 1829-1833), who brought Nellie Seay to Nashville, where she made her home by 1839, the year she became a member of Nashville's First Baptist Church (white).

During her youth, Frankie Seay received her education at the John G. McKee Freedmen's School, established as a Presbyterian mission in Nashville. After Frankie married and became Mrs. Pierce, she spent a number of years living out of state. After the death of her husband, she returned to Nashville to live with her mother, Nellie Seay. As her mother before her, J. Frankie Seay Pierce became involved in community life. Following her vision to create community unity, she was a founder of the Negro Women's Reconstruction Service League and joined her mother to become a mainstay of the First Colored Baptist Church on Eighth Avenue, North (Capitol Hill, which became the headquarters in 1958 and through the early 1960s for the nonviolent sit-in protests of the modern civil rights movement).

In the early 1900s, she organized the City Federation of Colored Women's Clubs, of which she served as president, and helped organize the Tennessee Federation of Colored Women's Clubs. Through her involvement and leadership in these civic groups, she began a campaign to accomplish a long-held goal: to establish a vocational training school for delinquent black girls. The need for such a school in Tennessee had become clear to Frankie Pierce when she observed facilities of this nature in several Southern states. She also was influenced by her friendship with a probation officer, who reluctantly took delinquent black girls to jail because the law would not permit them to enter institutions for white delinquent girls. Enlisting the support of her sister community activists, Frankie Pierce mounted a broad-based, unified effort to lobby for enabling legislation to create a state-supported vocational school for black girls. Thus, while her contemporaries, Ida B. Wells-Barnett and Mary Church Terrell, were earning national attention with their bold campaigns for equal rights, J. Frankie Pierce was gaining ground in Tennessee with arduous grass-roots crusades for equality.

One such crusade, conducted long before passage of any public-accommodations laws, was for restroom facilities for black women shopping in downtown Nashville. With other members of the City Federation of Colored Women's Clubs, she marched to the mayor's office, where they presented their demands. As a result, Montgomery Ward became the first store in the city to install restroom facilities for women of color.

Woman suffrage was another cause that won early support from Frankie Pierce. The value of that support was recognized by seasoned suffragists when the struggle for ratification of the 19th Amendment placed Tennessee in the national spotlight. In the spring of 1920, Catherine Talty Kenny, one of Nashville's influential and innovative suffrage strategists, decided to act. The state's newly re-named suffrage organization, the Tennessee League of Women Voters, was to hold its organizational meeting on May 18 in the House chambers at the Capitol, and Mrs. Kenny, reaching out across the color line, had invited Mrs. Pierce to be one of the speakers. After brief introductory remarks, J. Frankie Pierce mounted the podium and began her address to a rapt audience. Her assigned topic was, "What Will the Negro Woman Do With The Vote?" Her response, in part, was:

> What will the Negro woman do with the Vote? Yes, we will stand by the white women. We are optimistic because we have faith in the best white women of the country, of Nashville. We are going to make you proud of us and yourselves.

Then, speaking her deepest convictions, Frankie Pierce continued:

> We are interested in the same moral uplift of the community in which we live as you are. We are asking only one thing — a square deal. It remained for the war to show what the Negroes could do. We bought bonds, we gave money, we made comfort kits, we prayed…. We want recognition in all forms of government…. We want a state vocational school and a child welfare department of the state, and more room in state schools.

Frankie Pierce was, at last, close to reaching her long-cherished goal. After the 19th Amendment was ratified on August 18 by the Tennessee General Assembly, making woman suffrage effective throughout the nation, Frankie Pierce built upon the momentum of women's empowerment to press her campaign. Vocational schools became part of the legislative agenda for the Tennessee League of Women Voters and this support, in concert with Mrs. Pierce's extensive lobbying efforts, resulted in the bill creating the Tennessee Vocational School for Colored Girls being passed by the General Assembly on April 7, 1921. When the school opened its doors two years later on October 9, 1923, she was its first superintendent. To sustain support for the school, which accepted girls between the ages of 12 and 15 from juvenile courts across the state, and was located on a 66-acre campus near Tennessee Agricultural and Industrial State College in Nashville, she held annual breakfasts for state legislators and other community leaders, so they could see the school in operation.

The vocational school continued to evolve over the years and, after Mrs. Pierce's retirement in 1939, her dream was shared by a succession of superintendents. The school offered academic and vocational training for girls from elementary grades through secondary school, provided psychological counseling, increased staff, gained accreditation, and formed affiliations with local and national organizations. In 1966, the school was integrated, and from

1971 until it closed in 1979, it was known as the Tennessee Reception and Guidance Center for Juveniles.

On April 10, 1950, a testimonial dinner for J. Frankie Pierce was held at Tennessee A&I College (now Tennessee State University), and an array of state and local dignitaries paid tribute to her as church woman, educator, civil rights and suffrage leader, politician, businesswoman, and friend. Following her death in 1954, J. Frankie Pierce was eulogized as a woman of vision who possessed the perseverance, determination, and courage to provide the leadership to make her community vision a community reality.

— Compiled from research and writings by Virginia Edmondson, Linda T. Wynn, Ilene Jones-Cornwell, and Carol Lynn Yellin.

Charter members of Fisk University Auxiliary, Nashville Chapter, American Red Cross

Those in the group are: Misses Abigail Jackson, Chairman, Instructor in Mathematics, Felina G. Blaine, Velda T. Brown, Lucy Brewer, Helen M. Burrell, Grace B. Broyles, Mabel E. Campbell, Emmie F. Drake, Tommie Sue A. Fosta, Pearl C. Hayes, Flay M. Henderson, Arah L. Horton, Florence B. Jackson, Clara W. Johnson, Clara L. Langrum, Ada B. Lewis, Ferris W. Lewis, Andrades S. Lindsay, Alma A. Oakes, Manila L. Owens, Poselyn L. Purdy, Nellie A. Randolph, Altamese C. Roberts, Ruth I. Rowan, Valda E. Sanders, Margaret A. Slater, Moirselles M. Stewart, Ethelynde J. Sutton, Alice M. Thomas, Isabel B. Walden, Annie G. Quick, Mrs. Tilla W. Brown, Dean of Women, and Mrs. M. L. Crosthwait, Registar.

This bas-relief sculpture by Alan LeQuire commemorates the suffragists' 1920 victory and hangs on the second floor of the Tennessee State Capitol.

Showdown in Tennessee

by Carol Lynn Yellin

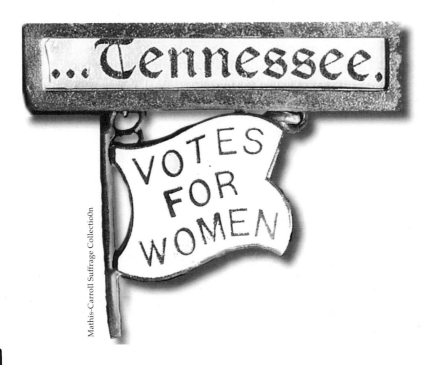

Mathis-Carroll Suffrage Collectio0n

At 5 p.m. on June 4, 1919, when the Sixty-sixth Congress yielded up the two-thirds majority required for passage of the 19th Amendment to the Constitution of the United States, a victory celebration among American woman suffragists seemed in order. After all, 21 successive Congresses had previously rejected this federal Suffrage Amendment, and it had taken over 70 years of petitioning, lobbying, politicking, and, most recently, picketing by four generations of right-to-vote crusaders to bring the struggle for enfranchisement of women to this high ground.

But the battle-weary, campaign-wise suffrage forces did not celebrate. In the headquarters of Carrie Chapman Catt's National American Woman Suffrage Association at 171 Madison Avenue, New York, the joy was restrained. The NAWSA women remembered how often their brave labors to win full suffrage state by state through amendments to state constitutions had met with heartbreak; they remembered how regularly their stubborn skirmishes to win the half-a-loaf of partial suffrage (voting only in presidential or municipal elections that was sometimes possible through state legislative enactment) had ended in disappointment; they remembered how all of this had led inevitably to the concerted push for federal amendment action. Remembering, they knew that total victory had not yet been won.

In the headquarters of the National Woman's Party just off Lafayette Park in Washington on that June night, there was business as usual among Alice Paul's select, young, banner-bearing color guards. They remembered how their silent and dramatic pro-amendment demonstrations in the halls of Congress

A Suffrage Timetable, Country by Country

At the moment Tennessee's ratification of the 19th Amendment to the U.S. Constitution granted American women the right to vote, woman suffrage had already become a reality in 26 other countries — beginning, fittingly enough, with the Isle of Man, in 1881. This chronological listing, country by country and year by year, of the order in which women were enfranchised, was reported in The New York Times, *August 19, 1920.*

1.	Isle of Man	1881
2.	New Zealand	1893
3.	Australia	1902
4.	Finland	1906
5.	Norway	1907
6.	Denmark	1915
7.	Mexico	1917
8.	Russia	1917
9.	Ireland	1918
10.	Wales	1918
11.	Canada	1918
12.	Germany	1918
13.	England	1918
14.	Poland	1918
15.	Scotland	1918
16.	Austria	1918
17.	Czechoslovakia	1918
18.	Hungary	1918
19.	Holland	1919
20.	British East Africa	1919
21.	Luxemburg	1919
22.	Uruguay	1919
23.	Belgium	1919
24.	Rhodesia	1919
25.	Iceland	1919
26.	Sweden	1919

and at the gates of the White House had outraged, then intrigued, and finally touched the conscience of the American public; they remembered how this had helped overcome the last bastions of congressional resistance. And yet they knew they could not pause to celebrate.

For the long-fought-for passage of the 19th Amendment by Congress in June, 1919, meant only the capture of a beachhead. The final campaign in this nation's longest and most civil "war," the campaign for ratification of the 19th Amendment, still lay ahead. And up the 48 hills once more, all the way — that battle must be won in the states. State by state. To complete adoption of the amendment now being submitted by Congress to the 48 states required ratification by legislatures in three-fourths of those states.

The Suffs, as headline writers liked to call them, had to win in no fewer than 36 legislatures, while their opponents, the entrenched and well-heeled Antis, could kill the amendment by squashing it in just 13 legislatures. And behind the Antis' formally organized battalions — a National Association Opposed to Woman Suffrage (for ladies) and the American Constitutional League (for gentlemen) — stood the suffragists' real and most powerful enemies, a shadowy conglomerate of special interests referred to by the suffragists as the whiskey ring, the railroad trust, and the manufacturers' lobby. Suffragist historian Ida Husted Harper once explained the how and why of their sinister manipulations:

> The hand of the great moneyed corporations is on the lever of the party 'machines.' They can calculate to a nicety how many voters must be bought, how many candidates must be 'fixed,' how many officials must be owned. The entrance of woman in the field would upset all calculations, add to the expenses if she were corruptible, and spoil the plans if she were not.

Although no time limit for completion of ratification had been written into the 19th Amendment (cynics were already predicting it would take 20 years), there was no time to lose if women's votes were to count in the upcoming 1920 elections, a matter, as the Suffs often proclaimed, of patriotic pride no less than simple justice. In a world we had helped make so safe for democracy, democratic Americans could not lag behind. Women already voted in 26 other nations. (Including Germany! Including Russia!!) More than that, the memory of American women's contributions to Allied victory in World War I — their crucial work on farms and in offices, hospitals, and munitions factories was rapidly fading, and with the country longing to return to what would soon be labeled "normalcy," suffrage forces knew that, psychologically, it was action now or never.

Thus it was that at 6 p.m. on Wednesday, June 4, 1919, just one hour after the decisive U.S. Senate vote on the 19th Amendment, the redoubtable, twice-widowed 60-year-old Carrie Chapman Catt, heiress to the mantle of Elizabeth Cady Stanton and Susan B. Anthony, veteran of more than 30 years in the suffrage movement and leader of its 2,000,000-member "traditional" wing, was hard at work in her office at NAWSA headquarters. She was methodically sending out telegrams to governors of all states where legislatures had already adjourned in that off-year of 1919, urging them to call special sessions to act on ratification as soon as possible. By midnight, the serenely efficient Mrs. Catt also had dispatched messages to each of the 48 state suffrage auxiliaries, exhorting them to put their long-planned ratification campaigns into high gear and reminding them, where necessary, to keep after their governors. Only when all of her own telegrams had gone out did Mrs. Catt read the congratulatory messages pouring in, among them a two-word cable from President Woodrow Wilson, in France for the Paris Peace Commission: "Glory Hallelujah!"

Alice Paul, too, was pushing on with single-minded intensity that Wednesday night. But the quiet, dedicated, 35-year-old Quaker social worker, who had gone to prison as an activist convert to the votes-for-women cause in England a decade earlier and now was leader of an estimated 25,000 women in the "militant" wing of the American movement, was not to be found in her office. She had boarded a train and was heading west to join her fieldworkers in a whirlwind tour of the several states where legislatures were still in session and where, beginning early the next morning, suffragists would be demanding immediate ratification.

In years gone by, Carrie Chapman Catt and Alice Paul had been contending rivals for the allegiance of American suffragists. The groups they led — the sprawling, well-established, persevering NAWSA, and the smaller, more maneuverable, less predictable Woman's Party — had only recently been bitterly divided over tactics, particularly over the effectiveness of White House picketing to "educate" an initially reluctant President Wilson on the need for a federal Suffrage Amendment and the responsibility of party

National Woman's Party

Alice Paul toasting suffrage victory.

leadership to achieve it. Now, however, their strategies meshing by unpremeditated design, the rivals seemed to be taking this last giant step for womankind together.

It augured well for the climactic struggle ahead.

The first six ratifications came in an eight-day period: Wisconsin, Michigan, Kansas, Ohio, New York, Illinois. Letter-writing and lobbying, speech-making and fund-raising intensified. In the next seven weeks, another seven states ratified. As sum-

The Suffrage Map Early in August, 1920

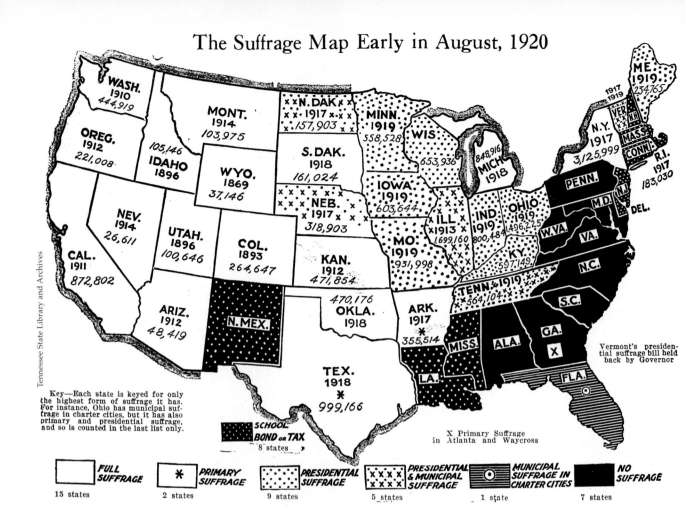

Key—Each state is keyed for only the highest form of suffrage it has. For instance, Ohio has municipal suffrage in charter cities, but it has also primary and presidential suffrage, and so is counted in the last list only.

WASH. 1910 *444,919*
OREG. 1912 *221,008*
105,146 IDAHO 1896
MONT. 1914 *103,975*
N. DAK. 1917 *157,903*
MINN. 1919 *558,528*
WIS 653,936
MICH 1918 848,916
ME 1919 234,765
1917 1919 VER. N.H.
N.Y. 1917 3,125,999
MASS. CONN.
R.I. 1917 183,030

NEV. 1914 26,611
UTAH. 1896 100,646
WYO. 1869 37,146
S. DAK. 1918 161,024
IOWA 1919 603,644
NEB. 1917 318,903
ILL 1913 1,699,160
IND. 1919 800,484
OHIO 1919 1,496,225
PENN.
N.J.
M.D.
DEL.
W.VA.
VA.

CAL. 1911 *872,802*
ARIZ. 1912 48,419
COL. 1893 264,647
N. MEX.
KAN. 1912 471,854
MO. 1919 931,998
KY. 597,149
N.C.

OKLA. 1918 470,176
ARK. 1917 * 355,514
TENN. 1919 564,104
S.C.
GA. X

TEX. 1918 * 999,166
MISS.
ALA.
LA.
FLA.

Vermont's presidential suffrage bill held back by Governor

X Primary Suffrage in Atlanta and Waycross

SCHOOL, BOND or TAX
8 states

FULL SUFFRAGE 15 states	PRIMARY SUFFRAGE 2 states	PRESIDENTIAL SUFFRAGE 9 states	PRESIDENTIAL & MUNICIPAL SUFFRAGE 5 states	MUNICIPAL SUFFRAGE IN CHARTER CITIES 1 state	NO SUFFRAGE 7 states

mer wore on, still the Suffs campaigned — staging rallies, conducting polls, issuing press releases. The Antis mobilized in kind. A corps of impassioned lady orators, headed by a woman attorney named Charlotte Rowe from Yonkers, New York, charged to state capitals to warn the populace in general and legislators in particular that ratification was the first step toward socialism, free love, and the breakup of the American family. One Southern governor, Ruffin G. Pleasant of Louisiana, publicly sought a union of 13 Anti states to prevent ratification.

By mid-September, the pace of ratification had slackened. The suffragists were particularly distressed by the failure of Far Western states, whose own female citizens had long enjoyed full suffrage, to come to the aid of voteless women elsewhere. Of these, only Montana had ratified. So the Suffs, as was their habit when coping with disappointment, redoubled their efforts — more meetings with party leaders, more pleas for special sessions, more volunteers out rounding up pledges of support among more thousands of legislators.

By New Year's Day, 1920, the total had reached 22 hard-won ratifications. Then, in late January and early February, there came a bouquet of 10 more ratifications, clustered as if to celebrate the 100th anniversary of the birth of Susan B. Anthony on February 15. (It was Susan B. Anthony, most venerated and undeviating of suffrage leaders, who had put on paper the exact words of the federal Suffrage Amendment when it was first introduced in the Forty-fifth Congress in 1878 and then had watched its regular defeat in each session thereafter until her death in 1906 — murmuring, according to suffragist mythology, " Failure is impossible!") Only four more states to go! Yet it was still too soon to celebrate. Or relax.

The opposition was growing ever grimmer, the odds longer, the gains more costly. In Oklahoma, Miss Aloysius Larch-Miller, a prominent and gifted young suffragist, ill with influenza, disregarded her doctor's orders and left her sickbed to debate the state's leading anti-suffrage politician at a state Democratic convention. Two days later she was dead. But her eloquence (plus her sacrifice) had won some decisive switchover votes in the Democratic-controlled state legislature. On February 27, Oklahoma became the 33rd state to ratify.

Meanwhile, once-promising West Virginia was now hopelessly deadlocked. Restive Antis demanded that the legislature close up shop and go home. But an absent pro-suffrage legislator, Senator Jesse A. Bloch, rushed back home by special train from California — five days across the continent while his embattled colleagues fought adjournment and the country watched and waited — to break a tie vote in the state Senate on March 20 and make West Virginia the 34th ratifying state. On March 22, news was flashed across the country that the legislature of the state of Washington, called into special session at long last by a dilatory governor, had unanimously completed ratification number 35. Where was number 36?

It was just here, with final victory so amazingly and tantalizingly close, that the ratification campaign stalled.

Six states, all Southern, had already rejected the amendment. Only seven states had not yet acted, and three of these Florida, Louisiana, and North Carolina were also from the Deep and Democratic South. No chance there, where memories of federally-controlled elections during the dark days of Reconstruction still rankled, and the 19th Amendment, with its Section 2 granting enforcement powers to Congress, was anathema. (Shades of the oppressive Fourteenth Amendment! And worse yet, the Fifteenth giving the vote to Negroes! Well, Negro men, at any rate!)

Nor was there much hope up in New England in the two rock-ribbed Republican holdout states of Connecticut and Vermont. Both had strong anti-suffrage governors who had proven granite-like in their refusal even to consider calling their reportedly pro-suffrage legislators into special session. This meant that the Suffs would have to find their "Perfect 36," as cartoonists had labeled the elusive thirty-sixth ratification, in one of just two states, Delaware or Tennessee. And the border state of Tennessee was decidedly a question mark.

Incumbent Tennessee legislators, in the session just adjourned, somewhat surprisingly had granted women voters partial suffrage in presidential and municipal elections, the first of the old Confederacy states to do so. But full, federally-imposed woman suffrage was a mare of a different color. In any case, Tennessee was hemmed in by a provision in its own state constitution requiring that any federal amendment be acted upon only by a legislature that "shall have been elected after such amendment is submit-

ted." This clearly meant after the 1920 elections. For this reason, Tennessee's Democratic Governor Albert H. Roberts (whose own suffrage sentiments were still unclear) claimed he could not call a special session of the current Tennessee legislature to act on ratification.

Which left only Delaware. In 1787, Delaware had been the first state to ratify the Constitution itself, and for a time that spring of 1920, it promised to be the last and deciding state to ratify the Constitution's 19th Amendment. Delaware's fervently pro-suffrage Republican Governor John G. Townsend had called the Republican-controlled legislature into special session on March 22, the very day of the 35th ratification out in Washington. Since comfortable Republican majorities in both legislative houses had long since pledged their votes for ratification, suffragists confidently expected instant action. But Delaware Republicans were in the midst of a fierce party feud. An almost equal division between pro-Townsend and anti-Townsend factions ensured that whatever the governor favored, his political rivals would oppose. In such circumstances pledges were forgotten and, amidst charges of vote-swapping, bribe-taking, and double-cross, the possibility of achieving stable pro-ratification majorities in both houses of the legislature slipped away. Weeks dragged by. March turned to April, April to May. The legislature remained in session, but no action was taken. Chances for victory in Republican Delaware receded with each passing day.

Then, most ominous of all, came the danger that some of the already-certified ratifications might be "recalled." In Ohio, one of the first states to act favorably on the amendment, petitions had been filed for a statewide referendum in which voters could confirm or reject their legislature's ratification. A recently-adopted article in Ohio's own state constitution specifically allowed such a referendum. The U.S. Constitution, on the other hand, with its straightforward requirement for amendment ratification by state legislatures, is equally specific in not providing for a recall referendum. So the validity of the Ohio referendum provision was being contested in an appeal to the U.S. Supreme Court. But the Antis, reveling in the legal havoc being created, were busily circulating petitions for similar post-ratification referendums in Missouri, Nebraska, Maine, and Massachusetts, with more to come. The ratification campaign had not just stalled. It was threatening to shift into reverse.

June 2, 1920, was the day of decision in Delaware's legislature. Ratification lost. Worried Republicans wondered if their party would be blamed nationally for the debacle. They didn't have long to wonder. The following week, when the Republican National Convention of 1920 opened in the Coliseum in Chicago — a convention from whose "smoke-filled rooms" Senator Warren G. Harding of Ohio would emerge as nominee for president — a long line of women, dressed in white and wearing the suffragists' emblematic yellow sashes, marched on the Coliseum. They carried the purple, white, and gold tri-color of the Woman's Party, and their banners read: REPUBLICANS, WE ARE HERE. WHERE IS THE 36th STATE?

The convention hastily inserted a plank in its platform expressing the "earnest hope that Republican legislatures in States which have not yet acted upon the Suffrage Amendment will ratify...."

In the Coliseum, the suffragists hung a banner from the balcony reading: WE DO NOT WANT PLANKS. WE DEMAND THE 36th STATE. Republican leaders beseiged the anti-ratificationist Republican governors of Vermont and Connecticut with pleas to relent and call special sessions. Suffragists in both states beseeched with letters, telegrams, delegations. This massive pressure brought continued massive resistance. Governor Percival W. Clement of Vermont announced after due reflection that he "did not care to make a decision at once." Governor Marcus A. Holcomb of Connecticut declared that no one had proved to him "the existence of a 'special emergency'" so he must decline.

Fortunately, however, June 2 had also been a day of decision in the U.S. Supreme Court. And there, ratification had won. Or at least it had been rescued from uncertain limbo. The Court's ruling on the Ohio referendum case declared flatly, "The Federal Constitution, and not the constitutions of several States, controls the method by which the U.S. Constitution may be amended."

This decision did more than free the 19th Amendment from the legal entanglements of threatened referenda. It also inspired careful study of one particular state constitution by the suffragists. And it spurred urgent and frenzied activity by the Democrats.

"Of course, you've heard the good news that Tennessee may be the 'perfect 36.' Wouldn't it be glorious to have the 36th state come from way down here in suffrage country where the mossbacks stay?" So began the letter NAWSA's national headquarters, postmarked Nashville, dated June 21, 1920, and signed by Catherine Talty Kenny, Chairman of Ratification, Tennessee League of Women Voters. (Having just won partial suffrage in 1919, the Tennessee Equal Suffrage League, in a burst of self- congratulatory exuberance, had recently adopted a change of name.) In New York, the letter was read with avid interest. A band of outstanding women over the years had molded Tennessee's suffrage movement in their own image — lively, determined, resourceful. Catherine Kenny was one of them.

A natural choice for the key post of state ratification chairman, Mrs. Kenny was a cheerful, motherly-looking woman who, serving the cause, had done everything from throwing out the first ball at the Nashville baseball park one spring day when players adorned their uniforms with sashes of suffrage yellow and played a Suffrage Day game, to traveling across the state making speeches from the rear platform of a train known as the "Tennessee Suffrage Special." (On that trip, when a heckler kept shouting that the ladies should all go home because, in

the watchword of the era, "Home is woman's sphere," Mrs. Kenny's apt rejoinder had silenced him: "Woman's sphere," she declared, "is the world.")

Now, with Tennessee moving into the ratification spotlight, and in the absence of two of the state's foremost suffragist leaders, Mrs. Guilford Dudley of Nashville, a NAWSA national vice president, and Mrs. George Fort Milton of Chattanooga, the Tennessee League president, were en route to San Francisco where a Democratic National Convention would, for the first time, be welcoming women delegates. Catherine Kenny was holding center stage in Nashville, and loving every minute of it. She had opened a Ratification Headquarters for her committee at the famous old Maxwell House, long a favorite hangout for state politicians, and her June 21 letter to NAWSA headquarters brimmed with confidence: "The Ohio decision seems to cover our case in the opinion of every lawyer who has read it." She offered analysis: "Tennessee is the best bet for ratification by a Democratic state because we have partial suffrage and that gives us the whip hand." And she proposed a strategy for overcoming what she saw as the main obstacle — Tennessee's Governor Roberts, a mild-mannered, deliberate, teacher-turned-lawyer, whose principal backers and advisors were hopelessly split on the question of ratification, whose main interest was tax reform, and whose main worry was renomination, which in normally Democratic Tennessee was tantamount to re-election. She continued:

…But alas our Governor is running for re-election and they are about to get his scalp. He is afraid to call the session because he can't afford to take time off from his campaign before the primary Aug. 5. Now here is our hope: In Tennessee we all swear by Woodrow Wilson, exhausting every adjective in our voluminous Southern vocabulary to praise and glorify his every word and deed… Yesterday I conceived the idea of having the President wire Governor Roberts a loving message telling him to deliver the 36th state for the Democrats. I've sent a telegram to the President tonight signed by our entire State Executive Board League of Women Voters (32 names). If you know any way in the world to get that telegram by Mr. Tumulty to the President, for the love of Mike help…

Someone at NAWSA evidently did know how to circumvent (or wheedle) Joe Tumulty, White House watchdog for the now-ailing president, exhausted by his vain efforts to sell Americans on membership in the League of Nations. And Wilson, who hoped women voters would favor the League of Nations, found it politic to pay heed. On June 12, 1920, just hours after Mrs. Kenny's letter arrived in New York, the Department of Justice in Washington was asked by President Wilson to render an opinion concerning application of the Supreme Court's Ohio referendum decision to the constitution of Tennessee. Mrs. Kenny's lawyer friends contended that the provision postponing legislative action on a federal amendment until after the state's next election made that election itself a referendum in everything but name. The U.S. Attorney General, John L. Frierson, himself a Tennessee Democrat, agreed. His instant opinion, delivered that afternoon on behalf of the Justice Department, declared, "If the people of a State through their Constitution can delay action on an amendment until after an election, there is no reason why they cannot delay it until after two elections or five elections…thus practically nullifying the article of the Federal Constitution providing for amendment."

Later that same day, June 23, 1920, Woodrow Wilson telegraphed Governor Roberts just the sort of "loving message" Mrs. Kenny had envisioned:

> It would be a real service to the party and to the nation if it is possible for you, under the peculiar provision of your State Constitution, having in mind the recent decision of the Supreme Court in the Ohio case, to call a special session of the Legislature of Tennessee to consider the Suffrage Amendment. Allow me to urge this most earnestly.

But the governor still hesitated, wiring the president on June 24 that he had to consult his own state attorney general in Tennessee, to see "if ratification can now be made." And with that, Governor Roberts became, for the next few days, the target of an unprecedented barrage of messages, opinions, supplications — most of which were announced to the press even before they reached his desk in Nashville.

In New York, NAWSA made public the opinion of their distinguished chief counsel, no less an authority than the Honorable Charles Evans Hughes, a former U.S. Supreme Court Justice and Republi-

can nominee (and still-to-be Secretary of State and Chief Justice), who announced that the Tennessee legislature "has, in my judgment, full authority to ratify."

From San Francisco as their convention was getting underway, the Democratic National Committee's chairman, Homer S. Cummings, telephoned Nashville long-distance to urge Governor Roberts to convene the legislature. Then followed a series of telegrams from San Francisco to the governor — from all members of the DNC, from the full roster of women delegates to the convention, from the entire Tennessee delegation, men and women — each demanding a special session for the good of party, state and nation. The state's own U.S. Senator Kenneth McKellar, serving on the convention's platform committee, sponsored a plank specifically urging Tennessee's Democratic governor and legislators "to unite in an effort to complete ratification."

Back home, meanwhile, anti-suffragists from all over Tennessee, many of them the governor's own supporters, had bestirred themselves and were bombarding Roberts with threats of defeat in the primary if he dared to call a special session. But his main opponent in the primary, a Colonel W. F. Crabtree, who

was strongly backed by two of the state's most influential news papers, the *Nashville Tennessean* and *The Chattanooga News*, warned what would happen if Roberts did not call the session: "Some Republican state will ratify and rob Tennessee of its chance for glory…." And, to top it off, Frank M. Thompson, Attorney General of Tennessee, handed the governor an elaborate opinion which boiled down to this: No legal barrier to an extra session now existed.

The harried governor acted. In Nashville, on Monday, June 28, he announced his promise to formally call the Tennessee legislature into special session. Not immediately — he still hoped to defuse ratification as an issue in the August 5 primary — but on August 9, "in ample time for women to vote in the 1920 elections."

When the news reached San Francisco, the convened Democrats were euphoric. The "Perfect 36" had just been delivered to them and along with it (so it was believed) the women's vote and victory in November. From that moment, until they all went home a week later to begin campaigning for their chosen candidates — Ohio's Governor James Cox for President and a handsome young New Yorker named Franklin D. Roosevelt for Vice President —

Anne Dallas Dudley with her children.

and an idealistic young Congressman from Middle Tennessee named Cordell Hull — was almost irrelevant.

The convention's most spontaneous outburst came when Mrs. Guilford Dudley, delegate-at-large from Tennessee, rose to make a seconding speech for one of the nominees. The special qualities of this lovely, blue-eyed Nashville blueblood had long been proclaimed in her own state.

Anne Dallas Dudley had marched in suffrage parades with her wealthy husband's encouragement and her two beautiful young children in tow; she had lobbied most effectively for female enfranchisement in a day when the Antis liked to label all Suffs as "she-males." As an orator, her spellbinding charm had been prominently displayed and, according to many Tennessee suffragists, her name and visible presence had alone been enough to make their state movement not only respectable but fashionable. Since she had recently graduated to national leadership as Third Vice President of NAWSA, her wit and eloquence had become legendary. (She once demolished an Anti debater's argument that, because only men bear arms, only men should vote, with the observation, "Yes, but women bear armies.")

Now, as Anne Dallas Dudley mounted the podium in San Francisco, the band musicians down on the floor took one look at her and swung into the familiar measures of a popular song hit of the day. Soon, the entire Democratic National Convention joined in, singing, "Oh, You Beautiful Doll!"

However, it was still too soon to hail victory. No one knew this better than Carrie Chapman Catt. This veteran white-haired campaigner had dispatched a four-page, single-spaced letter to Catherine Kenny in Nashville, "not so much to congratulate you as to warn you of the pitfalls which surely lie between this date and the 9th of August." Mrs. Catt then proceeded to outline, point by point, the sort of practical knowledge suffragists had been sharing with each other for almost three-quarters of a century:

LITERATURE CAMPAIGN: The anti-suffragists will flood Tennessee with the most outrageous literature it has ever been your lot to read…outright lies, innuendoes and near-truths which are more damaging than lies. The "nigger question" will be put forth in ways to arouse the greatest possible prejudice. If there is any exception to the case of Tennessee, it will be the first state to escape this kind of dirty, lying tac-

the Democrats repeatedly demonstrated their new-found convictions that women voters could do no wrong, and Tennessee was a state without blemish.

Their platform included every plank asked for by women delegates. When Senator Carter Glass of Virginia finished presenting this document to the convention, he leaned forward and ad-libbed, "And if there's anything else the women want, we're for it." They named a woman, for the first time, as vice chairman of the Democratic National Committee — a Tennessee woman, of course. The fact that their choice, Miss Charl Ormond Williams, was a capable administrator, eminently qualified for the job by talent, tact, experience, and political know-how — she had served six years as Shelby County Superintendent of Schools and had been named Tennessee's Democratic National Committeewoman with the backing of such diverse politicians in her own state as the emerging "boss" of Memphis, E. H. Crump,

The Melting Pot: Women contribute jewelry to the "cause."

tics. Therefore, we entreat you to begin at once a campaign to antidote it…a great many people really think us suffragists to be exactly what the Antis tell them we are. We enclose a few samples of literature we could send you without cost for distributing by mail…if there are picnics or Chautauquas, enlist the services of your friends for circulation of literature and enlistment of further helpers….

PRESS WORK: A very vigorous press campaign should be conducted. A letter should go to every newspaper in Tennessee asking each to take your bulletins and to help you with editorials. Urge an answer so that you may find how your press stands….

POLL OF THE LEGISLATURE: I want to warn you against accepting as positive and final any report given by anyone except your own bonafide workers. More, if a man is considered doubtful, his position must be confirmed by more than one person. So many women are inclined to accept a complimentary word as a positive pledge….

HOW TO DO POLITICAL WORK: No matter how well the women may work, ratification in Tennessee will go through the work and action of men, and the great motive that will finally put it through will be political and nothing else. We have long since recovered from our previous faith in the action of men based upon a love of justice. Therefore, if you have not done so, secure a Men's Ratification Committee, the biggest and most important men of the state, men of every political faction, representative of all classes. Do it quick before the opposition has made it impossible. Not less than one hundred men, more if you can. Print all their names on your stationery — West Virginia did it on the back of their stationery — no matter what it costs….

Early the following week, the now beleaguered Mrs. Kenny, still minding the store alone in Nashville, wired NAWSA requesting assistance with press and public relations work. Mrs. Catt immediately dispatched to Nashville one of her able young lieutenants, Marjorie Shuler, experienced in fieldwork in state ratification campaigns.

Two days later Miss Shuler wired headquarters: "Political situation here just like Delaware, only worse."

Marjorie Shuler had recognized that ratification in Tennessee was already in big trouble. In a state famous for its " fightin' and feudin'," the current fracas involving Democrats, their governor, and their primary campaign would inevitably affect the ratification vote in the legislature — "just like Delaware." More troubling still, Tennessee's factionalism seemed built-in. The state was trisected by its very geography into three "grand divisions" as the mountains of East Tennessee rolled down into the hills of Middle Tennessee, and on toward the flat, delta, cotton fields of West Tennessee. History had also emphasized a bisectional division when East Tennessee's mountaineers, for the most part, had remained loyal to the Union after Tennessee voted to secede during the "War Between the States." Divisiveness was further nurtured in politics (especially in the legislature) where Republicans from East Tennessee, though usually outvoted by Democrats from Middle and West Tennessee, were always alert for rifts in the Democratic ranks and ready to make a deal with one or another of the opposing factions. Added to this was an urban/rural split, pitting larger cities such as Memphis, Chattanooga, Knoxville and Nashville against the "red handkerchief boys" from

QUESTION IS WILL THEY GET THROUGH IN TIME FOR THE PRESIDENTIAL ELECTION?

hollows, hills and hamlets. Then there was the wet/ dry split, a matter not to be taken lightly at a time when the Eighteenth Amendment's Prohibition laws had just gone into effect, and in a state where, a few years earlier, an anti-saloon-inclined candidate for governor had been gunned down on the streets of Nashville by an anti-prohibitionist. Finally, there was the suffrage/anti-suffrage split which seemed to cut across and betwixt the grain of all the other divisions. And even the suffragists themselves had known the sort of internal friction which, in 1918, had caused several officers of the Tennessee Equal Suffrage League to resign and establish a branch of the National Woman's Party in Tennessee.

But the most alarming thing Miss Shuler had learned during her two days in Nashville was that Governor Roberts, miffed because editorial attacks on him were continuing unabated in certain pro-ratification newspapers that opposed his renomination, was refusing to work with Catherine Kenny and other officers of NAWSA's state auxiliary, the Tennessee League of Women Voters. There was more logic than paranoia in his reasoning. The publisher of one such paper, *The Chattanooga News*, was none other than George Fort Milton, husband of the League's energetic and attractive state president, Abby Crawford Milton, now back home again after the San Francisco convention. And the anti-Roberts *Nashville Tennessean*, sometimes referred to as the "official" suffragist paper in Tennessee, was published by Colonel Luke Lea, a former U.S. Senator and much-celebrated war hero. (Colonel Lea and a group of his men of the 114th Field Artillery, mostly Tennesseans, had gained worldwide attention at the end of World War I with a spectacular, near-successful attempt to capture Germany's Kaiser Wilhelm.) A member of one of the state's pioneer families, Colonel Luke Lea happened also to be a close family friend of Catherine Kenny, the League's ratification chairman.

To avoid dealing with Mrs. Milton and Mrs. Kenny, the governor, on July 1, had appointed the League's popular and respected immediate past president, Mrs. Leslie Warner of Nashville, as chairman of *his* ratification committee. Kate Burch Warner, a woman of penetrating intelligence and Vassar education, had opened a headquarters at Nashville's newest and grandest hotel, The Hermitage, located strategically at the foot of Capitol Hill. She had set about selecting a Committee of 100 — to afford representation for at least one woman from each of

Tennessee's 95 counties. But she soon realized, to her consternation, that the committee she headed was expected to supercede the committee headed by Mrs. Kenny, with whom she had no quarrel. Still, Mrs. Warner hesitated to resign for fear of offending the governor — especially since the latest rumor had the governor so disturbed by the Suff alliance with his press enemies that he was threatening to renege entirely on his promise to call the special session in August. It was then that Carrie Chapman Catt dipped her pen into this embroiling pot, writing sharp letters of exhortation to all the women involved:

July 8, to Mrs. Dudley, Mrs. Milton and Mrs. Kenny:

> I judge from some things we have heard that some of you are not friendly to the Governor, and therefore you may not like to work with a committee of his appointment…. The need of ratification in Tennessee is so important that all differences should be forgotten and an absolute united optimistic front turned toward the enemy. Do not underestimate the power of the opposition which will be applied to the thirty-sixth state….

July 12, to two women members of that Democratic Party's State Executive Committee who had joined Mrs. Warner's "official" ratification committee:

> We are Governor Roberts' friends and acknowledge his right to appoint his committee. We, however, must acknowledge the right of our own auxiliary to work for the thing to which it has sworn its allegiance for many a year. It seems to me that these two committees can work side by side….

July 12, to Abby Crawford Milton:

> I know you are not the Governor's friend. That is alright. But upon the Governor will fall the blame of failure to ratify and the blame of opponents if the Legislature does ratify. Therefore, he must not be fought on the appointment of this committee… I venture to suggest that we in this office recognize the Governor's Committee and your Ratification Committee, and that we urge the Republican women to form a Republican Ratification Committee, and that all three go ahead with their work, keeping

Where Three's a Crowd

out of each other's way as much as possible…. It is so delicate a situation that it calls for very high-class behavior….

July 12, to Anne Dallas Dudley:

> I am writing this confidential letter to you. At this time I do not believe there is a ghost of a chance for ratification in Tennessee…it was factions which defeated us in Delaware. The opposition will know how to arouse these antagonisms anew…. The women who are suffragists in Tennessee, if they want to serve the women of the Nation, must neither pause nor sleep until ratification is over. If they are Democrats and anxious to serve their party, they will not even take a nap….

July 16, to Kate Burch Warner, on vacation in Michigan:

> I am going to Tennessee today, and my sole object in going is to see whether there can be any compromise between the Governor and his opponents in reference to this ratification business. You were quite right that we must have the Governor and his friends, but unless the Tennessee legislature is wholly unlike any other in the country, we must also have his enemies…it is

in an attempt to enlist them both that I am going to Nashville…. Now, my dear Mrs. Warner, if you tell the men that Mrs. Kenny is fighting you, and she tells them that you are fighting her, the only result will be that the men will call it a women's fight and find plenty of excuses for declining to ratify….

On July 17, a steamy, humid Saturday, Carrie Chapman Catt stepped off the train in Nashville and went to work. She had brought just one small traveling bag, expecting to stay only a few days. It would be six weeks before she returned to New York — what one of her biographers, Mary Gray Peck, would later call "the last and most harrowing six weeks of the whole 72 years that women had to fight for the ballot in these 'free and equal' United States."

During her first 36 hours in the state, the old campaigner set a brisk pace. She persuaded Luke Lea, the publisher of the *Tennessean,* to withhold for the good of the suffrage cause a planned attack lampooning Governor Roberts and *his* committee. She caught the campaigning governor "between trains," and they agreed on mutual recognition of both Mrs. Kenny's and Mrs. Warner's committees. Then she scheduled meetings with Republican suffragists to suggest formation of a Republican Ratification Committee.

Her Tennessee comrades were no less idle. Mrs. Warner was rushing home from Michigan and due momentarily. Mrs. Kenny was readying the first results of a legislative poll. Mrs. Milton would be motoring in from Chattanooga in the next day or two, and hoped personally to chauffeur Mrs. Catt and Miss Shuler across the state on a speaking tour to garner publicity and allow conferences with volunteers from some of Tennessee's more than 75 local suffrage clubs. (By 1920, many of these local groups boasted several hundred members, and clubs in the larger towns and cities counted their members in thousands.)

Late Sunday evening, just before she settled down in her hotel room, palm leaf fan in hand, to cool off, Mrs. Catt dispatched a night letter to NAWSA headquarters in New York: "Tennessee promising. Sending details by letter. Must stay indefinitely. Address Hermitage Hotel, Suite 309."

That same weekend, on Saturday, the moment Mrs. Catt's presence in the city became known, another telegram went off from Nashville — this one to Miss Josephine Anderson Pearson of Monteagle,

Josephine Anderson Pearson

Tennessee, the state president of the Tennessee Association Opposed to Woman Suffrage: "Mrs. Catt arrived. Extra session imminent. Our forces being notified to rally at once. Send orders and come immediately."

Fifty-two-year-old Josephine Pearson, educator, elocutionist, and pamphleteer extraordinaire, had been the recognized leader of women Antis in Tennessee for the past half-decade — ever since she had resigned as dean of an obscure women's college in Missouri, and returned home to the mountains of Tennessee to care for her aging parents, a retired Methodist minister and his temperance worker wife. As a child, little Josephine had recited poetic diatribes against the evils of drink at her mother's local Woman's Christian Temperance Union meetings, and it was from her mother that she derived an overwrought antipathy toward both whiskey and woman suffrage. Most temperance workers, following a tradition established by the WCTU's founding mother, Frances E. Willard, were devout suffragists as well — a fact that no doubt explained the consistently generous backing by the liquor interests of the anti-suffrage cause. But her mother was different. She believed that God, with admirable impartiality,

88

condemned both booze for men and ballots for women. Shortly before she died in 1915, Mother Pearson had elicited a vow from her daughter that, should consideration of the Susan B. Anthony Amendment ever come to Tennessee, Josephine would work against its passage. Miss Pearson later recalled how that deathbed promise, plus her reading in a local newspaper the infuriating suggestion that anti-suffragists were in league with the Whiskey Ring, had changed her life. By 1920, she was taking "paying guests" in the old Monteagle family home to make ends meet so that she could pour her full and considerable energies into anti-suffrage work.

On that sweltering Saturday afternoon of July 17, responding to the telegraphed summons, Josephine Pearson came down off her cool mountain and took the train to Nashville. She checked in at the Hermitage Hotel, asking for the cheapest room, and at the same time engaged the hotel's mezzanine assembly rooms as campaign headquarters for the Antis. That night she was unable to sleep in her sticky little room. "The only way I could endure the heat," she later wrote, "was to stand all night under the cool shower, from whence I composed telegrams to send out to Anti leaders all over the nation. Came promptly the official assurance from New York and Boston, 'our forces en route.'" When representatives of the national anti-suffrage organization arrived the next day, their first action was to move their Tennessee chapter president to Room 708, a larger and cooler corner room commanding a view of the turreted dome of Tennessee's handsome State Capitol Building, a few blocks away.

Now battle lines were drawn. For three weeks they waited, Suffs and Antis, tension mounting, for Tennessee to finish its primary fight and get on with the main event — the ratification battle. New combatants joined the ranks daily. Strategies took shape as

maneuver met counter-maneuver.

The Anti's first decision — calculated to point up Mrs. Catt's "outside agitator" status — was to change the name and affiliation of their state organization. On newly-printed stationery of the Tennessee Division of the Southern Women's Rejection League for the Rejection of the Susan B. Anthony Amendment — soon known simply as the Southern Women's Rejection League — President Josephine Pearson wrote to "representative women" throughout Tennessee, appealing not for financial aid, but for "active moral backing" to fight three "deadly principles" lurking in the 19th Amendment: 1. Surrender of state sovereignty. 2. Negro woman suffrage. 3. Race equality.

Meanwhile, Mrs. Catt, in a letter to her League of Women Voters troops, reported that the legislative poll, conducted by Mrs. Kenny and "card-indexed in a most efficient fashion," showed a large number of uncommitted legislators. She exhorted League members to "collect a group of earnest and well-informed local women — the larger the deputation the more impressive it will be — and visit these men yourself." In her book, *Woman Suffrage and Politics*, published in 1923, Mrs. Catt told how Tennessee suffragists responded:

The Southern summer heat was merciless, and many legislators lived in remote villages or on farms miles from any town. Yet the women trailed these legislators, by train, by motor, by wagons and on foot, often in great discomfort, frequently at considerable expense to themselves. They went without meals, were drenched in unexpected rains, and met with "tire troubles," yet no woman faltered....

On Sunday, July 25, the Tennessee League of Women Voters announced that their legislative poll, based in most cases on signed pledges from the members, showed an assured majority for ratification in both houses of the General Assembly. And this despite the admitted uncertainty of eventual voting patterns for a dozen vacancies in the legislature — the result of

Tennessee State Library and Archives

89

F.T.RICHARDS.

Mass Meeting
TONIGHT

Ryman Auditorium
8 O'CLOCK
TO SAVE THE SOUTH
FROM THE SUSAN B. ANTHONY AMENDMENT
AND FEDERAL SUFFRAGE FORCE BILLS

Senator Oscar W. Underwood, of Alabama, and Ex-Gov. Ruffin G. Pleasant, of Louisiana, Have Been Invited to Speak

MAJ. E. B. STAHLMAN
MISS CHARLOTTE E. ROWE
HON. FRANK P. BOND
AND
PROF. GUS DYER
WILL SPEAK
MRS. THOMAS H. MALONE, JR.
WILL SING
JUDGE J. C. HIGGINS
WILL PRESIDE
EVERYBODY INVITED

anybody's guess.

"They call us the 'Home, Heaven, and Mother Crowd' in derision," Miss Rowe told a reporter. That was all right with her, she said, because her concern was to show how "being down into the mire of politics cheapens women." She described her disgust watching the behavior of suffrage leaders at the recent Democratic Convention in San Francisco when adoption of the suffrage plank was announced. She saw them "jump upon desks and permit men to hoist them to their shoulders, and one even went so far as to do an Indian war dance in front of the speaker's stand." Such scenes, declared Miss Rowe, were enough to convince anyone that woman suffrage was a menace to womanhood.

To offset these offensives, the Suffs announced formation of their Men's Ratification Committee an impressive list of 207 names, headed by former Democratic Governor Tom C. Rye, and including former Republican Governor Ben Hooper, plus a notable array of judges, doctors, lawyers, mayors, business men, military men and labor leaders. As proof that their alliance with the incumbent governor had not come unglued, ratification leaders proudly pointed out that the list included not only Governor Roberts himself, but also two important Roberts backers: first, House Speaker Seth Walker, an engaging and influential legislator whose involvement would be crucial; and second, Major E. B. Stahlman, the powerful, irascible, 76-year-old owner of the conservative *Nashville Banner*. Stahlman's support meant that both Nashville newspapers now favored ratification, and Middle Tennessee was shaping up nicely for the cause.

The Antis countered with a Tennessee Constitutional League for men, formed under the direction of Everett P. Wheeler, the New York lawyer who headed the American Constitutional League and had come to Nashville with a large staff of paid workers to keep the legal cauldron boiling. Signing on with him as state president was local Judge Joseph C. Higgins, plus a nice scattering of Vanderbilt University professors, a host of Nashville attorneys, and enough Tennessee politicians and legislators to cause uneasiness in the ratification camp. The uneasiness increased when *The Chattanooga Times*, quite as stiff-necked an editorial foe of woman suffrage as was its sibling, *The New York Times*, printed an extraordinary legal opinion. Any legislator who voted for ratification during the special session, according to the *Times*, would be violating his oath of office to up-

the death or resignation of members after adjournment of the regular session — which were to be filled in a special election at the time of the August 5 primaries.

Miss Josephine Pearson, undaunted, summoned the faithful to Anti headquarters at the Hermitage Hotel to prepare exhibits, mail out literature, and plan garden parties. Headlines on the women's pages announced that "Social Leaders Oppose Vote," and a press release proclaimed the arrival of Mrs. James S. Pinckard of Montgomery, Alabama, President-General of the Southern Women's Rejection League, fresh from the victory in Baton Rouge, Louisiana, where another Southern legislature, with befitting regional decorum, had just rejected ratification. Mrs. Pinckard, "grandniece of John C. Calhoun," a former Vice President and pride of the South, would now aid Tennessee's Antis. Also, the Antis' star orator, the quick-witted, sharp-tongued Miss Charlotte Rowe, was down from New York to work the crowds in neighboring North Carolina where rejection of ratification was moving along on schedule, and in Tennessee, which was still

Governor A.H. Roberts and Kate Burch Warner (seated) with Tennessee suffrage leaders.

hold his state constitution and all its existing provisions — even, it was declared, provisions which federal courts had held to be invalid, such as the one postponing legislative consideration of ratification. Obviously crafted to provide a face-saving excuse for vote-switching legislators who might be persuaded to repudiate their pledges for ratification, this remarkable claim was widely reprinted and discussed. The reasoning, like the arguments, daily grew more rarified and confusing. Suffragists slyly suggested that a vote against ratification could also be a violation of a legislator's oath; Antis replied, very well, let the legislature take no action when it is called into extra session. One Anti lawyer from Camden, Tennessee, firm in his belief that the state's women were overwhelmingly opposed to their own enfranchisement, suggested in a letter to his local editor that the best solution was to bypass the legislature entirely: "Let the women vote on this question of whether they have the right to vote or not."

Mrs. Catt was now motoring across the state on her speaking tour with Abby Crawford Milton. Endeavoring to clear the air, she tackled the "oath issue" wherever she appeared — at luncheons with the Memphis Chamber of Commerce or the Nashville Kiwanis Club, at conferences with elected officials in Jackson, at citizens' meetings in Knoxville and Chattanooga. She reminded Tennesseans that "every legislator takes an oath of loyalty to two Constitutions, an obligation that comes from the Federal Constitution (Article VI, Section 3). The possibility of conflict between the two was foreseen and the Federal Constitution (Article VI, Section 2) declares that to be the supreme law of the land."

Meanwhile, there was action on the national scene which, in that summer of 1920, meant Ohio, home state of the presidential nominees of both parties. From all over the country, veteran suffragists skilled in the parry and thrust of congressional lobbying, along with one-time White House pickets, many wearing as badges of honor their "prison pins" which spoke of time served in the workhouse, showed up on the doorsteps of both candidates to urge them to apply pressure to Tennessee legislators. From his front porch in Marion, Senator Harding greeted a delegation of Woman's Party marchers led by one of Tennessee's own pioneer suffragists, 70-year-old Lizzie Crozier French, and carrying a street-wide banner inscribed with the question: WILL THE REPUBLICANS CARRY OUT THEIR PLATFORM BY GIVING A UNANIMOUS VOTE IN TENNESSEE FOR SUFFRAGE? Harding

assured them that he did, indeed, support their aim. And in Columbus, Governor Cox promised visiting delegations that he would go to Tennessee, if necessary, to campaign for ratification among Democratic legislators. Late in July, both Harding and Cox sent approving telegrams to Mrs. Catt which said, with what must have been heartfelt sincerity, how glad they were that she was in Tennessee.

The issue, however, would not go away. From Anti headquarters in Nashville, President-General Mrs. Pinckard of the Southern Women's Rejection League wrote to Governor Cox to prepare the way for an Ohio-bound group of "home-loving women of the South, who do not picket, card-index or blackmail candidates." She appealed to Cox, Democrat to Democrat, to pay heed to the views of these women on such matters as States' Rights, the Solid South, and the "Federalist Empire" which was trying to thrust into the hands of women the unwanted "weapon of the ballot." Cox hurriedly scheduled an appointment for the delegation which was led by the vice president of the Rejection League's Tennessee Division — the improbably-named Mrs. George Washington.

AN ANNOYING DELAY

TENNESSEE LEGISLATURE

UNIVERSAL SUFFRAGE

By August 1, still another ratification headquarters was operating in Nashville. The National Woman's Party had set up shop at the Tulane Hotel, and while Alice Paul, their national chairman, remained in Washington to orchestrate further pressure on party leaders, a select corps of attractive young Woman's Party crusaders appeared in Tennessee to work with Sue Shelton White, their politically sagacious state chairman.

At 33, "Miss Sue," a slender, brown-eyed, curly-haired native of Henderson, Tennessee, was one of the state's most level-headed, dedicated, and effective suffragists. For 10 years she had been a court reporter in Jackson, one of the first women in Tennessee to hold such a post. And her remarkable success as organizer of Jackson's Equal Suffrage League had recently been summed up by a newspaperwoman's review of changing local attitudes toward the idea of votes for women: "Hostility in 1913, ridicule in 1914, tolerance in 1915, frank approval in 1916."

Miss Sue had helped organize other Equal Suffrage Leagues throughout the state before breaking ranks with NAWSA during World War I over the wisdom of continuing pro-suffrage demonstrations during wartime, and the legality of the arrests that ensued. Sue Shelton White was convinced that a basic constitutional principle of free speech was at risk, and, before the war ended, would herself spend five days in jail for taking part in a White House demonstration. But, in 1917, she expressed her convictions by joining with the venerable Lizzie Crozier French, founder of Knoxville's Equal Suffrage League, and several other influential NAWSA dissidents who shared her reluctance to abandon the suffrage cause, even if there was a war going on, to form a small but active Tennessee branch of the National Woman's Party. As it turned out, that action would greatly improve the suffragists' ultimate chances for victory. Though the schism at first threatened to fragment Tennessee's established suffrage movement, the rivalries it created ended up honing the skills, stimulating the zeal, and increasing the number of suffrage crusaders in the state. By the time the ratification fight came to Nashville in 1920, Tennessee's reunited Suffs would be ready to do battle.

The high-spirited young Woman's Party fieldworkers who joined Sue Shelton White in Tennessee that August got busy, adopting the local cus-

Sue Shelton White

tom of dividing the state into three parts. A tiny and tireless South Carolinian named Anita Pollitzer went out beating the bushes for more pledges from East Tennessee legislators. Miss Sue took charge of Middle Tennessee. Miss Betty Gram of Portland, Oregon, a pert, smiling young woman with peaches-and-cream complexion, descended upon West Tennessee, ending up in populous Shelby County where soon appeared this headline: "110 Pounds of Femininity Hits Memphis." (A few years later, Betty Gram would make headlines again when she married a newsman and future radio commentator named Raymond Swing and he, to endorse her feminist beliefs, officially adopted her maiden name as his middle name, making them Mr. and Mrs. Raymond Gram Swing.)

In careful interviews with every legislator in the Shelby County delegation, Betty Gram uncovered an amazing unanimity — not a single vote, House or Senate, against ratification! Memphis, for many decades, had been a bastion of pro-suffrage senti-

ment in Tennessee, turning out big, reliably responsive audiences for touring national suffrage leaders. In years past, three pioneering Memphis suffragists — Elizabeth Avery Meriwether, Elizabeth Lisle Saxon, and Martha Moore Allen — had served as national presidents of woman suffrage organizations. Currently, both daily newspapers, *The Commercial Appeal* and the *Memphis News-Scimitar*, both favored votes for women. But, as Betty Gram soon gleaned, the Shelby County delegation's comforting pro-ratification consensus was due not just to the honored traditions of local history, but also to the artful manipulations of the local political boss.

Edward H. Crump, known simply as "Mister Crump," was blessed with an uncanny ability to recognize, attract, and utilize any and all potential blocks of voters. Meanwhile, Crump regularly achieved unanimity among Shelby County legislators in support of various issues that came before the legislature by imposing a so-called "unit vote rule" on lawmakers whose election he had sponsored — generally the entire delegation. This practice had earned power for Mister Crump in state Democratic circles, but had accumulated enmity for "Big Shelby" among small-town and rural legislators.

Betty Gram's optimistic report to Nashville noted that even the two existing vacancies in Shelby's legislative delegation would be filled by staunch ratificationists running unopposed in the August 5 primary. T. K. Riddick, an eminent Memphis attorney known as "the million-dollar lawyer" because of his courtroom eloquence, had often been mentioned as a likely candidate for United States Senator or Representative. For the good of the cause, Riddick not only had agreed to run for a seat in the Tennessee legislature, but also had volunteered to serve as floor leader for ratification forces in the House. And a 30-year-old bachelor, former legislator, and still-struggling lawyer, Joseph Hanover, was running to reclaim his own House seat, recently given up following adjournment so he could spend more time on his legal career.

Joe Hanover was as ardent a male advocate of votes for women as any female suffragist could have hoped to encounter. Brought to America at the age of five by penniless, immigrant Jewish parents who were fleeing from pogroms in their native Poland, Joe had grown up in Memphis where his father, through good sense and hard work, had managed to acquire a small dry-goods store. The elder

Tennessee General Assembly 1919-1920

Hanover had given his four sons daily instructions on the wonders of America and the glories of democracy. Young Joe, knowing that only in America were such things possible, had worked his way through night law school, then run for election to the Tennessee legislature in 1919 as an independent — which meant he hadn't consulted Mister Crump about it. To the amazement of all, including Crump, Joe Hanover had won. He had gone to Nashville, listened to the floor debate on the granting of partial suffrage to women, and reflected on what it meant to be born female — even in democratic America, the land of the free and the home of the brave. On the day the partial suffrage bill came to a vote in the House, the freshman lawmaker, speaking as one of only two Jews in the 61st General Assembly, poured out his thoughts and feelings in a patriotic speech that had touched the hearts of suffragists and had even changed a few Anti votes.

Now, in the summer of 1920, with ratification of the federal Suffrage Amendment up for grabs in the extra session, Joe Hanover knew he had to run again. He had to be there to help win justice and equal rights, not only for Tennessee women, but for all the women of the United States.

It was Anita Pollitzer, working for the Woman's Party in the back country of the Great Smoky Mountains, who discovered the first cracks in the Tennessee dam. Votes pledged for ratification in East Tennessee were beginning to drop away; defections were particularly noticeable among Republican legislators who were citing the "oath" excuse. And the responses of Republicans still marked "uncertain" or "unpledged" in the polls were disturbingly imprecise.

Take, for example, Harry Burn, serving his first term as representative from McMinn County and, at 24, the youngest Tennessee legislator. Anita Pollitzer was unable to get up to the remote village of Niota where Harry Burn lived with his widowed mother and his younger brother and sister. But she had gone to Athens, the McMinn County seat, to see the Republican county chairman who, after telephoning Harry Burn in her presence, had assured her the suffragists could count on Harry's vote. All of which was fine — until she later learned that this same Republican chairman's strong political ally was the district's state senator, H.M. Candler, a leading and vocal anti-suffragist. And Harry Burn, who was reading law under Candler's tutelage, was said to be the senator's political protégé.

Confronted with such contradictions and uncertainties, Anita Pollitzer called on Republican ex-Governor Ben Hooper, a longtime friend of suffrage. (In 1914, while welcoming delegates to NAWSA's national convention held in Nashville, Governor Hooper had won the assembly's heartiest applause by introducing his young daughter, Anna, with the declaration that, when woman suffrage became a reality, his greatest pleasure would derive "from the joy and exultation of my little daughter, who has been a positive, pronounced and persistent suffragist since she was nine-years-old.") Now, Hooper spent a full day telephoning wavering Republican lawmakers; he also sent a telegram to candidate Harding in Ohio to say the situation in Tennessee was critical and help was needed to bring legislators back in line.

Meanwhile, Carrie Chapman Catt, winding up her cross-state tour of East Tennessee, had also heard persistent and disconcerting rumors about a plot hatched by out-of-state Antis to firm up a solid Republican adverse vote, using the argument that, should Tennessee ratify, "the Democrats would get the credit." Worse still, one Republican leader with whom these Antis were said to be dealing was a certain James Beasley — whose wife had just been named state chairman of the Republican Women's Ratification Committee. In a handwritten message to Will H. Hayes, the chairman of the Republican National Committee, Mrs. Catt asked for help, noting, in a well-calculated afterthought, "The Democrats may be able to put the amendment through without the Republicans, and if they do they will certainly crow loud and long."

By the time Mrs. Catt got back to the Hermitage Hotel in Nashville on the afternoon of primary day, August 5, Chairman Hayes had wired his reply. The Republican National Committee's new vice chairman, Harriet Taylor Upton, would be coming to Nashville at once to help straighten things out. The exhausted suffrage leader must have heaved a sigh of relief at that news. For many years, Mrs. Upton, her good and trusted friend, had been the treasurer of NAWSA. Like Carrie Chapman Catt herself, she had done battle against every weapon in the Antis' arsenal.

Tennessee awoke on August 6 to the news that Governor Roberts had won renomination in the Democratic primary. On Saturday, August 7, true to his promise, the governor issued a proclamation calling the 61st Tennessee General Assembly into extraordinary session in the State Capitol at noon on the following Monday. Suffs and Antis alike spent the rest of the weekend in last-minute rallies for that high noon.

The legislators had started arriving at Nashville's Union Station early Saturday morning. They were a mixed bag of Southern gentlemen, run-of-the-courthouse politicians, small-town merchants, good old country boys, and earnest Bible Belt fundamentalists — the sort who would pass laws like the one prohibiting the teaching of the theory of evolution in public schools which, a few years hence, would again bring national attention to Tennessee during the famous Scopes "Monkey Trial." The moment they stepped off their cinder-gritted trains, the men were buttonholed, quite literally, by sweet-talking, flower-dispensing Southern ladies laden with bouquets from their flourishing summer gardens. Antis handed out American Beauty red roses as their emblem; Suffs offered their symbolic yellow roses. Boutonnieres blossomed as men agreed to show their colors, and Tennessee's ratification fight would henceforth be known as the War of the Roses.

There were more arrivals. U.S. Senator Kenneth McKellar was in from Washington, huddling with the Suffs, bringing encouragement from the Wilson administration. The Democratic National Committee's popular new vice chairman, Charl Ormond Williams, had arrived from Shelby County, pledging to spend "every hour of every day" working for passage of the ratification resolution. And well she might, for Governor Roberts had telephoned her privately, asking if he might arrange some way for her to apply her much-admired administrative talents to the fragmented chaos now evident in ratification efforts. Since the DNC had asked her to do just that, Miss Williams readily agreed.

Another new arrival was Mrs. Ruffin G. Pleasant, wife of Louisiana's crusading anti-ratification ex-governor, and, according to Miss Josephine Pearson's press release, "the daughter of Major General Ector, C. S. A., who had three horses shot out from under him at the battle of Lookout Mountain." A still greater coup for the Antis was the presence in Nashville of Miss Kate Gordon of New Orleans and Miss Laura Clay of Kentucky, both revered veteran suffragists and former national officers of NAWSA,

The Federal Suffrage Amendment

WILL NEVER BE RATIFIED

IF THE PEOPLE OF TENNESSEE

GUARD THEIR RIGHTS

The Susan B. Anthony Federal Suffrage Amendment has NOT been ratified. The Tennessee Constitution PROHIBITS ratification of ANY Federal Amendment until the PEOPLE ELECT a NEW Legislature. ANY GOOD LAWYER who has ever heard of the Haire vs. Rice Case, 204 United States Reports, KNOWS that the attempted and so-called ratification by an illegal and insufficient PART of the present Tennessee Legislature (less than a legal quorum) was NULL AND VOID, ILLEGAL AND UNCONSTITUTIONAL.

NOBODY but the United States Supreme Court has a right to say that the Tennessee Constitution is in conflict with the United States Constitution. It is NOT IN CONFLICT, and CANNOT be in conflict, unless the UNITED STATES SUPREME COURT DECIDES THAT IT IS.

GOV. JAMES M. COX, Democratic Candidate for President, says: "Most lawyers to whom I have talked believe that it is not in conflict. It is a very good provision that ought to be in every State Constitution."

If it is NOT in conflict, then every attempt to EVADE and OVERRIDE the Constitution of Tennessee is plain LAWBREAKING and VIOLATION of their OATHS OF OFFICE by every official who solemnly swore, with God as a witness, to uphold the Constitution of Tennessee.

Such men ought to be IMPEACHED, as well as ENJOINED.

A man who deliberately CONSPIRES with lobbyists to break the SUPREME LAW of the State of Tennessee is in the same class with the BOOTLEGGER and the BOLSHEVIST. The PEOPLE must see to it that OFFICIAL LAWBREAKERS are dealt with BY THE COURTS, just as any OTHER LAWBREAKERS.

ABLE LAWYERS and Tennessee citizens have already ENJOINED officials who want to DEFY and OVERRIDE the CONSTITUTION and the PEOPLE OF TENNESSEE.

DO YOUR BIT, ORGANIZE MASS MEETINGS, Circulate Petitions, and we will UPHOLD the Constitutional Rights of the People.

Suffragists marching in a May, 1919, parade in Nashville down West End Avenue to Centennial Park.

who had once hobnobbed with Susan B. Anthony herself. But because they believed in suffrage through state action only, both had resigned when NAWSA endorsed the federal amendment. Now, for the greater glory of states' rights, Misses Gordon and Clay would join the Antis in distributing pamphlets that accused all suffragists of being "atheistic feminists who rewrote the Bible," who "destroyed the home," and "blackened the honor of Robert E. Lee."

If Nashville was, as a local slogan claimed, the "dimple of the Universe," then the high-vaulted, marbled lobby of the Hermitage Hotel, by mid-afternoon on Saturday, August 7, had become the vortex of the dimple. Under the lobby's stained-glass skylight, milling around in suffocating numbers, were men and women, Suffs and Antis, legislators and politicians, Republicans and Democrats — all panting to learn what all the others were up to. Mixing in the melee were certain "mystery men," the sort who had appeared in every state capital where ratification had been considered. Old campaigners easily spotted numerous representatives of the textile manufacturers, mostly Southern mill owners who believed an inevitable result of woman suffrage

would be demands for higher wages for women workers or, more inconvenient still, the enactment of child labor laws. Also on hand were familiar lobbyists for the railroad companies such as the L. & N. (Louisville & Nashville), who were known for their obliging natures and past favors, which included free railroad passes issued to every legislator upon election, and "retainers" paid to legislators who practiced law — the rationale being that railroad-crossing accidents might occur in the lawmakers' hometowns.

Late that afternoon, some of the crowd moved upstairs to the mezzanine for the welcoming reception at Anti headquarters. As ceiling fans labored to redistribute the sultry Southern air and red roses wilted on perspiring Southern bosoms, ladies of impeccable Confederate lineage thanked the legislators in advance for protecting Southern womanhood from the perils of enfranchisement. Some legislators, however, remained ambivalent. State Senator Lon McFarland from the bluegrass hills of Middle Tennessee showed up in his white linen suit, black string tie, Panama hat, and a boutonniere that confounded his hostesses — it was a small talisman rosebud showing a bit of anti-suffrage red tinged with about the same amount of suffrage yellow. The senator remained noncommittal throughout but, on leaving the Antis' affair, McFarland was heard to murmur to a friend a remark that became instant legend among the Suffs: "That bunch of fillies was the longest on pedigree and the shortest on looks that I ever saw."

As the evening wore on, more and more legislators, single and in small groups, were observed making their way to the elevators and requesting passage to the eighth floor. Word had gone around that in a certain eighth-floor suite, in guarded privacy as discretion and 18th Amendment enforcement laws demanded, legislators would find available and free in any quantity desired their choice of bourbon, moonshine whiskey, or Tennessee's favorite Jack Daniel's "in the raw." By midnight, many of the state's lawmakers could be seen and heard, reeling happily up and down the halls of the hotel. Though some of them were singing the Anti's theme song, "Keep the Home Fires Burning," it was clear to every waking suffragist that the pros and cons of ratification were of little or no concern to any of them.

Governor Roberts, meanwhile, was proving to be the most committed ratificationist of all. He had named State Superintendent of Public Instruction Albert Williams as his legislative liaison and opened up an unofficial caucus room in the State Capitol for legislators favoring the resolution. Early Sunday morning, August 8, Albert Williams and several of the governor's aides met there to analyze the latest information about the leanings of the 99 House members and 33 state senators. House Speaker Seth Walker, the governor's trusted political ally, had amiably agreed the previous week to give the resolution of ratification added impetus by introducing it in the House himself, and Williams had asked him to come that morning to help cross-check the various poll results. It was mid-morning before Seth Walker appeared. He entered the caucus room and told the governor's men that he had undergone a change of conviction. He warned them that Governor Roberts was courting political disaster unless he could be persuaded by his friends to oppose ratification. Then he left.

For Albert Williams and the others, the question was: How many pledged votes had walked out the door with Seth Walker?

A highlight of Nashville's summer social season occurred that Sunday afternoon. Mr. and Mrs. George Washington entertained a group of Anti dignitaries (including Antis from out of state, locally prominent ladies and gentlemen of the Anti persuasion, and all the sympathizing legislators they could lay hands on) with a garden party at their country home in nearby Cedar Hill, Tennessee. Miss Josephine Pearson later reported in a handwritten notation on a group photograph taken on the steps of the Southern mansion that day: "More than forty automobiles gathered in front of the Hermitage Hotel to collect passengers, and then motored out to Washington Hall for a lovely party, enjoyed by all."

That night, in Mrs. Catt's suite at the Hermitage, suffrage leaders representing both NAWSA and the Woman's Party, compared session-eve notes. The Senate was safe with votes to spare, even after a couple of men who had been tabbed as "bribable" were discounted. The real battle would be in the House. Sixty-two of the 99 House members had pledged for ratification — 12 more than the 50-vote constitutional majority required for passage. But no one felt secure. Davidson County's six-man delegation from Nashville, as well as Shelby County's eight-man Memphis delegation, had been counted true-blue in the House polls. But now there were waverings in Davidson County. The representative from rural Meigs County had signed up for ratification back in June in Mrs. Kenny's poll with the assurance that "Anything you League of Women Voters want of me, command me. I will vote for women every time I have a chance until the Roll is called up Yonder." He had become the first confirmed dropout and was now working openly for the Antis.

Then there was the devastating perfidy of House Speaker Seth Walker! It was obviously taking its toll. Final count in the House showed only 55 in favor of ratification, 44 against. Still, suffragist spirits revived briefly when they heard how Betty Gram had challenged Walker in the crowded lobby of the Hermitage earlier that evening. In full view and hearing of everyone present, she had demanded: "What brought about your change? The Louisville & Nashville Railroad?" To which the chagrined Speaker had responded, "That's an insult!" and stalked off. (Rumor later had it that two of the more ardent pro-suffrage representatives were so delighted by her bold questioning of their defecting Speaker's motives they had proposed marriage to Betty Gram.)

The meeting in Mrs. Catt's room finally broke up in the early morning hours. In an agony of suspense, the suffragists went to bed, but not to sleep. There could be no turning back. Armageddon was at hand.

Day One, Capitol Hill, Monday, August 9, 1920:

Tennessee legislature convenes at noon in extra session. Galleries packed with ladies wearing red or yellow roses. Governor's message urging ratification "in justice to the womanhood of America" is read. Legislature adjourns for the day.

On this first day, everyone was biding time. Back at the Hermitage (now being referred to as the "third House"), Republican legislators held an afternoon caucus, heard ex-Governor Hooper urge them to vote for ratification, and agreed to vote their consciences. At a two-hour conference in Governor Roberts' offices at the Capitol, the Suff forces unanimously decided that all ratification committees would unite under a steering committee headed by Charl Ormond Williams. For strategic and public-relations reasons (and in line with a shrewd "graciousness is our watchword" policy first adopted by the gentleladies of the Nashville Equal Suffrage League way back in 1911), it was recommended that only Tennessee women, familiar with the male sensibilities and Southern antipathies of their Tennessee menfolk, should lobby on Capitol Hill.

As if to demonstrate proper application of this tactic, a cable addressed to the men of the Tennessee legislature had arrived that day from London from the celebrated one-time Southern belle, Lady Nancy Astor, *nee* Langhorne, of Virginia. In 1919, Lady Astor, famous as both socialite and suffragist, had become the first woman to sit in the British Parliament; now, in her gracious cable to her fellow lawmakers in Tennessee, Lady Astor couched her plea for a favorable vote on ratification wholly in terms of her confidence in the enduring and endearing nature of Southern chivalry.

Day Two, Capitol Hill, Tuesday, August 10, 1920:

Legislature convenes in morning. Capitol corridors are decked with yellow bunting. Joint resolution of ratification is introduced in Senate by Presiding Officer Andrew L. Todd and in House by the entire Shelby County delegation. Referred to Committees on Constitutional Amendments. On motion by Antis in each house, joint public hearing is set for night of August 12. Both houses adjourn for day.

Suspicion that the Antis were using a strategy of delay made the Suffs nervous. They contained their nervousness as best they could. Sue Shelton White and Betty Gram had discovered a watermelon stand on the outskirts of Nashville and regular forays there by streetcar began. Others, more daring, made their way to the room of Mrs. Isaac B. Reese, a 60-year-old Memphis suffragist, both aristocratic and flamboyant, who had been active in both NAWSA and the Woman's Party. Lulu Colyar Reese had been famous for years for the "Parisian salons" held in her home, where lively assortments of persons with varied backgrounds met for conversation and interaction, and where Mrs. Reese herself had been known to smoke an occasional cigar. Her room at the Hermitage now served as safe territory for suffragists wanting to sneak a quick cigarette.

The Antis, meanwhile, busied themselves with sterner matters. Judge Joseph C. Higgins, president of the Tennessee Constitutional League, called reporters in to issue a warning that, if ratification should be voted in Tennessee, the League "would be constrained to go into court and inhibit the Secretary of State from certifying it."

Day Three, Capitol Hill, Wednesday, August 11, 1920:

Resolution by Antis in House to delay consideration of ratification until "the will of the people can be heard" in county conventions is tabled by a vote of 50 – 37. No other action. In this first test of strength, the Suffs had won — but without a single vote to spare, for in future tallies they could not count on any of the absent or abstaining legislators to put the pro-ratification count above that bare constitutional majority of 50. They must now be prepared to ride herd on all pledged members every hour of every day, watching, guarding, personally escorting. Word was sent out, reserves called in, assignments made. From this day on, bewildered Tennessee legislators would be overwhelmed by the flattering attentions of gracious Tennessee suffragists.

That night, as always, at their strategy meetings in Mrs. Catt's suite at the Hermitage, there was news and gossip to share, including another Lon McFarland story. Anne Dallas Dudley had been solicitously straightening the uncommitted senator's black string tie while explaining why his vote for

Suffrage strategists: U.S. Sen. McKellar, State Sen. Haston, Sue Shelton White, Gov. Roberts, Rep. Hanover

ratification was needed. Without a word, Senator McFarland had whipped out his pen-knife, cut himself free, and walked away, leaving Mrs. Dudley standing, tie in hand, in the Capitol corridor. There were rumors of discontent among pro-ratification House members over the choice of high-falutin' Memphis attorney T. K. Riddick as floor leader; he was too new and inexperienced a legislator for the old-timers, too Democratic for the Republicans, and too rich for the blood of the country boys. Another rumor was that Albert Williams, the governor's liaison, had hired a private detective to check up on reported bribe offers. Joe Hanover, whose third-floor room was just down the hall from Mrs. Catt's suite, had now become a regular at the Suffs' nightly sessions, and he had good news: pro-suffrage men were now passing the hat to raise much-needed suffrage cash.

Day Four, Capitol Hill, Thursday, August 12, 1920:

Resolution sponsored by Antis declaring any action by the House, for or against ratification, would "violate the spirit" of the State Constitution, is tabled, again by vote of 50 – 37. Both houses adjourn until evening's joint committee public hearing.

The biggest crowd ever assembled in the Capitol attended the suffrage hearing that night in the hall of the House of Representatives. Among those speaking for the Suffs — all Tennesseans — were Charl Ormond Williams, Anne Dallas Dudley, Senator McKellar. The Antis led off with Charlotte Rowe, followed by a congressman, two judges, and the big (and for suffragists, ominous) surprise. It came in the person of old Major E. B. Stahlman, the German-born newspaper publisher who, starting as an immigrant railroad construction worker, had risen through the ranks to become vice president of the L. & N. Railroad before he quit and bought the *Nashville Banner*. When Stahlman, one-time member of the Men's Ratification Committee, rose and told the crowd that he (and his newspaper) were now unalterably opposed to ratification, elated Anti ladies waved red roses and discouraged Suffs fought back tears.

To counteract this shock, the Senate Committee on Constitutional Amendments gallantly went into emergency session on the spot, right after the hearing, and voted 8 – 2 to report the 19th Amendment favorably in the State Senate the very next day. The Suffs could take comfort from this; their Senate floor leader for ratification, Senator E. N. Haston, was still

"Truth crushed to the earth will rise again." Mrs. James S. Pinckard, President-General of the Southern Women's League for the Rejection of the Susan B. Anthony Amendment unfurls the Confederate flag. To her left are a Confederate veteran and Josephine A. Pearson, State President of the Tennessee Association Opposed to Woman Suffrage.

confident they had a shoo-in. Then someone remembered — the next day was *Friday the Thirteenth*.

Day Five, Capitol Hill, Friday, August 13, 1920:

State Senate, after three hours of debate, passes resolution of ratification with 25 ayes, 4 nays, 2 not voting. Resolution is referred to the House. Both houses adjourn until Monday. When Tennessee suffragists hurried down to the Hermitage, where Mrs. Catt, Mrs. Upton, and other national leaders banished from Capitol Hill were waiting for news, they scarcely mentioned the unexpectedly wide margin of victory in the Senate. They were still spluttering about the remarks of Senator H. M. Candler, paradigmatic of every anti-suffrage oration ever made. They reported how Candler had railed against "petticoat government," causing one of his fellow senators to gleefully announce that "the ladies don't wear

petticoats anymore." (This remark, in turn, had inspired a parade of pro-suffrage ladies to form just outside the Senate chamber when the session was over and daintily lift their skirts to show just enough petticoat to prove him wrong.) Candler had gone on to denounce "low-neck, high-skirt suffragists who know not what it is to go down in the shade of the valley and bring forth children." (At this point, an indignant, yellow-sashed Nashville matron had interrupted from the gallery: "I've got six children!") And, finally, Candler had concluded with a tirade against "an old woman down here at the Hermitage Hotel, whose name is Catt — I think her husband's name is Tom — trying to dictate to Tennessee's lawmakers."

The women finally calmed down long enough to report with some relish how another senator, card-indexed as an Anti, had nevertheless voted for ratification of the 19th Amendment — because, he explained during the debate, he wanted to get back at the North for those diabolical Fourteenth and Fifteenth Amendments. And still wearing his talisman rose, noncommittal to the end, Senator Lon McFarland was one of the two abstainers.

The weekend had brought new perils. Until the House reconvened on Monday, not a single ratification-inclined member could be permitted time to sneak home, fall ill, or turn coat. In a frenzy of solicitude, the Suffs invited their assigned legislators to go for long automobile drives in the country, to take in a movie ("Old Wives for New" was showing at the Crescent), or to have dinner at the club. Some legislators, catching the spirit, volunteered themselves to spend time in the company of various pretty, young suffragists. One House member was amazed to find himself at the posh Belle Meade Country Club, the guest of a Mrs. Stahlman, who happened to be the *Banner* publisher's suffragist daughter-in-law.

"Beware! Men of the South! Heed not the song of the suffrage siren!" Thus began one of the pamphlets Josephine Pearson and her helpers were now distributing. In a further appeal to Southern pride and prejudice, she and another Anti leader posed for photographs with a weathered old Confederate veteran just outside their mezzanine headquarters at the Hermitage, which was bedecked with red roses and flags

— the Stars and Stripes and the Stars and Bars. The frail-looking old soldier was holding a tattered battle standard he had once carried as a scout for Tennessee's most popular Civil War hero, General Nathan Bedford Forrest — whose latter-day fame (or notoriety, according to many) would derive from his role as principal founder of the Ku Klux Klan.

Meanwhile, Antis had placed an advertisement in Nashville newspapers announcing a shocking new exhibition now on display at their headquarters — a copy of the so-called "Woman's Bible," a commentary published in the 1890s by prominent suffrage leaders (mostly deceased) and edited by the legendary Elizabeth Cady Stanton. The big news was that Carrie Chapman Catt was listed as a member of the Revising Committee.

To illustrate how the offending volume denigrated "the Christian Bible, the Christian Religion and the Christian Ministry," quotations were offered:

"The Bible has been and will continue to be a stumbling block in the way of the truest civilization…. The Bible has always been, and is at present, one of the greatest obstacles in the way of emancipation and advancement of the sex…."

And the question was posed: "Are you willing for women who hold these views to become political powers in our country?" Such was the turn the campaign was now taking.

Later that weekend, in a letter to a suffragist friend in Washington, Carrie Chapman Catt reported, "We are up to our last half of a state…. It is hot, muggy, nasty, and this last battle is desperate. Even if we win, we who have been here will never remember it with anything but a shudder!"

Tension was not confined to Nashville. Woodrow Wilson wired to remind Seth Walker that he favored ratification. From Ohio, Governor Cox kept calling Governor Roberts to emphasize how enthusiastically he supported ratification. And Senator Harding had again announced that he was pro-ratification. But Harding had also written, in a letter to a Republican Anti which was now being widely circulated, that

THE PESSIMIST AND THE OPTIMIST.

he could understand how an oath-taking Tennessee legislator with "a very conscientious belief that there is a constitutional inhibition" might vote against ratification. Mrs. Upton, trying to check with party leaders on this disquieting development, had one of her telegrams stolen somewhere between her room and the hotel's front desk, and it was reprinted in the next day's papers.

Mrs. Catt, meanwhile, was sure her telephone was tapped. And her fears of enemy treachery were compounded when, on retiring to her bedroom for a much-needed afternoon nap, she was startled to discover a bottle of whiskey hidden under her pillow. Obviously, this was an Anti plot to embarrass and discredit her. How could she get rid of the stuff before it was discovered by some prearranged search party? Flush it down the toilet? The smell would linger. Hide it in her suitcase? That's the first place they'd look. In a state of near-panic, she heard someone enter her sitting room! The raiding party had arrived!

Then she realized it was only her friend, Harriet, who was soon able to calm her fears. Mrs. Upton knew all about the whiskey bottle. It had been left in their suite for safekeeping by a friendly newspaperwoman. No need to worry. Still, Mrs. Catt did worry. Later that afternoon, she insisted on being taken for a long drive out into the countryside; only after she saw the bottle of whiskey hidden away in a crevice of a stone wall covered with poison ivy was she able to rest easy.

To foil the many eavesdroppers found lurking in corridors outside their rooms as the long weekend wore on, some suffragists took to closing their door transoms, despite the unrelenting heat. In a retaliatory mood, Anita Pollitzer and Sue Shelton White volunteered to go listen in on the goings-on up in the convivial "Jack Daniel's suite." Their expedition became front-page news. A story in *The Chattanooga Times*, datelined Nashville and headlined "Two Women Spies Caught In Hotel," told how "two wily, militant suffragists undertook to snatch information from the anti-suffrage forces on the eighth floor of the Hermitage." After determining that the "spies" had no legitimate business on the eighth floor, the sergeant-at-arms of the House, according to the *Times*, asked them "in a mild manner" to leave the vicinity. Instead, the unwelcome visitors calmly took seats in the elevator lobby, "within earshot of the headquarters." A clerk was called but the offending Suffs still refused to move,

and the matter was not resolved until "the proprietor came, and in none too gentle a way led the women to a waiting elevator, closed the door, and ordered the car lowered."

Sometime that weekend, a key question was settled. Joe Hanover had emerged as the suffragists' (and Mrs. Catt's) choice to take over the duties of floor leader for ratification in the House, replacing the respected but unpopular Representative T. K. Riddick. Hanover was quoted in the Sunday edition of *The Commercial Appeal* as saying he was confident the amendment would be ratified. When a reporter asked if he feared vote-trading, he had replied, "I am prepared for that."

Indeed he was. Joe Hanover had even found an effective way to handle the bribery menace which the Suffs, because of high principles and low cash reserves, were unable to answer in kind. As a young and accommodating lawyer, Hanover often had been consulted by older legislators of lesser education who needed help in drafting bills they wanted to introduce in the House. Mostly out of friendship for Joe, one such representative, an old fiddle-playing farmer from the hills, had been voting faithfully with the ratificationists in this special session, and his vote was counted safe. But early this Sunday morning he showed up at Hanover's door, bleary-eyed but happy, to announce, "Sorry, Joe, but I'm going to have to leave you suffrage boys. The Antis just paid me three hundred dollars." Hanover did not even pause before delivering his alleged reply: "Well, you're a pretty cheap vote — I hear they're paying the others a thousand." "Why, those dirty crooks!" cried the old farmer. He had become, on the instant, a true believer in the wickedness of the Antis, and would vote accordingly.

Day Six, Capitol Hill, Monday, August 16, 1920:

House postpones action, awaiting report of its Committee on Constitutional Amendments, scheduled to meet in night executive session.

Lobbyists were now working boldly, feverishly, offering business loans, lucrative jobs, political appointments; these failing, they threatened foreclosure on loans, loss of jobs, withdrawal of political favors. Polls, checked and rechecked daily, had become useless. No one knew where anyone stood. There were puzzlers like Representative Jacob Simpson of Humphreys County, carried as an Anti on all the polls, yet consistently voting for the Suffs.

Then there was young Harry Burn of McMinn County. His lapel was regularly decorated with a red rose, but he had recently told Anita Pollitzer, "My vote will never hurt you." Seth Walker was wielding his power as Speaker to bring his legislative friends, mostly "Roberts men," to his side, but they were under equal pressure from Capitol Hill to keep faith with the Democratic governor. Representative Banks Turner, a party regular from Gibson County in West Tennessee, seemed especially torn by conflicting loyalties, but thus far Turner had voted with Speaker Walker.

Neither Suffs nor Antis were sure enough of their votes at this point to hazard a showdown. Even the House committee's night executive session turned out to be a cliffhanger. A deadlock was averted only after two absent members, both pledged for ratification, were rounded up by alert suffragists and marched into the meeting to make the vote 10 – 8 to report the amendment favorably in the House the next day. By the next day, those two men had jumped the fence and come out for the Antis.

Day Seven, Capitol Hill, Tuesday, August 17, 1920:

Motion that House concur in Senate's adoption of the Senate Joint Resolution Number 1, ratifying the proposed 19th Amendment, is offered by Representative Riddick of Memphis. Debate cut off in mid-afternoon by Speaker Walker's motion to adjourn until next morning. Motion carried, 52 - 44.

What did the 52 - 44 vote mean? Did the Antis now control the House? If so, why hadn't they called for a vote on the resolution itself? Could Suff forces survive another night of suspense? On this day, in neighboring North Carolina, the legislature had rejected ratification of the 19th Amendment, and the Antis would be celebrating. Suffragists decided to set up all-night patrols of hotel corridors and of Union Station to forestall unwarranted departures or disappearances. Ratificationists were being summoned home by fake messages telling of illness in the family. Rumors of kidnapings, actual or threatened, abounded. Joe Hanover had been jostled in the elevator, and publicly denounced as a "Bolshevist" in the Hermitage lobby. Sultry-voiced females, purporting to be suffragists, were telephoning his room to invite him to compromising midnight trysts; anonymous male voices were telephoning threats on his life.

Word of this had reached Governor Roberts, and

ALL READY BUT THE LAST BUTTON.

late that afternoon Hanover was called to the governor's offices. There he was introduced to a tall, handsome captain of the Nashville police force, Paul Bush, now reassigned, courtesy of the State of Tennessee, as Joe Hanover's bodyguard. Captain Bush, henceforth, would monitor Hanover's phone calls, check his mail, and occupy a connecting room at the Hermitage. Later that same night, Governor Roberts himself was threatened. Men representing a group of pro-Roberts, anti-suffrage newspapers called on the governor to warn that, unless "his men" straightened out and voted right in the legislature's balloting next day, they would switch their editorial support to his Republican opponent and work to defeat him in the November election.

"There is one more thing we can do — only one," said Carrie Chapman Catt as the suffragists' strategy meeting broke up that night. "We can pray."

103

Day Eight, Capitol Hill, Wednesday, August 18, 1920:

The crowds began to gather early. Suffragists showed up in white dresses with yellow sashes — their marching clothes. Antis came, responding to the big ad in the morning's *Tennessean*, appealing for a show of red-rose strength at the Capitol. A few women factory workers came, wearing red roses and enjoying a day off, both courtesy of their employers. There were young and old, men and women, the curious and the concerned, reporters, politicians, preachers, bartenders, students, grandmothers — all hoping to get into the House galleries, all hoping to see history made that day.

They hurried up Capitol Hill, past the equestrian statue of Tennessee's own President Andrew Jackson. They passed the tombs of Tennessee's own President James K. Polk and Tennessee-born First Lady Sarah Childress Polk — the couple who had been residents in the White House in 1848 when Elizabeth Cady Stanton and Lucretia Mott had started this whole suffrage business with their Women's Rights Convention in Seneca Falls, New York. They ran, climbed, and hobbled up the 72 steps to the Capitol's main entrance — as if each succeeding step, in some strange unremarked symbolism, signified another year in the 72-year-long struggle of American women to win voting rights. They traveled down the wide Capitol corridor, then up the grand stairway, their fingers running lightly over the chipped marble of the bullet-scarred balustrade, a relic of the gun-fight that had marked the stormy debate over Tennessee's ratification of the Fourteenth Amendment in 1866.

By 9:30 a.m., the Capitol was jammed and the crowds were spilling out onto the surrounding lawns. Inside the House chamber, yellow banners hung between tall columns, and a yellow sunflower had been lashed to the spread eagle mounting guard above the Speaker's chair. But as the members began drifting in, Suffs standing in the galleries saw an ominous number of red roses on the floor below. Anita Pollitzer caught a glimpse of red in Harry Burn's lapel and sadly marked him off her "hopeful" list. But what she could not see was the turmoil in Harry Burn's mind or the letter in his pocket.

The letter had arrived that morning. It was from his mother, Mrs. J. L. Burn of Niota, Tennessee. As a widowed, land-owning, non-voting taxpayer, Febb Ensminger Burn had felt first-hand the need for representation; although she had never been an activist, she believed instinctively in woman suffrage. Reading the reports of the special session in the papers, she had been disappointed to see that her son Harry had taken no stand, even though she understood why. The sentiment against ratification had become fierce in McMinn County, especially since Senator Candler's "bearcat" of a speech in the Senate, and she knew Harry had been hearing from his constituents. Mrs. Burn had decided to write, too:

Dear Son:

Hurrah, and vote for suffrage! Don't keep them in doubt. I notice some of the speeches against. They were bitter. I have been watching to see how you stood, but have not noticed anything yet.

Don't forget to be a good boy and help Mrs. Catt put the "rat" in ratification.

Your Mother.

(This last was a reference to one of the many newspaper cartoons about Tennessee's legislative battle that Mrs. Burn was sure Harry had seen — a drawing of an old woman with a broom, chasing after the letters R-A-T which, in turn, were lagging behind the letters I-F-I-C-A-T-I-O-N.)

As he made his way to his desk, Harry Burn was still weighing in his own mind his duty to represent his constituents against his duty to vote his own (and his mother's) suffragist convictions.

Down on the floor, Dr. J. Frank Griffin arrived — back home from California in time to swell the suffrage vote. A cheer went up from the Suffs when another ratificationist, R. L. Dowlen of Pleasant View, just out of the hospital following an operation, was assisted to his desk. That meant tally sheets were consulted — only three of the 99 House members would be absent. But even when Griffin and Dowlen were included, the Suffs' last, best poll estimates showed they could count on only 47 votes. With 96 members present and voting, that was not enough. The Antis would have 49.

Speaker Walker's gavel pounded at 10:30 a.m. Suffs, Antis, and several dozen lobbyists who were on the floor, in flagrant violation of House rules, making last-minute offers and appeals, were moved to the rear of the hall by the sergeant-at-arms. They took their places behind a railing and stood, tally sheets in hand, pencils poised, ready to check off names as the roll was called on yesterday's motion to concur in the Senate's ratification. But debate was the first order of the day.

Oration after oration reviewed 72 years of familiar arguments until, abruptly, a self-assured Speaker

MISS ELSA McGILL, ONE OF THE MOST ARDENT SUFFRAGISTS

GOV. ROBERTS, MRS. LESLIE WARNER (SEATED) AND A GROUP OF SUFFRAGISTS.

SUFFRAGE SCENES and LEADERS

REPRESENTATIVE, HARRY BURN, THE MAN WHOSE CHANGE OF VOTE MADE RATIFICATION POSSIBLE. IN HIS HAND IS A SHEAF OF TELEGRAMS OF CONGRATULATIONS UPON HIS ACTION.

REPRESENTATIVE, JOE HANOVER, OF MEMPHIS, FLOOR LEADER OF THE SUFFRAGE FORCES.

MRS. CARRIE CHAPMAN CATT, PRESIDENT OF THE NATIONAL AMERICAN WOMAN SUFFRAGE ASSOCIATION

REPRESENTATIVE SIMPSON, OF HUMPHREYS COUNTY, WHO STOOD FIRM FOR THE SUFFRAGE RESOLUTION IN SPITE OF THE MOST TERRIFIC PRESSURE.

SETH WALKER SPEAKER OF THE HOUSE OF REPRESENTATIVES.

THE HOUSE IN ACTION

Walker turned over his gavel to Representative William Overton, another staunch Anti, then made his way down to the House floor and asked to be recognized. With melodramatic flourish, Seth Walker was making it known that the Antis, just as suffragists had calculated, had at least 49 sure votes, a majority of those present and voting.

"The hour has come," Walker declared. "The battle has been fought and won, and I move you, Mr. Speaker, that the motion to concur in the Senate action goes where it belongs — to the table." And now his strategy was clear. As double insurance, Walker was moving to kill the amendment by tabling it. Any still-uneasy fence-sitters could more easily justify a temporizing vote to table than an outright vote against.

Antis chorused "Second the motion." Suffragists clamored for recognition. Representative Overton ordered the roll call to begin. There were no surprises. Harry Burn's name came early in the roll; he voted in favor of tabling. Other members answered according to expectation until the name Banks Turner was called. Turner did not answer. That morning, shortly before the House convened, Turner had been in Governor Roberts' office just down the hall, listening to the voice of Governor Cox, his party's presidential nominee, telephoning from Ohio. The pleas of both governors still echoed in his ears; the long pause continued, then the roll call went on. But before the final vote could be announced — most had already added up their own totals at 48 - 47 in favor, with one abstention — Turner arose.

"I wish to be recorded as against the motion to table," he announced.

Suffragists gasped in joy. On a tie vote, 48 - 48, the motion to table was defeated. The 19th Amendment was still alive in Tennessee.

Seth Walker, unwilling to accept his good friend's decision as final, demanded a recount. He made his way to Banks Turner's desk, sat down, and put his arm around Turner's shoulder. While the clerk's voice again droned each name, and each answer came back as before, the Speaker of the House whispered urgent pleadings in Turner's ear. For ratificationists, it was an excruciating moment, seeing the arm of the most powerful man in the legislature resting on the shoulders of a man who had voted both ways. They waited in silence for Turner's name to be called again. When it was, Turner threw off Walker's arm, arose again, and again voted "Nay." The roll call was finished. So was the motion to table.

The suffragists cheered.

But not for long. The motion to table had failed on a tie vote. It seemed certain that the original motion to concur in the Senate's ratification would do likewise. Realizing this, Seth Walker immediately called for a vote on the original motion. Once more the terrible suspense of the roll call began. And this was the vote that counted. Even if Banks Turner stuck with them, the ratificationists must still find one more vote to have a majority of 49.

An East Tennessee mountaineer named Anderson was first on the list. He had been instructed by suffrage leaders to shout his answer, and his "Aye" came loud and clear. Another "Aye" followed. Then came four "Nays," two of them from the faithless Davidson County delegation. Harry Burn's name was seventh on the roll call, and his "Aye" came so quickly, so unexpectedly, that many present did not catch it. Others thought perhaps the young lawmaker had become confused, made a mistake. Then, as the meaning of what they had heard sank in, a murmurous wave of amazement swept the House chamber. Had it happened? Had Harry Burn cast the last deciding vote, the vote that would enfranchise one-half the adult population of the United States?

The answer could not be certain until this third roll call of the day ended — until the strength of Banks Turner's new-found suffragist faith was put to the test one more time. In breathless silence, even their waving fans motionless in the heavy, hot air of the galleries, the crowd waited for the clerk to get to the T's. This time Banks Turner fairly shouted his "Aye!" The resolution was carried, 49 - 47. But even before the clerk could announce the result, a white-faced Seth Walker was on his feet to play out one last, desperate but well-worn parliamentary maneuver: "I change my vote from 'Nay' to 'Aye,' and move to reconsider."

If Walker's vote were recorded with the suffragist majority, he might be able to buy time for the Antis somehow to erode that majority. Only a legislator voting on the prevailing side can bring up a motion to reconsider. That member then controls the measure for the next 72 hours — in this case, until noon on Saturday, August 21. He alone can call it to a vote, and he can make that call at any moment when he believes he has present and voting the votes to win. It was not until later that the irony emerged: This change of vote by Seth Walker, made for parliamentary expediency, had given the ratification resolu-

106

tion an unchallengeable constitutional majority — 50 of the total House membership of 99. Walker unwittingly had cut off one line of legal attack upon the validity of Tennessee ratification already being prepared by Anti lawyers. At that moment, however, the uproar in the House chamber had become so great that the clerk's announcement that the resolution to ratify had carried — by a vote of 50 - 46 — was never heard.

Pandemonium prevailed. Women were screaming, weeping, singing. They threw their arms about each other and danced, so far as it was possible, in the jam-packed aisles. Suffragist legislators tore off their yellow boutonnieres and threw them into the air to meet the gentle rain of yellow rose petals floating down from the galleries above.

The jubilation spread to the Capitol corridors, to the Capitol lawns, and the cheers of the pro-ratification multitudes could be clearly heard in the suite at the Hermitage Hotel where Carrie Chapman Catt and Harriet Taylor Upton sat waiting, in an agony of suspense, for news.

No one had to tell them. The time had come to celebrate!

What followed, though it seemed important at the time, was mostly anticlimax — or, as many claimed, comic opera.

Now, predictably, it was the Antis who charged their enemies with bribery, double-dealing, and general chicanery. There were speculations, rumors, accusations: Joe Hanover had bribed Harry Burn; the governor's secretary had gotten to Harry Burn; Kate Burch Warner had said in the presence of Harry Burn that she would pay $10,000 for just one more vote for ratification. One elaborate and convoluted theory even had Seth Walker publicly playing the role of an Anti for reasons best known to himself, while remaining at heart a true ratificationist who knew exactly what he was doing when he changed his vote to give the suffragists their unbudgeable constitutional majority. But this theory never gained

much currency, even in later years when the L. & N. Railroad named Seth Walker their legal counsel in Nashville.

In any case, young Harry Burn put himself forever above suspicion or censure when he rose in the House chamber the day after the vote to explain his decision to change sides: "I know that a mother's advice is always safest for her boy to follow, and my mother wanted me to vote for ratification."

As the politicians and the public waited for Seth Walker's motion to reconsider to expire on Saturday, the drama played itself out. In order to "build fires" under the legislators who had voted for ratification and reduce their voting strength, the Antis held mass rallies ("To Save the South!") all over Tennessee. In Nashville, meanwhile, the suffragists' legislators were being tested with new and unalloyed threats and temptations and facing other unforeseen hazards. But no weak brethren turned up among the "Sterling 49," as the Suffs now called their steadfast

Southern Chivalry

Tennessee State Library and Archives

legislative supporters. None fell by the wayside drunk or disabled, not even the representative from Putnam County who was shot in the leg on Thursday night while attending a somewhat raucous party; on Friday he reported he would be there when the vote came up the next day. Antis had hoped that one Knox County representative, a Seventh-Day Adventist, would be absent, but on Friday afternoon he announced he intended to attend the Sabbath session without qualms, on the ground that "the ox was in the ditch" and circumstances altered cases. Another worried East Tennessee legislator, whose baby had become ill, agreed to remain for the voting when suffrage leaders promised to charter a special train (at a cost of $615.00) to get him to Chattanooga in time to make a connection with the only train that could get him home for the rest of the weekend.

Thus it was, that on Saturday, August 21, the "Sterling 49" showed up in the House, ready to vote full force against any reconsideration of ratification. But they found only nine Antis in attendance that morning. The others had skipped town. In one of the more bizarre filibusters on record, 38 Tennessee lawmakers — Antis called them the "Red Rose Brigade" — had stolen away in little groups of two or three in the middle of the previous night, gone to a small railway flag stop south of town, and taken the train over the state line to Decatur, Alabama, where they were hiding out rather publicly in the lobby of the local hotel. But there were not enough of them to achieve their aim: to prevent the assembling of the crucial quorum in the Tennessee House and thus prevent action on reconsideration.

But the "Sterling 49" proceeded joyfully to do business without them. (The House's anti-suffrage chaplain added to their merriment when he opened the morning's session with a prayer that "God's richest blessings be granted to our absent ones.") As soon as the noon deadline ended Seth Walker's control of the pending motion to reconsider, they called it up and voted it down. The ratified amendment was returned to the Senate. From there it went to the governor for certification, to be followed by delivery to Washington. But the battle still was not over.

Suspense was prolonged by several more days of last-gasp Anti maneuvers — injunctions, briefs, writs of *certiorare et supersedeas*, threats of grand jury indictments, more injunctions. (The repercussions of these legal shenanigans would not be disposed of until February, 1922, when the U.S. Supreme Court dismissed the last of the appeals on 19th Amendment ratification cases.)

On Tuesday, August 24, Governor Roberts shook himself free of all such impediments. He signed, sealed, and sent off by special delivery registered mail the certificate of Tennessee's ratification to Secretary of State Bainbridge Colby.

That same day, Carrie Chapman Catt, Harriet Taylor Upton, and Charl Ormond Williams boarded the train to Washington, hoping to be on hand for the ceremonies when the Secretary issued his proclamation — the final, formal confirmation of the suffragists' prized victory. But when they arrived, early on the morning of August 26, 1920, it was all over. The certificate had preceded them by a few hours, and Secretary Colby, to preclude any further last-ditch legal obstructionism by the Antis, had issued his proclamation on the instant, before breakfast. While most of the country was in bed, asleep or otherwise occupied, votes for women had become the law of the land.

Nashville Tennessean

The spectacular fight for woman suffrage ended when Gov. A. H. Roberts affixed his signature to the paper that certified Tennessee's ratification. Looking on is Charl Ormond Williams of Memphis, vice chairman of the Democratic Executive Committee and one of the leaders of the Tennessee suffrage struggle.

October 28, 1920

Life

Vol. 76.   Copyright, 1920, Life Publishing Company   No. 1982

Price 15 Cents

"Congratulations"

A Suffrage Timetable, State By State

By August, 1920, when the Tennessee legislature's deciding ratification of the 19th Amendment to the U. S. Constitution made it official — □Vtes for Women had become the law of the land — □35 other legislatures had already ratified. This listing, state by state and date by date, of the order in which states had ratified appeared in The New York Times, *August 19, 1920.*

1. Wisconsin ....June 10, 1919
2. Michigan ....June 10, 1919
3. Kansas ....June 13, 1919
4. Ohio ....June 14, 1919
5. New York ....June 16, 1919
6. Illinois ....June 17, 1919
7. Pennsylvania ....June 24, 1919
8. Massachusetts ....June 25, 1919
9. Texas ....June 28, 1919
10. Iowa .... July 2, 1919
11. Missouri .... July 3, 1919
12. Arkansas .... July 20, 1919
13. Montana .... July 30, 1919
14. Nebraska .... August 2, 1919
15. Minnesota ....September 8, 1919
16. New Hampshire ....September 10, 1919
17. Utah ....September 30, 1919
18. California ....November 1, 1919
19. Maine ....November 5, 1919
20. North Dakota...................................December 1, 1919
21. South Dakota ....December 4, 1919
22. Colorado ....December 12, 1919
23. Rhode Island....................................January 6, 1920
24. Kentucky ....January 6, 1920
25. Oregon..January 12, 1920
26. Indiana ....January 16, 1920
27. Wyoming...January 27, 1920
28. Nevada .... February 7, 1920
29. New Jersey .... February 10, 1920
30. Idaho ....February 11, 1920
31. Arizona .... February 12, 1920
32. New Mexico.................................... February 19, 1920
33. Oklahoma .... February 27, 1920
34. West Virginia .... March 10, 1920
35. Washington .... March 22, 1920
36. Tennessee .... August 18, 1920

Meanwhile, the legislatures in nine other states, acting in the following order, had already rejected the amendment.

1. Georgia .... July 24, 1919
2. Alabama .... September 2, 1919
3. Mississippi .... January 21, 1920
4. South Carolina .... January 21, 1920
5. Virginia .... February 12, 1920
6. Maryland .... February 17, 1920
7. Delaware .... June 2, 1920
8. Louisiana....................................... June 15, 1920
9. North Carolina .... August 17, 1920

No action on the amendment had been taken by legislatures in the three remaining states:

Connecticut   Vermont   Florida

National Woman's Party

National Woman's Party leader Alice Paul unfurls the tri-color suffrage flag bearing 36 stars in Washington, D.C.

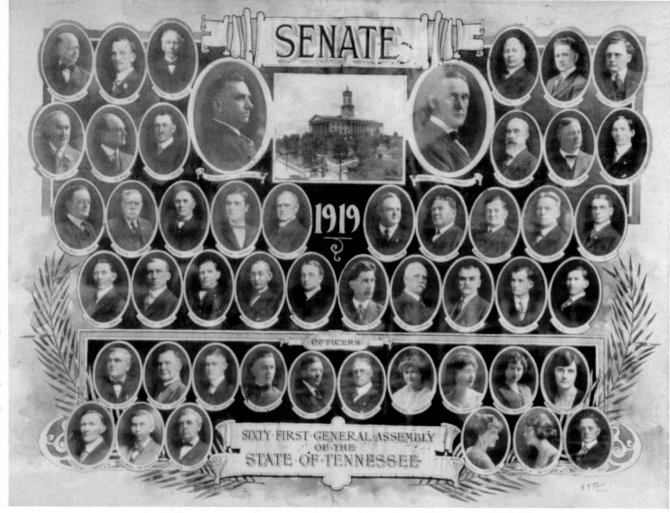

61st Tennessee General Assembly, Extraordinary Session, Convened August 9, 1920, called by Governor A.H. Roberts to consider Resolution 1 (19thAmendment) to the U.S. Constitution. Senate voted August 13; House voted August 18, 1920.

SENATE "AYE" VOTES = 25

V.A. Bradley	John C. Houk
David A. Burkhalter	Thomas C. Long
John D. Caldwell	J. Walter McMahan
F. Thomas Carter	Wm. J. Matthews
Thomas L. Coleman	Wm. P. Monroe
C.C. Collins	John W. Murrey
M.H. Copenhaver	E. Eugene Patton
Finley M. Dorris	Frank J. Rice
Frank D. Fuller	Robert Lee Stockard
L. Estes Gwinn	Thomas J. Whitby
John H. Harber	Douglas Wikle
Ernest N. Haston	Andrew L. Todd, Speaker
Albert E. Hill	

HOUSE "AYE" VOTES = 50

Wyatt K. Anderson	Charles W. Longhurst
Ernest S. Bell	Emerson O. Luther
Harry T. Burn	Charles E. Lynn
George A. Canale	Charles McCalman
Sidney F. Carr	J. Madison Martin
Joe Seb Crawford	L.D. Miller
Brown Davis	A.M. Moose
T.A. Dodson	John E. Morgan
Robert Lee Dowlen	Joseph F. Odle
U.S. Grant Ellis	W.R.H. Phelan
Robert T. Fisher	Felix H. Phillips
P. Preston Fitzhugh	Wm.W. Phillips
Walter K. Foster	J.H. Rector
J. Frank Griffin	Thomas K. Riddick
Joseph Hanover	Wm. A. Shoaf, Jr.
Joseph C. Harris	Jacob H. Simpson
A. J. Hickman, Jr.	Thomas O. Simpson
James A. Howard	S. Edgar Stovall
T. Jefferson Jeter	R.B. Swink
B.L. Johnson	F.G. Tallant
Aubrey M. Kahn	Edward A. Travis
Grover H. Keaton	Wesley S. Tucker
Carl A. Larsen	B.P. Turner
Samuel M. Leath	Joseph E. Wade
Wm. M. Light	Seth M. Walker, Speaker

HOUSE "NO" VOTES = 46

W.W. Bond	A.S. Montgomery
Joseph S. Boyd	Robert Orr, III
C. Fulton Boyer	E.C. Norvell
Robert W. Bratton	E.R. Oldham
C. Conrad Carter	W. Austin Overton
John E. Cassady	James J. Rucker
Charles L. Cheek	Wm. J. Russell
James B. Cole	Percy Sharpe
Hugh P. Crawford	John P. Sipes
Wm. A. Dunlap	A. Jackson Skidmore
John M. Forsythe	Thomas J. Smith
George E. Francisco	W.F. Story
Stephen E. Frogge	Wm. T. Swift
James H. Galbraith	W.C. Thorneberry
F. Sampson Hall	Charles A. Travis
G. Cleveland Harvill	John T. Vinson
Samuel A. Hays	Wm. E. Weldon
Lawrence M. Jackson	Larkin M.Whitaker
A.G. Keisling	M.E. Whitaker
Martin F. Long	John T. Whitfield
James D. McMurry	W.C. Wilson
James O. Martin	Daniel Wolfenbarger
C.F. Milliken	J.H. Womack

SENATE "NO" VOTES = 4

H.M. Candler
Roy H. Parks
James W. Rice
J.B. Summers

SENATE ABSTAINED = 2

L.P. McFarland
Wm. R. Miller

HOUSE ABSENT = 3

C.W. Brooks
J.G. Harris
J.C. Rowan

House of REPRESENTATIVES 61ST GENERAL ASSEMBLY.
TENN. 1919.

SPEAKER
GOVERNOR

A young Joe Hanover (center) poses with his family: (l-r) his father, Wolf, brother Benjamin, brother Morris, and his mother, Esther.

A Suffrage Sampler

News and views, amusements and amazements — a collection of brief items culled from many sources to provide some vivid footnotes to the story of Tennessee's fateful, decades-long encounter with the question of woman suffrage.

Joe Hanover

The Man Who Took Democracy Seriously

The cause of woman suffrage may never have had a more passionate advocate than young Joe Hanover, a 30-year-old bachelor lawyer from Memphis who, in an August 1920 election, had run for (and won) a seat in the special session of Tennessee's General Assembly for the sole purpose of voting for ratification. In Nashville, with the outcome becoming ever more uncertain, Joe Hanover's zealous support attracted the attention of the harried suffrage leader, Carrie Chapman Catt. She invited him to attend strategy meetings at the Hermitage Hotel, and eventually asked him to assume the role of legislative floor leader for the embattled suffrage forces.

Mrs. Catt's confidence was not misplaced. Soon, Joe was working all hours, covering all bases, tracking down undecided votes, reclaiming backsliders, receiving threats on his life, and getting an ulcer. Before the session ended, he had lost 20 pounds and was existing on a diet that consisted mostly of zwieback, a commonly used teething biscuit for toddlers, which he carried in his pockets.

Years later, in semi-retirement after a career of more than 50 years as a Memphis attorney, civic leader, and humanitarian, Joe Hanover reminisced about why a young, unmarried legislator would campaign so hard for votes for women.

"I guess my main reason goes all the way back to when I was born," he said. "A lot of people don't know it, but I was actually born in Poland, and came to America with my mother at the age of five." Memories of that adventure were still fresh in his mind. Joe's father, fleeing oppression of Jews in Poland, had earlier made his way across an ocean and half a continent before settling in Memphis, where he established a small dry-goods business. Determined to rescue his family from the frequent pogroms in Poland, he saved every penny he could and, in 1895, sent his wife second-class steamship tickets to America on a Holland Line steamship, and $500 to pay "bootleggers" to guide the family out of Poland.

For five-year-old Joe, the youngest of three Hanover brothers, getting safely across the border was the most frightening, but also the most exciting part of the journey. Little Joe was carried on a Polish guide's back across a frozen lake in the dead of winter, tucked away in a sort of gunny sack with a hole cut for his head. As for the sea voyage, Joe remembered the ship's captain sending food down to his mother, who was seasick the whole time. But his favorite memory was of making his way up to the first-class deck where he danced ("sort of a tap dance," he recalled) to the music of a big orchestra, and was surprised to find the passengers throwing money to him.

While growing up and going to school in Memphis in the early 1900s, Joe Hanover, influenced by his parents' love of freedom and their gratitude for the haven offered by their new country, began to read and study the Declaration of Independence and the U.S. Constitution. That was when he first wondered why, in democratic America, women seemed left out.

"If I had been female," he declared, "I would have felt that I had no voice, that I was shut out." His parents were a case in point. Even after they became citizens, his mother, unlike his father, was unable to vote. "And I knew that wasn't right. So, you see," he concluded, "I always believed women should be equal."

Thus, it was somehow inevitable that young Joe Hanover, after finishing his night school law studies and getting elected to the Tennessee legislature, would campaign ceaselessly for the 36th ratification of the 19th Amendment. For a man who grew up loving democracy, it was a simple matter of helping America take care of its unfinished business.

— Based on a series of interviews with Joe Hanover by Carol Lynn Yellin, in Memphis, Tennessee, 1978-1979.

Mother Proud of Boy Who Cinched Suffrage Victory

Burns Happy Tho Vote May End Political Career.

MADE OWN CHOICE

Changed Vote After Reading Mother's Plea.

The Mother's Son Who Made It Happen

On the morning of August 18, 1920, a young Tennessee lawmaker from the village of Mouse Creek (now Niota), changed his "Nay" vote to "Yea" during the legislature's crucial final ballot on ratification of the 19th Amendment to the U.S. Constitution. That action, giving suffragists the elusive victory they had sought for 72 years, enraged suffrage opponents. It also won for 24-year-old Harry T. Burn and his widowed mother, Febb Ensminger Burn, who had written him a letter telling him to "be a good boy and vote for suffrage," a secure place in American history. Many years later, in magazine and television interviews, Harry Burn shared his reminiscences of the crucial ratification struggle, and its aftermath. The story begins at his moment of decision:

The huge chamber was hushed as anti-suffragists, in a test of strength, made a motion to table the amendment, tantamount to its death. The vote was taken. It proved a tie: 48–48.

Sitting in the third row to the right of the rostrum was Harry T. Burn, an apple-cheeked youngster among legislators. His constituents back home in East Tennessee were divided on woman suffrage. But not so Harry's mother, from whom he had received a letter that morning.

A slightly built farm wife, Febb Ensminger Burn found time to read a dozen magazines, books, and four newspapers between milking cows, churning butter, cleaning and mending for her family. "Suffrage has interested me for years," she told a reporter at the time. "I like the suffrage militants as well as the others…. After I read the bitter speeches suffrage opponents had made, I sat down on that little chair on the front porch and penned a few lines to my son."

In Nashville, Harry Burn faced a dilemma as he read and re-read his mother's words: "Dear Son: Hurrah and vote for suffrage. Don't keep them in doubt...be a good boy and help Mrs. Catt put the 'rat' in ratification." He was seeking reelection. Was his duty to vociferous Anti voters back home, or to his own (and his mother's) political ideals? "I had voted to table the amendment," he explained, "not in opposition but in hopes that it would come up again at the next session after election day."

But the issue was not to be avoided. Anti-suffragists now called for a vote on the amendment itself. When the clerk, droning the roll call, reached the name of Harry T. Burn, there was a moment of hesitation. Then, in a clear voice, Burn called "Aye." The tie was shattered! Tennessee's ratification of the 19th Amendment, granting 27,000,000 women the right to vote in national elections, had passed!

Reaction was immediate. There were attacks and threats, mainly against young Harry Burn. He was accused of accepting a bribe, threatened with prosecution. But he showed no signs of retreating. On the floor of the House the day after the vote, he expressed his resentment over the "veiled intimations and accusations regarding my vote." Then, referring to the letter from his mother, he declared: "I want to state that I changed my vote in favor of ratification, because I believe in full suffrage as a right...and my mother wanted me to vote for ratification. I knew that a mother's advice is always safest for her boy to follow."

Back home in East Tennessee, his troubles were not over. "People from all over the country went into my county," he recalled. "They held indignation meetings, passed resolutions…. When I went home for a weekend I would generally keep a bodyguard around so that no one would attack me."

Even Mrs. Burn was visited at her farm by anti-suffrage partisans who urged her to disavow her letter to her son. But Febb Ensminger Burn, like her son, was not one to wilt under fire. She wired the suffrage headquarters: "I stand squarely behind suffrage and request my son to stick until the end." In the end, voters in his home county gave Harry Burn a vote of vindication by reelecting him to a second term in the legislature.

Years later, in semi-retirement from a career as a successful banker and gentleman farmer, Harry Burn was still proud that he helped American women win the vote. "I had always believed that women had an inherent right to vote. It was a logical attitude from my standpoint. My mother was a college woman, a student of national and international affairs who took an interest in all public issues. She could not vote. Yet the tenant farmers on our farm, some of whom were illiterate, could vote. On that roll call, confronted with the fact that I was going to go on record for time and eternity on the merits of the question, I had to vote for ratification."

— *Based on a "Twentieth Century" television documentary on woman suffrage, CBS-TV, 1962, and on "The Man Whose Vote Gave Women The Vote" by William Cahn,* Look *magazine, August 25, 1970.*

THE NEW FREEDOM

Dateline: Bygone Days

Louisville, Kentucky, June 7, 1877. Mrs. Elizabeth Avery Meriwether of Memphis spoke here at the invitation of the Ladies' Physiological Society, a liberal group devoted to intellectual pursuits. She was told that Henry Watterson, editor of the *Louisville Courier-Journal*, was so opposed to woman suffrage that he would write a savage review. Nevertheless, Mrs. Meriwether made the venture before a crowded house, and apparently won Watterson over completely. Wrote he: "Mrs. Meriwether's lecture on 'Women Before the Law' was one of the ablest and most eloquent appeals on the subject that has ever been made…. Those who doubt the ability of women to think with vigor and express themselves with eloquence and force would be convinced by listening to Mrs. Meriwether of Memphis."

— *Quoted in "News of Bygone Days" column,* The Commercial Appeal, *June 7, 1977.*

"PLEASE!"

Nashville, Tennessee, October 27, 1897. A featured speaker at the convention of the National Council of Women of the United States, meeting in Nashville, was the outstanding feminist, Susan B. Anthony. She told her audience that she had become interested in woman's rights many years earlier when she was not allowed to speak at a temperance meeting because she was a woman. Her zeal was later intensified when a national statesman informed her that an equal suffrage petition signed by 20,000 women was not important because the signers were "only women." She took a solemn vow then and there, she said, that she would not rest until a woman's name and a woman's opinion were worth as much as a man's, and that meant the ballot. Editorial comment on Susan B. Anthony's speech was complimentary but not encouraging. The editor of the *Nashville American* called her a distinguished and influential woman, but had little confidence in the cause she was championing: "We believe that natural laws will settle these questions…. Sooner or later they [the suffragists] will retrace their steps and come to that place which the laws of nature and nature's God intended for them."

— *Adapted from* The Woman Suffrage Movement in Tennessee *by A. Elizabeth Taylor.*

Memphis, Tennessee, April 21, 1900. Mrs. Carrie Chapman Catt, the most eloquent proponent of woman suffrage, delivered an address last night at the Grand Opera House. "Women put their hopes, ambitions and prayers in the outcome of the ballot just as men do," she said. "Why shouldn't the hopes and prayers of women be counted like those of men? Women put virtue not vice into the ballot box." Mrs. Catt pointed out that the public school systems in the United States were founded for boys, with the idea that the schools should educate future citizens. Girls, who would not function as citizens, were not allowed to go to school in the early years, or were allowed to go only from 6 to 8 in the morning before the boys awoke.

— *Quoted in "News of Bygone Days" column,* The Commercial Appeal, *April 21, 1975.*

118

Rhymes and Reasons

The Suffs and the Antis, creative souls all, liked to state their arguments in verse or set them to music. Their works were recited at rallies, sung at meetings, printed in pamphlets, and submitted to newspapers. And on both sides, as is evident in the examples presented below, ridicule and satire were favorite weapons. We hear first from the Suffs, then from the Antis:

Woman Unsexed By The Vote

It doesn't unsex her to toil in a factory
Minding the looms from the dawn till the night;
To deal with a schoolful of children refractory
Doesn't unsex her in anyone's sight;
Work in a store — where her back aches
  inhumanly —
Doesn't unsex her at all, you will note,
But think how exceedingly rough and
  unwomanly
Woman would be if she happened to vote!

To sweat in a laundry that's torrid and torrider
Doesn't subtract from her womanly charm;
And scrubbing the flags in an echoing corridor
Doesn't unsex her — so where is the harm?

It doesn't unsex her to nurse us with bravery,
Loosing death's hand from its grip in the throat;
But ah! how the voices grow quivery, quavery,
Wailing: "Alas, 'twill unsex her to vote!"

She's feminine still, when she juggles the
  crockery,
Bringing you blithely the order you give;
Toil in a sweatshop where life is a mockery
Just for the pittance on which she can live —
That doesn't seem to unsex her a particle
"Labor is noble" — so somebody wrote —
But ballots are known as a dangerous article
Woman's unsexed if you give her the vote!

— Alice Duer Miller, "Poet Laureate" of the suffrage movement, quoted in Tennessee Women, Past and Present *by Wilma Dykeman.*

A Suffrage Love Song

Suffragette, suffragette
Won't you be mine?
I much prefer you to a
Weak "clinging vine."

I want to be sure of
My three meals a day
And when you're a voter
We'll have equal pay.

I want to feel certain
When I'm sick and pale,
You'll have to support me
Or else go to jail.

You can help pay the house rent
And take care of me;
And when we're divorced
Pay me alimony.

— From Woman's Protest, *published by National Association Opposed to Woman Suffrage, 1917. Quoted in* The Woman Suffrage Movement in Tennessee *by A. Elizabeth Taylor.*

"WITH MY COMPLIMENTS, MADAM."

119

"BOMBS FOR THE WOMEN"

That headline appeared in The Chattanooga Times *in its coverage of the state convention of the Tennessee Equal Suffrage League being held in Morristown in October, 1913. The newspaper's correspondent gave the following account of "an Anti-Suffragette argument" which "was not strong enough to break up tonight's meeting."*

The hall was comfortably filled. During the address of Mrs. Guilford Dudley, president of the suffrage association of Nashville, delegates were alarmed by the crash of breaking glass. A heavy object smashed a window near the speaker and fell to the floor at her feet.

Mrs. Dudley calmly permitted herself to look at the object for a few seconds, asked, "Is that an anti-suffrage bomb?" and resumed her address. Miss Margaret Ervin of Chattanooga sprang from her seat and picked up the "bomb," throwing it out of the window through which it entered the room. It did not explode. Instead, the leaking can — it held about one-half a pint and did not seem to be fastened — permitted a thick sticky liquid to ooze through the opening. At once, a frightful odor permeated the room. One or two of the faint-hearted left, but a majority of the suffragettes were made of sterner stuff. True, handkerchiefs were more in evidence than faces, and there was a sudden epidemic of coughing, but they stuck it out and heard the program through. An analysis of the "bomb" brought the statement that it contained a concoction of some kind, made up mostly of sulphuric acid. Several citizens of Morristown tonight started a subscription fund to be used in an investigation of the "bomb-throwing."

— Condensed from a story datelined Morristown, Tenn., in The Chattanooga Times, *October 21, 1913.*

Davidson County Women

Anne Dallas Dudley

Getting Organized

When Tennessee's suffragists realized it was up to them to deliver the crucial 36th ratification of the Susan B. Anthony Amendment in 1920, they did not flinch. Thanks to the phenomenal growth of local equal suffrage leagues across the state during the preceding decade, as evidenced in the listings below, they were well prepared for the movement's final battle in Nashville that August.

The progress of the woman suffrage movement in Tennessee for many decades was steady but very slow. By 1911, only five equal suffrage leagues had been organized, with total membership of less than 150. But from 1912 to 1919, the movement rapidly gained momentum and there was considerable growth in favorable sentiment.

During this period, the number of leagues increased to more than 75, while individual societies made large gains in membership. Several leagues had hundreds, and in some cases thousands of members. Aggregate membership of all leagues reached an estimated total of more than 25,000.

There was at least one and sometimes two or more equal suffrage leagues in each of the following places: Memphis, Knoxville, Chattanooga, Morristown, Nashville, Jackson, Clarksville, Franklin, Gallatin, Murfreesboro, Bolivar, Brownsville, Centerville, Columbia, Dresden, Fayetteville, Hartsville, Hickerson Station, Johnson City, Madison, Manchester, McKenzie, Somerville, Tullahoma, Union City, Big Sandy, Collierville, Covington, Dixon Springs, Elizabethton, Humboldt, Huntingdon, Mountain City, Pulaski, Shelbyville, Trenton, Waverly, Whiteville, Alamo, Ashland City, Dyersburg, Gainesboro, Henderson, Lebanon, Livingston, McMinnville, Milan, Hohenwald, Lafayette, Lawrenceburg, Lewisburg, Lynchburg, Martin, Smithville, Watertown, Waynesboro, Woodbury, Athens, Bristol, Harriman, Jefferson City, Jonesboro, Lenoir City, Dickson, Paris, Lexington, and Sewanee.

— Adapted from The Woman Suffrage Movement in Tennessee *by A. Elizabeth Taylor.*

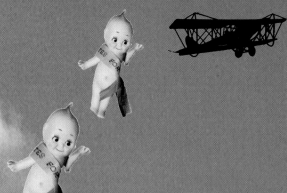

The Parachuting Kewpie Dolls

For Tennesseans, the publicity surrounding the National American Woman Suffrage Association's convention held in Nashville in November, 1914, marked a turning point in public sentiment concerning women's rights and capabilities in general, and woman suffrage, in particular. A Tennessee Men's Equal Suffrage League was organized during the meeting, and some 500 new converts declared their allegiance to the cause that autumn. One of the more persuasive and ingenious of the suffragists' public relations stunts took place at the Nashville fairgrounds.

The week after the convention, crowds braved north winds sweeping over the fairgrounds to see Miss Katherine Stinson in her airplane circle over the track and race her sister in a car below. According to news reports, there were long freezing waits before Miss Stinson "took her seat in the craft and was pushed into flight." Then, after a few turns, the plane "swept back in a descending curve" over the assembled crowd, and Miss Stinson let a shower of Kewpie dolls swathed in suffrage sashes float down on tiny yellow parachutes. Later that same day, she made several similar sensational flights over the city.

— *Adapted from "The Gracious Road to Battle" by Louise Davis*, The Nashville Tennessean Magazine, January 11, 1948.

"I am a suffragist because. . . ."

In 1914, a Nashville newspaper photographed very young children who were said to favor equal suffrage, and asked then to complete the statement, "I am a suffragist because..." One curly-haired two-year-old named Judith Folk [whose mother, Mrs. Reau E. Folk happened to be a leading Nashville suffragist] allegedly "prattled" her response as follows:

The female sect deserves respect.
The goose is grander than the gander,
And hens more knowing without their crowing,
Than any rooster I've been used to.

— *From a Special Suffrage Supplement of the* Nashville Tennessean, *August 20, 1914.*

The Publisher's Granddaughter Remembers

Here, recorded more than half a century later, are recollections by Mary Stahlman Douglas of her life as a "girl reporter" on the Nashville Banner, *the newspaper owned by her grandfather, Major E. B. Stahlman:*

I was a young reporter on the Banner in those days when women were tolerated and unwanted. They would never have considered sending a woman to cover the capital, for example. [But] I was the only staff member with a car, an antique Franklin that cost me dearly in down payments and repairs, and that enabled me to cover stories not otherwise possible.

She recalled a day in September, 1919, when some other reporters asked her if she had her car and did she want to go up in an airplane. Two U.S. Air Service pilots had been sent round the country to popularize flying by taking up newspaper persons free. Naturally adventurous, she said yes and drove them to the airport.

I was the only woman there, and the two planes took up all the men from the *Banner* and the *Tennessean,* then landed. Both flyers removed their goggles and helmets, as though through for the day which was fast waning. I rushed over to them, asked: "Aren't you going to take me up?" They were dumbfounded. They had orders not to take up women but agreed, after consultation, that if I would sign only my first and middle initials, in case of accident, they would take me up. I put on helmet and goggles and climbed in the rear cockpit of one of the planes, and off we sailed into the wild blue yonder, with dusk coming on and the Cumberland River lying coiled below like a great green serpent. When we tried to land, the trees were coming at us and up we went again. This happened three more times until finally, with dark approaching, no lights on plane or field, the trees only a few feet away, and the gas tank on empty, we landed safely. It was the thrill of a lifetime. Was the *Banner* interested in my account of the episode? Certainly

Yesterday's Nashville

Mary Stahlman Douglas

not. The woman's angle was not stressed in those days. It was not even considered.

Recalling the 1920 ratification campaign, Mary Stahlman Douglas wrote:

My grandfather was against suffrage, and my future husband, Boyd Douglas, a young lawyer who assisted Seth Walker [the Speaker of the House] was also against it. I look back, and fail to see how I could have been so unconcerned either way, for I am a very independent woman. Maybe it was my grandfather's influence, but I later regretted not taking sides.

She did, however, help the Banner *cover the campaign, and a number of women, both Suffs and Antis, came to the paper to give her interviews. But she was seldom assigned to cover their meetings. When she was, the usual happened:* In those days, when a reporter returned from a woman's club meeting the city editor asked: "Were they funny? Did they fight?" If both answers were negative, there was no story.

— From letters written to Carol Lynn Yellin by Mary Stahlman Douglas, December 12, 1977, and January 7, 1978.

"In memory of our fight for democracy..."

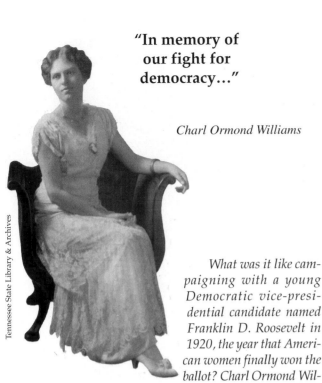

Charl Ormond Williams

What was it like campaigning with a young Democratic vice-presidential candidate named Franklin D. Roosevelt in 1920, the year that American women finally won the ballot? Charl Ormond Williams, the Tennessee woman who became the vice-chairman of the Democratic National Committee that year and went on to a distinguished career in public service in Washington, later recalled her experiences. In remarks made during the presentation of certain mementos to the Franklin D. Roosevelt Library in Hyde Park, New York, in 1947, two years after his death, she told a very personal story of one particular photograph:

In 1920, young Franklin D. Roosevelt resigned the position of Assistant Secretary of the Navy to become a candidate for vice president of the United States. With Governor James M. Cox as candidate for president, Mr. Roosevelt embarked on the arduous but unsuccessful campaign that followed. During the campaign, he, accompanied by Mrs. Roosevelt, was making a series of speeches in Indiana.

I had been elected that year as the first woman vice-chairman of the Democratic National Committee and, in my new party role, I was speaking also in Indiana — on the requested subject of Tennessee's just-delivered 36th ratification of the Woman Suffrage Amendment. (After the speech, I received a huge armful of yellow chrysanthemums, the suffrage colors, which I arranged to be presented later to Mrs. Roosevelt — but that's another story.) Being free on the next day when Mr. Roosevelt was scheduled to speak in a nearby city, I traveled over to hear him and to meet his wife. Little prepared was I for what happened that day.

The square around the Court House was filled with eager men, women, and children — and the audience was growing restless. Finally, a telephone message came: The car in which Mr. and Mrs. Roosevelt were riding had broken down. They could not possibly arrive within an hour, perhaps two. Something had to be done. Someone discovered I was the "ranking" party official, so I had to substitute for Franklin Roosevelt. For more than an hour, I faced what seemed to me a sea of faces, speaking until our candidate arrived, smiling and apologetic, to take over.

Soon after the campaign was finished, Mr. Roosevelt sent to me, as I am sure he must have sent to others in the campaign, a photograph of himself autographed as follows:

"To Miss Charl Williams.
    In memory of our fight for real democracy.
        Franklin D. Roosevelt, 1920."

When I left Memphis in 1922, I packed away the unframed photograph of him with all my cherished belongings, and it was not until 1936 [the year Franklin D. Roosevelt was first re-elected as President] that I brought it to Washington and gave it the place of honor in my home. From the moment I had this fresh view of the photograph, that autograph of his took on new meaning for me.... Although I had not had an opportunity to converse with him personally for many years, I knew he remembered my "standing-in" for him — several times he told groups of people that "Miss Williams and I campaigned together." One day in 1940, Mrs. Roosevelt, at my request, arranged for me to have tea with the President in the second-floor living room of the White House. I sat beside him on a great sofa, and told him I had something to show him. I put into his hands the simple photograph of him, simply framed. After a long look at himself as he appeared in 1920, he said, "My, Miss Williams, doesn't that look snooty?" To which I replied, "As I remember you, Mr. President, that was a very good likeness."

Then I read aloud the autograph — "In memory of our fight for real democracy..." — and I said, "Mr. President, in view of all that you have done and are doing to preserve democracy, this autograph, with 'democracy' spelled with a little 'd,' has deep significance for me. And, I want to say that that pronoun 'our' is my only hope for some measure of immortality."

The Newspaper-Publishing Bridegrooms of Nashville

Much has been made of the contrasts in background and character between the feuding publishers of Nashville's two leading newspapers during the 1920 suffrage ratification struggle. But the two men shared in common that year one little-noted distinction — some might have said distraction: They both became bridegrooms for the second time.

The dashing Colonel Luke Lea, owner and publisher of the *Nashville Tennessean* and descendant of a wealthy and distinguished line of Tennessee soldiers and statesmen, was educated by private tutors, earned degrees from the University of the South at Sewanee and Columbia University in New York, and in 1906, married Nashville socialite Mary Louise Warner. He founded the immediately successful *Tennessean* in 1907, and in 1911, at age 33, he was elected to the U.S. Senate, at that time the youngest ever to serve in that body. He was also a World War I hero, still being lionized in 1920 for leading a select group of Tennesseans under his command in a daring, though futile, attempt to capture the German Kaiser.

In contrast, the stolid, hard-working Major E. B. Stahlman, owner and publisher of the *Nashville Banner*, was born in Germany, and at age 11, in 1854, migrated with his family to West Virginia, where the father soon died, leaving his wife and seven children destitute. To help support the family, young Edward began his long struggle upward working as a common laborer on the Baltimore & Ohio Railroad, even though a schoolroom accident had left him permanently crippled early in life. Recruited by the Louisville & Nashville Railroad in 1863 for repair work on a tunnel near Gallatin, Tennessee, he soon was serving as the superintendent's secretary, became manager of a company store where he survived a

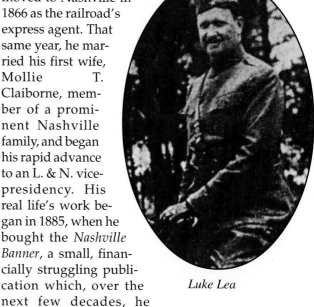

Luke Lea

Confederate raid, then moved to Nashville in 1866 as the railroad's express agent. That same year, he married his first wife, Mollie T. Claiborne, member of a prominent Nashville family, and began his rapid advance to an L. & N. vice-presidency. His real life's work began in 1885, when he bought the *Nashville Banner*, a small, financially struggling publication which, over the next few decades, he turned into one of the state's most influential and successful newspapers.

Major Stahlman's first wife, by whom he had three children, had died in 1915, and Colonel Lea's first wife, mother of two sons, died in 1919 while he was en route home from the war in Europe. But the rigors of the suffrage battle in Nashville the following year did not interfere with the widowed publishers' private lives. On May 1, 1920, 41-year-old Luke Lea married Percie Warner, the younger sister of his first wife, and they later became the parents of three children. Meanwhile, on August 23, 1920, just five days after the Tennessee legislature's pivotal ratification vote, and less than a month before his 77th birthday, the durable E. B. Stahlman got married in New York to his secretary, Sarah Shelton of Erin, Tennessee, by whom he later had a son.

— Based on newspaper obituaries of Luke Lea in the Nashville Tennessean, *Nov. 19, 1945, and of E. B. Stahlman in the* Nashville Banner, *August 12, 1930, and* Who's Who in America.

E. B. Stahlman

Mrs. Man

The time-honored custom of referring publicly to a married woman by use of her husband's first name, never her own, was still in full force in 1920, and was scrupulously adhered to by most newspapers in their coverage of Tennessee's ratification struggle. This could result in confusing misidentifications of Suffs and Antis alike. One ever-alert copy editor on the *Washington Times-Herald*, in an effort to conform to tradition, got tripped up twice in one story. According to the *Times-Herald*'s account of that day's goings-on in Nashville, it was a "Mrs. Charles Williams," not the leading suffragist Charl O. Williams, who had been announced as leader of the allied women's suffrage groups gathered in Tennessee. And a letter urging Governor Cox, the Democratic Presidential nominee, to declare himself against ratification of the suffrage amendment had been written, not by the prominent Anti, Josephine Pearson, but by one "Mrs. Joseph Pearson."

— *Based on coverage of the ratification story,* Washington Times-Herald, *August 10, 1920.*

Suffrage Day at the Tri-State Fair

In 1914, in an ongoing attempt to present innovative ideas to the public, the annual Tri-State Fair in Memphis added automobile races and a vaudeville act featuring the latest dance crazes, such as the Tango, Maxie, and the Hesitation. Bolder still was the specially designated Suffrage Day, celebrated for the first time that year. The 1914 Tri-State Fair promotional brochure justified the move as follows:

> No matter what one may individually think of Woman's Suffrage, the cause has many sincere advocates among men as well as women, and is bound to eventually triumph in America. The Fair, being an exponent of progressive ideas, is glad to welcome the women on Wednesday…when special exercises will be held on the grounds both day and night. Speakers of note will be present to address those interested.

— *Quoted in* A History of the Mid-South Fair, *by Emily Yellin.*

Affirmative Action, Affirmative Speech

On March 21, 1870, a United States Congressman from Columbia, Tennessee named Samuel Mayes Arnell, introduced a bill "to do justice to the female employees of the Government" in the House of Representatives. This early (perhaps earliest) version of Equal Employment Opportunity legislation, would have made "equal pay for equal work" an official government policy. It further decreed that "All job classification designations shall be held hereafter to apply to women as well as men," and that "No discrimination shall be made in favor of either sex." Though the act failed to gain any support in Congress, members of the National Woman Suffrage Association took notice. At their annual meeting the following year, held at the Apollo Hall in New York City, Congressman Arnell was an honored speaker. His remarks on that occasion did not disappoint his audience:

> In bringing the proposition before Congress to pay women the same price for the same work performed, I desired, not only to help those spirited, deserving women in the [government] Departments, but also to aid two-and-a-half millions of my working sisters in this country…. I greatly admire and respect either a working man or woman, for I devoutly believe that "to work is to pray," and I drew my best inspiration in this great contest for justice and freedom, from a bright, sunny-faced wife, who today is far away among the hills of Tennessee…. Ladies, the nobility of your work, far above all ridicule, misjudgment, slander and abuse even, is the emancipation and elevation of both man and woman. The Great Republic, of which you are citizens…can exist only as it is free, as it is just — two ideas that lie, as I understand it, at the bottom of your movement. The country must continue one-sided, ill-balanced, imperfect in its civilization, until woman is admitted to that individuality which of right belongs to every human being. Therefore, I bid you God-speed in your work.

— *Quoted by Elinor B. Bridges, in* The Wheel, *a monthly publication of Women's Resources Center of Memphis, Inc., September, 1977.*

Nashville Tennessean

The Senate Chamber in action under the watchful eyes of female suffragists on the floor.

VOTES FOR WOMEN

Tennessee Heroes: The Gallant Few

It was clear from the beginning that the men of Tennessee would decide, with their ballots, the fate of woman suffrage in their state. (Indeed, as it turned out, it was Tennessee men who ultimately decided its fate in the entire nation.) A vast majority of the state's male voters were initially opposed to the very notion of votes for women, and most remained so through the years. But there gradually developed a small cadre of Tennessee men willing to go against prevailing attitudes and able to convince others to join them in supporting the suffrage cause. What follows is an honor roll, incomplete though it may be, compiled to identify and pay tribute to the far-sighted and gallant Tennessee suffragists who happened to be male. Some whose names appear here became key players in the ongoing struggle for women's rights, and their role in winning the breathtaking ratification victory in 1920 was indispensable.

Acklen, Col. Joseph H. of Nashville — Prominent attorney who served as general legal counsel for Tennessee Equal Suffrage Association and its successor, the Tennessee League of Women Voters. A member of the Men's Ratification Committee, 1920, he urged members of the League to agitate for calling the special ratification session of the legislature.

Albright, Dr. James Alexander of Somerville — Member of Men's Ratification Committee, 1920. Later served two terms in the state Senate (1927-1929, 1931-1933); wrote as correspondent for the *Nashville Banner* for 30 years.

Anderson, Harry B. of Memphis — Spoke at Suffrage Day rally in Court Square, 1914.

Arnell, Samuel Mayes of Columbia — Congressman from Tennessee who, in 1870, introduced a bill in the U.S. House of Representatives to "do justice to the female employees of the Government" by guaranteeing that all government employees would be paid "irrespective of sex, according to the character and amount of services performed," and that "all job classification designations shall apply to women as well as men." One of the earliest versions of "equal pay for equal work" legislation, the bill did not pass.

Aust, John R. of Nashville — Member of Men's Ratification Committee, 1920.

Barnes, L. P. of Chattanooga — Featured speaker at second meeting of Nashville Equal Suffrage League, 1911.

Bates, Samuel Ogden of Memphis — State Senator in 60th Assembly who favored 1917 bill allowing women to vote in presidential and municipal elections.

Beasley, James S. of Nashville — Member of Men's Ratification Committee, 1920. Husband of chairman of Republican Women's Ratification Committee.

Bejach, Lois Dillard of Memphis — During his first

Memphis & Shelby County Library

term (1913-1915) in the state House, he was a proponent of women's rights and sponsored the Bejach Law, based upon the 1898-drafted bill to grant property rights to married women in Tennessee. Judge Bejach gave many speeches supporting woman suffrage in 1919-1920 and remained an ardent proponent of legislation emancipating women during his two terms in the House and one term in the Senate, as well as during his long service as Shelby County Attorney and as a court chancellor.

Bradley, Vernon Adolphus of Pleasant View — State Senator in the 61st Assembly who confessed during debate of 1919 limited suffrage bill that he had once believed in the "woman-stay-at home theory," but had outgrown this idea.

Brannan, Robert of Nashville — Described woman suffrage as "right, expedient, practical, just, respectable, respectful, and sure to win." *Nashville Tennessean* Suffrage Supplement, 1917.

Brown, O. E. of Nashville — Vanderbilt University professor who favored votes for women because "complete masculine domination was bad for society." *Nashville Tennessean* Suffrage Supplement, 1917.

Browning, Gordon of Huntingdon — Lawyer, judge. Member of Men's Ratification Committee, 1920. Twice elected Governor of Tennessee (1937, 1949).

Burn, Harry T. of Niota — Youngest Tennessee leg-

Nashville Tennessean

islator who, responding to pressure from his constituents, reluctantly voted with the anti-suffragists in the 1920 special session. When he realized, on August 18, that a 48 – 48 tie vote to table the ratification resolution would effectively kill the amendment, he changed his vote on final ballot — an action that gave suffragists their ultimate victory.

Caldwell, David P. of Union City — Two-term state Senator who opposed suffrage in 1917, but spoke and voted for it in special session, 1920.

Caldwell, John Dalton of Knoxville — Two-term state Senator, attorney and bachelor, who gave a number of speeches supporting equal suffrage — then cast his affirmative vote on August 13, 1920.

Caldwell, J. H. of Bristol — Member of Men's Ratification Committee, 1920.

Cameron, Walter Marvin of South Pittsburg — This 61st Assembly Senator gave a stirring speech to fellow senators in 1919 supporting woman suffrage and cast one of the 17 votes in the majority for passage of equal suffrage in municipal and presidential elections. He repeated his actions for the 1920 vote for the 19th Amendment.

Canale, George Anthony of Memphis — Representative from Shelby County in the 61st Assembly who spoke in favor of ratification in special session floor debate, 1920.

Carre, Henry Beach of Nashville — Vanderbilt University professor who wrote that government by men alone could meet "only a portion of humanity's needs." *Nashville Tennessean* Suffrage Supplement, 1917.

Carter, Finney Thomas of Chattanooga — State Senator in the 61st Assembly who spoke in favor of statewide suffrage in 1919 and for ratification in special session floor debate, 1920.

Cates, Charles A. Jr. of Knoxville — Speaker at public hearing of legislature's joint Committee of Constitutional Amendments, August 12, 1920; criticized out-of-state women there to oppose ratification.

Clements, H. H. of Knoxville — Republican State Chairman for Tennessee; urged all Republican members of legislature to vote for "immediate ratification of the Amendment," August, 1920.

Coleman, Thomas Lloyd of Lewisburg — During his first term in the state Senate, opposed suffrage (1919), but was member of committee recommending ratification of suffrage amendment, August 13, 1920.

Collins, Christian Carriger of Elizabethton — State Senator in the 61st Assembly and member of committee recommending ratification of suffrage amendment, August 13, 1920.

Cook, R. B. of Chattanooga — Helped form Men's Suffrage Club in Chattanooga, 1914.

Cooke, Dr. G. W. of Bolivar — Member of Men's Ratification Committee, 1920.

Copenhaver, M. H. of Sullivan County — Appointed and sworn in on August 10, 1920, to complete the unexpired term of ailing Senator J. J. Parks Worley of Bluff City (who had addressed the Senate in 1919 in opposition to equal suffrage). Three days later, Senator Copenhaver was among the committee members recommending ratification of the 19th Amendment. (Senator Copenhaver's actions apparently did not please his Sullivan County constituents. In a special election after Parks Worley's death on January 6, 1921, his widow, Anna L. Keys Worley, was elected — and qualified February 8, 1921 — to complete her late husband's senate term, thus becoming the first female to serve in the state legislature.)

Crabtree, William Riley of Chattanooga — Senate Speaker of 60th Assembly, he favored the 1917 bill giving women the ballot in presidential and municipal elections. Defeated by Governor A. H. Roberts in 1920 primary bid for Democratic gubernatorial nomination, but he urged calling of special session to ratify amendment so Tennessee could "perform an act of justice for the womanhood of America."

Crump, Edward Hull of Memphis — Mayor of Memphis and influential political "boss" of Shelby County. Strongly favored equal suffrage as early as 1913 in special suffrage edition of *The News-Scimitar*. Helped send unanimous pro-ratification Shelby delegation to special session, 1920. Member of Men's Ratification Committee, 1920.

The Commercial Appeal

Crutchfield, Thomas of Chattanooga — Having just married when he began service as a state representative, he spoke in floor debate on the 1917 limited suffrage bill, saying he believed women were entitled to the ballot by "all the laws of equity and justice."

Daughtry, Maj. C. L. of Nashville — Aide to Governor A. H. Roberts and member of Men's Ratification Committee, 1920.

Dodson, T. A. of Kingsport — Tennessee legislator who was called home from special session because his baby was dying. He left the train just as it was pulling out of Nashville after being notified by suffragist Newell Sanders that his vote for ratification was needed; he returned to the Capitol, voted, then was sent home on a specially-chartered private train to find his baby recovering.

Dorris, Finley Marborough of Nashville — Two-term state Senator who spoke in favor of suffrage in floor debate, August, 1920.

Douglas, Lee of Nashville — Favored suffrage in statement in *Nashville Tennessean* Suffrage Supplement, 1917.

Dowlen, Robert Lee of Pleasant View — This two-term pro-suffrage legislator, recovering from surgery, was carried into the legislative chamber to vote, August 18, 1920.

Dudley, Guilford of Nashville — Supported the dedicated suffrage work of his wife, Anne Dallas Dudley; member of Men's Ratification Committee, 1920.

Dyer, G. W. of Nashville — Vanderbilt University professor favored woman suffrage in *Nashville Tennessean* Suffrage Supplement, 1917.

Elkins, Louis Emerson of Dyer — State Representative, speaking in favor of 1917 limited suffrage bill, said it was time for women to take their place in government and "men might as well butt their brains against the Rock of Gibraltar as to oppose it."

Fineshriber, Rabbi W. H. of Memphis — Spoke at Suffrage Day rally in Court Square, 1914.

Fisher, Hubert Frederick of Memphis — Spoke at 1914 Suffrage Day rally in Court Square. Staunch supporter of woman suffrage both as Tennessee state Senator in 1913-15 and as a U.S. Congressman in 1920 (serving from 1917 to March 3, 1931).

Fitzhugh, Guston T. of Memphis — Longtime suffrage advocate, spoke at 1914 rally in Court Square. As State Representative, voted for 1917 limited suffrage bill and for ratification in special session in 1920.

Folk, Reau of Nashville — Member of Men's Ratification Committee, 1920.

Fowler, James A. of Nashville — Attorney who spoke in favor of ratification at legislature's public hearing of joint Committee on Constitutional Amendments, August 12, 1920.

Frierson, W. L. of Chattanooga — Member of Men's Ratification Committee, 1920.

Fuller, Frank Darwin of Memphis — Four-term state Senator; member of Democratic Steering Committee for Ratification, 1920.

Galloway, Jacob Scudder of Memphis — State Senator in the 43rd Assembly who introduced state's first woman suffrage bill in Tennessee legislature in 1883. The bill failed.

Gardner, H. C. of Nashville — Member, with his wife, of earliest woman suffrage association in Nashville, 1894.

Griffin, Dr. J. Frank of Tiptonville — Legislator who hastened home from California to vote for ratification during Tennessee legislature's special session in August, 1920.

Gwinn, Lambert Estes of Covington — State Senator in the 61st Assembly who supported successful 1919 limited suffrage bill; presented committee report recommending ratification of suffrage amendment, August 13, 1920.

Hanover, Joseph of Memphis — State Representative in 61st Assembly

Memphis & Shelby County Library

and fledgling attorney who argued eloquently and voted for limited suffrage bill in 1919. During the special session in August, 1920, he became floor leader in the House for suffrage forces; also a member of Carrie Chapman Catt's strategic planning group. Worked so tirelessly he lost 20 pounds, and his work was so effective that he became the target of anti-suffragist plots. Governor Roberts appointed a special bodyguard to protect him.

Haston, Ernest Nathaniel of Spencer — Two-term state Senator; Democratic Steering Committee for Ratification, 1920; member of committee recommending ratification of amendment, August 13, 1920. Floor leader for suffrage forces in the Senate.

Henry, Robert of Nashville — Assisted with arrangements for 1914 NAWSA Convention in Nashville.

Hibbett, Dr. W. E. of Nashville — Member of Men's Ratification Committee, 1920.

Hill, Albert E. of Nashville — Three-term state Senator who favored 1917 and 1919 limited suffrage bills; voted for ratification in 1920.

Hooper, Ben W. of Newport — Two-term Governor of Tennessee, 1911-1915; welcomed NAWSA Convention to Nashville, 1914. Member of Men's Ratification Committee, 1920.

Houk, John Chiles of Knoxville — Five-term state Senator who spoke in favor of 1917 bill granting equal suffrage in presidential and municipal elections: "It is the central right of an individual human being, whether male or female, to have a role in the making of the laws to govern a human being." Worked and voted for ratification in 1920.

Howse, Hilary of Nashville — Former state Senator (1905-1907, 1909-1911) and Mayor of Nashville (1909-1915), who welcomed NAWSA Convention to Nashville in 1914.

Hull, Cordell of Carthage — U.S. Representative from Tennessee, 1907-1921. Member of Men's Ratification Committee, 1920. Later elected U.S. Senator, 1930; appointed Secretary of State, 1933.

Johnson, William Allen of Ellendale — State Senator in the 59th and 60th Assemblies, he spoke in favor of 1917 limited suffrage bill.

Keating, J. M. of Memphis — Editor of *The Daily Appeal* who gave early support to equal suffrage. In 1888, he wrote, "The right of women to suffrage is no longer a subject of mockery, jibe, or jest. Intelligent people realize the injustice of withholding the ballot from women."

Keeble, John Bell of Nashville — Attorney and president of Men's Suffrage League formed during NAWSA convention in Nashville, 1914.

Kimbrough, D. T. of Nashville — Once called "One of the original unterrified (male) suffragists in Nashville." Advised finance committee of Nashville Equal Suffrage League.

Lea, Luke of Nashville — Member of pioneer

Memphis & Shelby County Library

Tennessee family, World War I hero, and a U.S. Senator from Tennessee, who was one of only three southern Senators to vote in favor of the federal suffrage amendment when it was defeated in Congress in 1914. As publisher of pro-suffrage *Nashville Tennessean*, he gave invaluable support to ratification campaign in 1920.

Lewinthal, Rabbi Isadore of Nashville — Favored woman suffrage in *Nashville Tennessean* Suffrage Supplement, 1917.

Lowry, J. B. F. of Chattanooga — Helped form Men's Suffrage Club in Chattanooga, 1914.

Mayfield, George of Nashville — Vanderbilt University professor, who wrote in favor of equal suffrage: "When I look at some of the men who are allowed to vote and then at some of the women who are not allowed to cast the ballot... I stand ready to give my heart and vote to the cause." *Nashville Tennessean* Suffrage Supplement, 1917.

McFarland, Lonsdale Porter of Lebanon — Longtime member of the Tennessee House; was serving in the Senate during the 61st Assembly, where he gave an enthusiastic speech in 1919 supporting statewide equal suffrage for women. Unfortunately, he abstained when the State Senate voted on the 19th Amendment.

McKellar, Kenneth D. of Memphis — Attorney and

Nashville Tennessean

influential pro-suffrage Democrat. Spoke at 1915 suffrage rally in Memphis, predicting women would improve politics and saying that working women needed the ballot for their own protection. As U.S. Senator from Tennessee, he voted for federal suffrage amendment in Congress in 1918; received telegram in August, 1920, in San Francisco (where he was vacationing) from President Wilson, instructing him to "go to Tennessee and aid in getting the Tennessee Legislature to ratify the Amendment." He departed for Nashville and was a key strategist for ratification during the special session.

McRee, Frank Johnson of Macon — State Representative in 59th and 60th Assemblies, who spoke in favor of 1917 limited suffrage bill, saying he had switched sides because of arguments which "could not be gotten around."

Mickell, Dr. H. L. of Nashville — Favored woman suffrage in statement in *Nashville Tennessean* Suffrage Supplement, 1917.

Miller, Leonidas D. of Chattanooga — House member of the 61st Assembly who made the final speech in the special session floor debate on August 18, 1920, strongly championing ratification and denouncing the "infamous gang of lobbyists" working against the suffrage amendment.

Mills, Robert Daniel of Nashville — State Representative in first session of the 61st Assembly who said he voted for successful 1919 limited suffrage bill because his wife and mother begged him to do so.

Milton, George Fort of Chattanooga — Founding member of Chattanooga Men's Suffrage Club, 1914;

publisher of pro-suffrage *Chattanooga News*; husband of Abby Crawford Milton, president of Tennessee League of Women Voters; member of Men's Ratification Committee, 1920.

Mims, Edwin of Nashville — Vanderbilt University professor who presided at public appearance of militant British suffragist Emmeline Pankhurst, brought to Nashville by Vanderbilt University Equal Suffrage League, 1916.

Mooney, C. P. J. of Memphis — Editor of *The Com-*

The Commercial Appeal

mercial Appeal, who gave steadfast support to equal suffrage in the years before and during ratification vote in 1920. Spoke at 1915 suffrage rally in Memphis, saying woman should be a "full partner in life and not a junior one."

Morgan, Dr. Carey of Nashville — Member of Men's Ratification Committee, 1920.

Morrison, Dr. W. J. of Nashville — Member of Men's Ratification Committee, 1920.

Murrey, John Woodall of Gallatin — State Senator replacing resigned Senator A. V. Louthan in special session; member of committee recommending ratification of suffrage amendment, August 13, 1920.

Neal, Maj. E. H. of Knoxville — Member of Men's Ratification Committee, 1920.

Odle, Joseph Fry of Camden — Three-term state Representative; supported successful limited suffrage bill in 1919. Spoke and worked for ratification during special session, 1920.

Overall, John W. of Nashville — Member of Men's Ratification Committee, 1920.

Paine, Rowlett of Memphis — Progressive Mayor of Memphis supported by majority of Memphis women in their first vote in municipal election, 1919.

Parker, James William of Alexandria — State Representative in 60th Assembly; spoke in favor of limited suffrage bill in 1917.

Parks, Judge J. B. of Fayetteville — Member of Men's Ratification Committee, 1920.

Patton, Erastus Eugene of Knoxille — "Patton Turned the Tide for Suffrage" proclaimed the April 15, 1919, headline of the *Knoxville Journal*. State Senator E. E. Patton's eloquent speech in favor of statewide equal suffrage for women in municipal and presidential elections "was the sensation of the session," according to fellow Senator John C. Houk. "He has been congratulated by many prominent men of the state on his presentation of the cause for equal suffrage." Patton remained steadfast in "the bitter fight over freedom for women" and in the summer of 1920, during floor debate in special session, he spoke in favor of ratification of the federal amendment. Later recalling the moment's drama, Patton wrote, "Mrs. Gilford [sic] Dudley led the fight in Nashville, and I can see and hear her scream when the vote was announced."

Peay, Austin, IV, of Clarksville — Member of Men's Ratification Committee, 1920. Three-term Governor of Tennessee, 1923-1927.

Puryear, Judge David B. of Memphis — Longtime  suffrage supporter, who introduced equal suffrage resolution at Tennessee Bar Association meeting. Accompanied his wife, who was first president of Memphis League of Women Voters, to Nashville in August, 1920, to lobby for ratification of suffrage amendment. He became a criminal court judge after a distinguished career in the legislature.

Rice, Frank Jr. of Memphis — Associate of Memphis political leader, E. H. Crump. Partial term as state Senator, 1920, and voted for suffrage amendment; member of Men's Ratification Committee, 1920.

Riddick, Thomas Kader of Memphis — Eminent  pro-suffrage attorney; spoke at 1915 suffrage rally in Memphis, accusing Antis of not considering women to be human beings. Chosen a state Representative in special election to fill vacancy in Shelby County delegation in August, 1920, having run for the office especially to vote for ratification. "To Mr. Riddick, more than to any other, the credit of Tennessee's ratifying the Woman Suffrage Amendment is due…. On the final vote, Mr. Riddick told me that with Burn's vote the Suffrage Amendment would be ratified, and without his vote it would not be ratified," wrote U.S. Senator Kenneth McKellar in 1942. "I immediately called [Newell] Sanders…and he immediately called Burn, and Burn cast the deciding vote in favor of ratification."

Roberts, Albert Houston of Livingston — Governor of Tennessee, 1919-1921. Signed limited suffrage bill passed by 61st General Assembly, April 17, 1919. Issued call for special session to vote on ratification of suffrage amendment August 9, 1920. Sent message to legislature supporting ratification, saying "Tennessee occupies a pivotal position upon this question; the eyes of all America are upon us. Millions of women are looking to the Tennessee Legislature to give them a voice and share in shaping the destiny of the Republic." On August 23, signed certificate of ratification and sent it on to the Secretary of State of the United States, who proclaimed the 19th Amendment part of the United States Constitution on August 26, 1920.

Roby, Prof. J. H. of Union City — Member of Men's Ratification Committee, 1920.

Rutherford, Judge A. J. of Nashville — Member of Men's Ratification Committee, 1920.

Rye, Thomas Clarke of Paris — Two-term Governor of Tennessee, 1915-1919. The 60th Assembly, in 1917, could not reach a consensus on woman suffrage, so suffragists began a push to gain statewide municipal and presidential suffrage (which could be granted by the legislature without a constitutional amendment). Led by the Tennessee Equal Suffrage Association, which held its convention in Nashville on January 30, 1917, they relentlessly lobbied legislators. They won the support of Governor Rye, who told the suffragists that he "hoped Tennessee will be the first Southern state to give votes to women." President Wilson enlisted suffrage leader Sue Shelton White to personally appeal to the state's Democratic leaders for support, and the House passed the bill by a 59-24 vote before recess on February 3. On February 26 — the first day of session after recess — the Senate defeated the bill, 21-12, and the work for woman suffrage in the following session began anew. Governor Rye served as chairman of the Men's Ratification Committee, 1920.

Saunders, Clarence of Memphis — Successful businessman and founder of innovative Piggly-Wiggly grocery stores, which introduced concept of self-service. Member of Men's Ratification Committee, 1920.

Sanders, Newell of Chattanooga — Republican former U.S. and state Senator, who was a strong advocate of woman suffrage and active in the fight for ratification of the 19th Amendment in 1920. He and several other ratificationists paid for a chartered train late on August 19 to transport Rep. T. A. Dodson home to Kingsport — he having halted his earlier homeward trip to be with his dying child (who rallied and recovered). Also credited by U.S. Senator Kenneth McKellar as having telephoned legislator Harry Burn to appeal for suffrage ratification, resulting in his influence being "responsible for one vote at the right time...because of the respect and esteem that Mr. Burn had for Senator Sanders."

Seay, Edward T. of Gallatin and Nashville — Former three-term state Senator from Gallatin and Senate Speaker, 1903-1905, who became a socially prominent attorney and jurist in Nashville after 1907. Quoted in *Nashville Tennessean* Suffrage Supplement, 1917, as favoring suffrage "because I find that the arguments against it are for the most part sentimental." Spoke in favor of ratification at public hearing of legislature's joint Committee of Constitutional Amendments, August 12, 1920.

Shook, Col. A. M. of Nashville — Member of Men's Ratification Committee, 1920.

Shropshire, Clyde of Nashville — Moved from Rome, Georgia, to Nashville in 1911 and served in state House during 1915-1919; Speaker of Tennessee House, 1917-1919. Consistent supporter of woman suffrage, who introduced 1917 bill to grant women the vote in presidential and municipal elections: "Let Tennessee be the first Southern state to stand out in the clear white light of this great movement."

Simpson, Jacob of Cleveland — Elected to replace

Nashville Tennessean

resigned Rep. Jacob Smith for extra session and who voted for ratification. Was challenged, at a mass protest meeting on August 26, 1920, to defend his action. This father of nine daughters said he was proud to vote "in behalf of the women of the nation," and called anti-ratification lobbyists "just about all the worst elements of society that could be herded together."

Smith, Blair of Nashville — Male member of Nashville Equal Suffrage League, 1911.

Smith, Rev. Wesley J. of Chattanooga — Male member of Chattanooga Equal Suffrage League, 1911.

Stephenson, J. H. of Nashville — Vanderbilt University professor spoke on "Equal Suffrage" to Housekeeper's Club of Nashville, 1911.

Taylor, Alfred A. of Happy Valley — Member of Men's Ratification Committee, 1920. Governor of Tennessee, 1921-1923, having served in the 1870s in the Tennessee House and in the U.S. House in the 1890s.

Terrell, Robert H. of Washington, D. C. — First black man appointed (1902) to a federal judgeship and husband of Mary Church Terrell of Memphis, who became an early proponent of woman suffrage when it was rare for men to support such a radical notion. The August, 1915, issue of the NAACP publication, *The Crisis,* included a special section, "Votes for Women: A Symposium by Leading Thinkers of Colored America," with essays by leading suffragists — and one was Robert H. Terrell.

Thompson, Gen. Frank of Nashville — Member of Men's Ratification Committee, 1920.

Tigrett, I. B. of Jackson — Member of Men's Ratification Committee, 1920.

Todd, Andrew Lee of Murfreesboro — Speaker of

Nashville Tennessean

Tennessee Senate in the 61st Assembly, 1919-1921, fought for passage of ratification of 19th Amendment; later served as president of Tennessee College for Women at Murfreesboro.

Turner, Banks Pearson of Yorkville — Legislator who resisted pressure from House Speaker Seth Walker to vote against ratification during final roll call at special session in August, 1920.

Walker, Seth M. of Lebanon — State Representative and Speaker in 61st Assembly; spoke and voted in favor of 1919 limited suffrage bill, saying, "It would be a crime and a shame if the women were not given this right." Had established legal practice and residence in Nashville before becoming an original member of Men's Ratification Committee, 1920. During special session, he changed sides and worked to defeat amendment, a betrayal suffragists attributed to pressure from railroad lobbyists.

Warner, Percy of Nashville — Member of socially prominent Nashville family and father-in-law of Luke Lea, publisher of *Nashville Tennessean.* Member of Men's Ratification Committee, 1920.

Watts, Rev. George O. of Jackson — Rector of St. Luke's Church who served as first vice-president of Jackson Equal Suffrage League in 1914.

West, Dr. Olin of Nashville — Member of Men's Ratification Committee, 1920.

Wikle, Douglas of Franklin — Two-term state Senator and member of Democratic Steering Committee for Ratification; member of committee recommending ratification of suffrage amendment, August 13, 1920.

Williams, Albert of Nashville — State superintendent of public instruction; appointed by Governor Roberts to serve as his legislative liaison to keep track of legislators' pledges to support ratification during special session, August, 1920.

Williams, Judge Joe V. of Chattanooga — Member of Men's Ratification Committee, 1920.

Wilson, Judge S. F. of Nashville — One-time member of Men's Ratification Committee, who switched sides and spoke against suffrage at public hearing of legislature's joint Committee on Constitutional Amendments, August 13, 1920.

"Man trusts woman with his name, his honor, and with the rearing of his children. There is no good reason he should not trust her with the ballot."

THE
CONSTITUTION

Tennessee Heroines: A Suffrage Roll of Honor

This is a tribute to the many Tennessee women whose dedication over the years to the suffrage cause helped win the great 1920 ratification victory in Nashville. It particularly honors some of the state's lesser-known suffragists, whose contributions to that triumph are seldom remembered today. In some cases, we are able to give names only, without hometowns. Identification is incomplete in other cases because, as this listing indicates, married women of the past, including suffragists, were seldom referred to publicly by their given names, but by the names of their husbands. There also are, sad to say, countless other Tennessee women whose names belong on this honor roll, but whose roles in the long, hard-fought battle for enfranchisement of women were never recorded or cannot now be recalled. Though their identities remain unknown, they, too, are honored here.

Adamson, Helen — Vanderbilt University Equal Suffrage League, 1917.

Aiken, Mrs. M. C. of Memphis — Corresponding secretary of Tennessee's first local Equal Suffrage Society, organized in Memphis in 1889.

Albright, Mettie White of Humboldt — While

Courtesy of Joan Albright

working as an engrossing clerk in the Tennessee legislature in 1919, the young Mettie White produced the hand-written House bill used the following summer when Tennessee ratified the 19th Amendment. An organizer of the Humboldt Business and Professional Women's Club, Mrs. Albright (1894-1994) became chief engrossing clerk of the Tennessee Senate in 1951.

Allen, Mrs. Martha Moore of Memphis — Member of Memphis Equal Suffrage Society in the early 1900s. President of Tennessee Equal Suffrage Association from 1906 to 1912. Active in the National American Woman Suffrage Association. An eloquent orator, she organized rallies, issued press releases, and led a successful campaign for admission of women to the Memphis Law School.

Anderson, Mrs. Harry B. of Memphis — Spoke at suffragists' 1915 May Day rally in Memphis. Testified before the judiciary committee of the Tennessee House of Representatives in 1917 in favor of the bill granting women the right to vote in municipal and presidential elections.

Anderson, Helen — Vanderbilt University Equal Suffrage League, 1917.

Aust, Mrs. John R. of Nashville — A committee chairman for League of Women Voters Ratification Committee, 1920.

Baker, Mrs. Charles of Nashville — Active member of Nashville Equal Suffrage League and "a member of a noted corps of writers who used their pens only for World War work" during 1917-1918. Served as chair of *Bulletins* for state Equal Suffrage Association and issued numerous newsletters "which kept the various county leagues in close co-operation with the State Department" during World War I.

Bang, Mrs. M. P. of Nashville — Nashville Equal Suffrage League, 1911.

Bangs, Mrs. W. F. of Nashville — Secretary of Davidson County Women's Christian Temperance Union. She gave the invocation at the suffragists' 1914 May Day Celebration in Nashville.

Barksdale, Cornelia of Nashville — Press secretary of Nashville Equal Suffrage League, 1918; secretary of Tennessee Woman Suffrage Association, 1918.

Barnes, Mrs. L. P. of Chattanooga — Spoke at second meeting of Nashville Equal Suffrage League in 1911.

Baxter, Mrs. Mary of Nashville — Member of the early, but short-lived, Nashville Equal Suffrage Association, 1894.

Baxter, Mrs. Perkins of Nashville — Helped establish Equal Suffrage League in Jackson in 1911. Member of executive committee of Tennessee Equal Suffrage Association in 1914.

Beasley, Mrs. James S. — Headed the state Republican Women's Committee for Ratification of Suffrage Amendment in 1920.

Beattie, Mrs. Robert — Vice president of Tennessee Woman Suffrage Association in the early 1900s.

Bell, Camille B. of Jackson — An organizer and the first president of Jackson Equal Suffrage League, 1911.

Betts, Mrs. Virginia Meriwether of Memphis — Daughter of suffrage pioneer Lide Meriwether, she was secretary of both Memphis and Tennessee Equal Suffrage Associations in the early 1900s. After she was widowed, she entered medical school, exhibiting the "personal independence" her mother had advocated.

Binford, Miss Elizabeth of Nashville — This school

teacher was corresponding secretary of the Nashville Equal Suffrage Association, 1914; also was a charter member, 1917, of the Equal Suffrage Auxiliary during the first Red Cross campaign of World War I.

Blanton, Miss Anna of Nashville — Member of hospitality committee for National American Woman Suffrage Association convention in Nashville, 1914; as a member of Equal Suffrage Association's Auxiliary was a lieutenant under Mrs. Harry W. Evans, commander, of the Emergency Canteen Service Committee, American Red Cross, begun in January, 1918.

Bloomstein, Miss Elizabeth ("Lizzie") Lee of Nash-

ville — Member of one of Nashville's prominent Jewish families, she was in the first graduating class of George Peabody College in 1877; she joined the faculty and served as head librarian until her death in 1927. An early advocate of women's rights, she was one of the unsung activists who helped set the stage for the suffrage ratification victory in Nashville in 1920.

Boyd, Pattie of Knoxville — Pioneer Tennessee newspaperwoman who reported news of suffragists in the *Knoxville Journal*.

Branch, Mae C. — One of the incorporators named in charter of Tennessee Equal Suffrage Association, 1914.

Breen, Elizabeth of Nashville — Chairman of literature committee of Nashville Equal Suffrage League in 1913, recording secretary in 1914.

Brown, Frances Fort of Chattanooga — A founding member of Chattanooga Equal Suffrage League, 1911.

Buchanan, Mrs. A. S. — Honorary president of the Tennessee Woman Suffrage Association, 1918.

Buckner, Claire B. of Fayetteville — President of Fayetteville Equal Suffrage League who reported in 1912, "We have much to contend with, much opposition, and a deadly indifference which is worse. But we hope that 'ere another year has passed we shall be able to report more accomplished and less 'hoped for.'"

Burn, Febb Ensminger of Niota — Widowed mother of young legislator Harry Burn who, as a property owner, objected to taxation without representation. She became a key player in the 1920 legislative struggle in Nashville when her last-minute message, "Be a good boy and help Mrs. Catt put the 'rat' in ratification" letter, caused her son to change his vote and give suffragists their one-vote victory.

Butler, Mary Ellis of Jackson — President of Jackson Equal Suffrage League in 1917. Reporting on the hard-earned progress of suffragists in Tennessee, she recalled that, in 1912, members of the newly-organized Jackson league were "looked upon as peculiar, to say the least, but by 1917 even the local Antis were saying, 'Suffrage is coming and nothing will stop it.'"

Caldwell, Mary French of Knoxville — A young newspaper reporter of suffragist sympathies who covered the 1920 ratification story for the *Knoxville Sentinel.* Since her father was a good friend of Governor Roberts, she had access to him and was able to serve, when needed, as a conduit of information between the suffragists and the governor.

Cannon, Mrs. E. C. of Murfreesboro — First vice president of the Murfreesboro Equal Suffrage League, established in June, 1914.

Chase, Elise — Vanderbilt University Equal Suffrage League, 1917.

Childers, Mrs. Ben of Pulaski — Auditor, Tennessee Equal Suffrage Association, 1915.

Chumbley, Miss Mabel — Treasurer, Tennessee Equal Suffrage Association, 1918.

Clark, Ida Clyde of Nashville — Worked with National American Woman Suffrage Association, and in 1911 was a founding member and press secretary of Nashville Equal Suffrage League.

Coleman, Mrs. Lewis of Chattanooga — A founding member of Chattanooga Equal Suffrage League, 1911.

Coleman, Mattie E. Howard of Nashville — A physician and early graduate of Meharry Medical College, and a suffragist, she was an influential leader among black women and was deeply involved in social reform and missionary work for the Christian Methodist Episcopal Church. She stated in the *Nashville Tennessean* in 1913 that woman suffrage was often discussed at meetings of black women,

but no organized suffrage work had yet been done among them.

Collier, Ada of McKenzie — District vice president, Tennessee Equal Suffrage Association, 1915.

Coonrood, Eleanor of Chattanooga — A lawyer who became the first woman member of the Tennessee Bar Association. She was secretary of the Chattanooga Equal Suffrage League, 1911.

Conner, Mrs. William — Auditor for the Tennessee Woman Suffrage Association, 1918.

Cope, Mrs. Emille B. of Chattanooga — A founding member of Chattanooga Equal Suffrage League, 1911.

Crawford, Mrs. J. A. of Memphis — The Memphis convention of the Southern Woman Suffrage Conference was held in her home in 1906.

Crickett, Lillian of Nashville — Member, Nashville Equal Suffrage League.

Croft, Margaret of Knoxville — Secretary, Knoxville Equal Suffrage League.

Crozier, Mary Hume of Knoxville — Like her suffragist sister, Lizzie Crozier French, she was active in the suffrage movement. She helped establish the Woman's Educational and Industrial Union in the 1890s, which worked to improve the lot of working women, and got Lizzie Crozier French appointed as the South's first police matron.

Dame, Mrs. M. L. of Harriman — Vice chairman of Tennessee Division of the Congressional Union, forerunner of National Woman's Party, 1916.

Daviess, Maria Thompson of Madison — Vice president of Nashville Equal Suffrage League, 1911, and close co-worker of Anne Dallas Dudley. Honorary President, Tennessee Equal Suffrage Association, 1915. The Madison Equal Suffrage League was founded at a barbecue at her home in 1915.

Denney, Jane Franklin Hommel (Mrs. G. W.) of Knoxville — Civic activist and social reformer in late 1890s and early 1900s; married to managing editor of Knoxville's *Journal and Tribune,* which published many articles on suffrage and women's rights. Early member of Tennessee Federation of Women's Clubs, founded in 1896, and was TFWC lobbyist for 1913 passage of state Married Women's Emancipation Act; president of TFWC, 1913-1917. Also lobbied for 1898-drafted bill to make women eligible to serve on school boards; act finally passed in 1915. Tennessee chairman of Women's Committee, Council of National Defense during

World War I; legislative activist/lobbyist for Tennessee Equal Suffrage Association.

Diehl, Mrs. Charles of Clarksville — Secretary of Clarksville Equal Suffrage League, 1914.

Dodson, Mary Lemire of Humboldt — President of Humboldt Equal Suffrage League, 1916.

Donelson, Bettie Mizell (Mrs. William A.) of Nashville — Member of a pio-

Tennessee State Library & Archives

neer Tennessee family, a prominent early suffragist and a dedicated temperance worker, she was elected secretary of Tennessee Equal Rights Association when it was organized in 1897, and became known as one of Tennessee's most forceful advocates for woman suffrage. She once complained that early suffragists had to withstand not only sarcasm and ridicule from cartoonists and editors, but also "sneers from the pulpit whence should have come their strongest support."

Dortch, Miss Della of Nashville — Chair of

Davidson County Women

Nashville's Equal Suffrage Auxiliary Committee for War Fund Campaign, 1917, and chair of Nashville Public School Teachers Auxiliary for the same campaign. For the Equal Suffrage Auxiliary, she organized the first Red Cross campaign for relief funds in 1917 with sister-suffragist Matilda Porter as chair for the city workers; in 1918, a subsequent Red Cross campaign she chaired raised $2,700 in relief funds. Speaker in 1918 at Nashville Equal Suffrage Association headquarters' rally for third Liberty Loan fund-raiser; described as a "Nashville suffrage leader who did exceptional war work." Member of advisory board, Democratic Ratification Committee, 1920; regional chair of national League of Women Voters, 1920.

Dudley, Anne Dallas (Mrs. Guilford) of Nashville — One of Tennessee's most influential suffragists, she founded the Nashville Equal Suffrage League in 1911, was president of the Tennessee Equal Suffrage League in 1915, vice president of the National American Woman Suffrage Association in 1917, and an indispensable campaigner for the 36th ratification of the suffrage amendment in Nashville in 1920. Her beauty, charm and eloquence made her the living refutation of the "she-male" label often given to suffragists by opponents of woman suffrage.

Dresser, Mrs. Prudence Simpson of Gallatin — Vice president for Middle Tennessee, Tennessee Equal Suffrage Association, 1918-1919. Organized local meeting for ratification of the suffrage amendment, 1920.

Dromgoole, Miss Will Allen of Murfreesboro and Nashville — Elected as en-

Davidson County Women

grossing clerk for Tennessee Senate, 1885 and 1887; became a published novelist, 1886, and feature writer for *Nashville Daily American*, 1890; a founding member of Tennessee Woman's Press and Authors Club,1899, (now Tennessee Media Women, Inc.) and staunch advocate of women's rights. She was the first woman to volunteer from Tennessee to enter military service, enlisting in the U.S. Navy on May 1, 1917; first operated the Nashville soldiers' canteen, then recruited enlistments in Maryland, Virginia, and North Carolina, and sent a column of "war news" to the *Nashville Banner* through 1918.

East, Mrs. E. H. of Nashville — Member of the early, but short-lived, Nashville Woman Suffrage Association, 1894.

Elcaro, Mrs. M. H. — Treasurer of the Tennessee Equal Suffrage Association, 1908.

Elliott, Sarah Barnwell of Sewanee — A well-known author, she circulated suffrage petitions to governor, legislators, mayors and other Tennessee office holders in 1912. She served two terms as president of Tennessee Equal Suffrage Association in 1912 and 1913; was responsible for inviting National American Woman Suffrage Association to hold its annual convention in Nashville in 1914.

Ellis, Margaret Crosby of Nashville — Member of the early, but short-lived, Nashville Woman Suffrage Association, 1894.

Epperson, Mrs. John Algood — Fourth district chairman of the Tennessee Equal Suffrage Association, 1914.

Ervin, Josephine of Chattanooga — Chattanooga Equal Suffrage League, 1911.

Ervin, Margaret of Chattanooga — Member of Chattanooga Equal Suffrage League, 1911. President of Tennessee Equal Suffrage Association, 1917. Testified before judiciary committee of the Tennessee General Assembly in 1917, urging the ballot for women in presidential and municipal elections. Organized defense corps of women to practice riflery during World War I. Secretary of Democratic Ratification Committee, 1920.

Eslick, Mrs. E. E. of Pulaski — Prominent in state suffrage work with Kate Burch Warner in the Tennessee Equal Suffrage Association; she was a featured speaker at the December 2, 1918, banquet in Nashville's Hermitage Hotel for New York's Mrs. Charles Tiffany, board member of the National Equal Suffrage Association.

Evans, Beverly of Chattanooga — Chattanooga Equal Suffrage League, 1911.

Ezzell, Fanny Moran of Newsom Station — Ninth

Davidson County Women

District Chairman of Tennessee Equal Suffrage Association, 1914; vice chairman, Democratic Ratification Committee, 1920.

Farrington, Mrs. William — First vice president of Tennessee Equal Suffrage Association, 1908.

Folk, Mrs. Reau E. of Nashville — Legislative committee, Tennessee Equal Suffrage Association; addressed suffragists' 1914 May Day Rally in Nashville on "Why the Mothers of Tennessee Want to Vote." With Mrs. Joseph A. Gray, was co-chair of the December 2, 1918, banquet in Nashville's Hermitage Hotel to honor New York's Mrs. Charles Tiffany, board member of the National Equal Suffrage Association.

Ford, Mrs. Zora of Chattanooga — Member of Chattanooga Equal Suffrage League, 1911.

Fox, Mrs. Lee of Murfreesboro — Organized local mass meeting for ratification of suffrage amendment, 1920.

Fraser (also spelled Frazer), Anita Lewis (Mrs. James S.) of Nashville —

Davidson County Women

Chaired organizational meeting at state Capitol, July 20, 1917, of the Division of Women's Committee, Council of National Defense; served until April, 1918. Board member, Democratic Ratification Committee, 1920.

Frazier, Miss Sarah of Chattanooga — Writer and lecturer; early member of Tennessee Woman's Press and Authors Club, founded in 1899; vice president and chair of state's Third District, Tennessee Equal Suffrage Association, 1918. Lobbied for suffrage ratification in the Tennessee legislature, August, 1920. Fourth woman elected to the Tennessee House of Representatives, 1927, and fifth woman to serve in the Tennessee General Assembly.

Frazer, Mrs. George of Nashville — Member of Nashville Equal Suffrage League, 1914. Chairman of automobile arrangements for 1914 NAWSA convention in Nashville.

French, Lizzie Crozier of Knoxville — Organizer

McClung Historical Collection, Knoxville

of Ossoli Circle, one of Tennessee's first women's clubs in 1885; founder of Knoxville Equal Suffrage Society in 1910; president of Tennessee Equal Suffrage Association, 1914. In 1920, at the age of 71, she campaigned for equal suffrage locally and nationally, and led a delegation of National Woman's Party members who marched to the Ohio home of Republican presidential nominee, Warren G. Harding, to demand a 36th ratification of the 19th Amendment. When registering to cast her first ballot in November, 1920, she listed "suffragist" as her occupation.

Friedman, Mrs. Ben of Memphis — Active suffragist and member of Memphis League of Women Voters. She organized Tennessee's first woman voter registration drive in Memphis, 1920.

Gardner, Mrs. H. C. of Nashville — Held first meeting of the early, but short-lived, Nashville Woman Suffrage Association at her home in 1894.

Garth, Janie — Vanderbilt University Equal Suffrage League, 1917.

Gillenwaters, Mrs. Edward of Knoxville — Treasurer of Tennessee chapter of National Woman's Party, 1920.

Gilmore, Rose Long (Mrs. John G.) of Nashville — Charter member of Nashville Equal Suffrage Association; state and Davidson County press chairman, National League for Women's Service in World War, 1917-1919; extensive service on many war-relief committees. Press chairman and member of Kate Burch Warner's statewide committee for the Tennessee Equal Suffrage Association's banquet at Nashville's Hermitage Hotel on December 2, 1918, to honor national board member Mrs. Charles Tiffany of New York. Member of advisory board, Democratic Ratification Committee, 1920. Rose Gilmore recorded the names of state and local officers and members of the Equal Suffrage Association (published in 1923 in *Davidson County Women in the World War, 1914-1919)*, which otherwise might have been lost to history.

Gray, Hilda of Nashville — Member of the early, but short-lived, Nashville Woman Suffrage Association, 1894.

Griffin, Miss Marion Scudder of Memphis and Bolivar — An ardent advocate  of women's rights and suffrage, she served in 1899 as a law clerk in the Memphis office of Judge Thomas M. Scruggs. She was certified by two sitting judges to practice law on February 15, 1900, but she was barred from the legal profession on the basis of her sex. After a lengthy campaign for a state law enabling women to practice law, a bill was passed on February 13, 1907, and M. Griffin was licensed and enrolled as a member of the Memphis bar on July 1, 1907, thus becoming the first woman licensed as an attorney in Tennessee. She ran for the state House of Representatives and was elected in 1922 to the 63rd Assembly, where she headed the Social Welfare Committee and sponsored legislation benefitting the lives of women and children.

Memphis & Shelby County Library

Hall, Agnes Grace of Nashville — Member of the early Nashville Woman Suffrage Association, 1894.

Hancock, Essie of Murfreesboro — Treasurer of Murfreesboro Equal Suffrage League, 1914.

Hardy, Mrs. Fred of Columbia — Seventh District chairman of the Tennessee Equal Suffrage Association in early 1900s.

Henry, Margaret — Secretary of Tennessee Equal Rights Association, 1900.

Henry, Mrs. R. A. of Nashville — Treasurer for NAWSA convention in Nashville, 1914.

Henderson, Elizabeth Lea Miller (Mrs. J. C.) of Bolivar — This youthful suffragist majored in law at Nashville's Peabody College, then "Lizzie" Miller became a legal aide c.1907 in her father's law office in Bolivar; she traveled with him when he served as chairman of the state Democratic Party. These early experiences shaped her into a staunch advocate of woman suffrage. After becoming Hardeman County's first female attorney in the early 1920s, she was elected in 1925 as the first female representative from the county; she was one of only two women (the other being Knoxville's Anne M. Davis) serving in the 64th General Assembly.

Herron, Louise — Vanderbilt University Equal Suffrage League, 1917.

Hickerson, Frances Maude of Hickerson Station — Corresponding Secretary, Tennessee Equal Suffrage Association, 1915.

Hillie, Mrs. O. G. of Nashville — Secretary of early, but short-lived, Nashville Woman Suffrage Association, 1894.

Hirsch, Mrs. J. H. of Jackson — Secretary of Jackson Equal Suffrage League, 1912.

Hixon, Mrs. C. T. of Nashville — Member of Nashville Equal Suffrage League, 1911.

Holder, Renamae W. of Gallatin — Treasurer of Gallatin Equal Suffrage League, 1914.

Hobson, Mrs. H. P. of Somerville — President of Somerville Equal Suffrage League, 1915. Helped organize a Whiteville suffrage league.

Horine, Dora C. of Chattanooga — National worker for suffrage; directed a "suffrage school" on parliamentary procedure and public speaking.

Howard, Mary of Chattanooga — Second vice chairman of Tennessee Division of Alice Paul's Congressional Union, 1916, which became the National Woman's Party, 1918.

Hughes, Mabel Williams of Memphis — The older sister of Charl Ormond Williams and an outstanding educator who served variously as Superintendent of Shelby County Schools, as first woman president of Tennessee Public School Officers Association, and as both state and national president of the Parent-Teacher Association. A campaigner for woman suffrage in 1920, she was later elected to three successive terms as a Tennessee state Senator from Shelby County.

Huntingdon, Mrs. Flora E. of Memphis — Secretary of Memphis Equal Suffrage Society in the 1890s. Spoke at state suffrage conference in Nashville in 1897, demanding the ballot for women "as a protection for the helpless widow and the great army of women who work to support themselves and, in many cases, worthless husbands."

Ingram, Miss Katherine Priscilla of Bolivar — Embracing the woman suffrage movement while a student at Randolph-Macon College in Virginia and at Nashville's George Peabody College for Teachers, she was a vocal proponent of women's rights. In 1922, she was appointed by the Hardeman County court as County Superintendent of Education, becoming the first and only woman to hold the position. In 1929, she became the first woman elected president of the Tennessee Education Association since its founding in 1865.

Jackson, Mrs. Walter C. of Murfreesboro — Secretary, Murfreesboro Equal Suffrage League, 1914. District chairman of Tennessee Equal Suffrage Association, 1915.

Jetton, Lillian of Murfreesboro — District vice president, Tennessee Equal Suffrage Association, 1915.

Johnson, Mary Hannah of Nashville — Member of Nashville Equal Suffrage League, 1911.

Jones, Mrs. Frederick of Knoxville — Treasurer of Knoxville Equal Suffrage League.

Jones, Mrs. K. P. of Maryville — Third vice chairman of Tennessee Division of Congressional Union, 1916, which later became the National Woman's Party.

Jones, Miss Lutie of Nashville — Member of Nashville Equal Suffrage Association and charter member, 1917, of Equal Suffrage Auxiliary for first Red Cross campaign; worked with sister-suffragists on muslin dressings at the Tulane Hotel workroom. Advisory board, Democratic Ratification Committee, 1920.

Davidson County Women

Kenny, Catherine Talty of Nashville — An enthusiastic suffrage campaigner, she served as vice president of Tennessee Equal Suffrage Association, 1914. Chairman of arrangements for NAWSA convention in Nashville, 1914. Presided over 1916 May Day rally in Nashville. A leading strategist for newly-renamed Tennessee League of Women Voters in 1920, she was their chairman of ratification during crucial months leading to final vote on the 19th Amendment in Nashville.

Kimbrough, Caroline of Nashville — An incorporator and treasurer of Tennessee Equal Suffrage Association, 1914. Active on legislative committee.

Kuhn, Agnes of Nashville — Corresponding secretary and literature chairman, Nashville Equal Suffrage League, 1912.

Lackey, Mrs. W. M. of Gallatin — Vice president of Gallatin Equal Suffrage League, 1914.

Lamb, Margaret — Vanderbilt University Equal Suffrage League, 1917.

Landrum, Mrs. L. of Memphis — Treasurer of Tennessee's first Equal Suffrage Society, organized in Memphis in 1889.

Langstaff, Mrs. A. D. of Memphis — Recording secretary of state's first Equal Suffrage Society which held its organizational meeting in her Memphis home in 1889.

Lewis, Marie L. — An incorporator of Tennessee Equal Suffrage Association, 1914.

Lillie, Mrs. Pryor of Franklin — President of Franklin Equal Suffrage League, 1914.

Lindsey, Louise G. of Nashville — Entertainment committee for NAWSA convention in Nashville, 1914.

Lipe, Miss Mary of Nashville — As co-chairman of automobile arrangements for NAWSA convention in Nashville in 1914, she commandeered 300 cars to meet and transport delegates. In the Automobile Show in June, 1918, she was in charge of the Equal Suffrage Association's booth and sold $850 in war-relief Thrift Stamps. Chaired all bond sales for all drives through the Association; speaker at the headquarters' rally, 1918, for third Liberty Loan drive, which raised $86,000 for war relief.

Lusky, Jennie Lowenheim (Mrs. J. C.) of Nashville

— Social reformer and suffrage proponent, who was a member of the Equal Suffrage Association and a charter member in June, 1917, of the Council of Jewish Women's Auxiliary, chaired by Mrs. Henry Teitlebaum. She served as chair of the Fourth, Fifth, and Sixth Wards of Davidson County during the World War I Thrift Stamp drive, 1918; state chair of the Women's Division of Jewish Welfare of the United War Work Campaign in November, 1918, after just serving extensive hours as a volunteer nurse and social worker during the influenza epidemic at the Bertha Fensterwald Settlement House in October.

Lusky, Lettie Nassauer (Mrs. Lou) of Nashville —

Like her sister-in-law, Jennie Lowenheim Lusky, she was a charter member in June, 1917, of the Council of Jewish Women's Auxiliary, chaired by Mrs. Henry Teitlebaum; also a charter member of the Nashville Equal Suffrage Association and charter member in May, 1917, of the Tennessee Mothers' Congress and Parent-Teachers Auxiliary for the first Red Cross campaign. She chaired all Association war activities, including sales of Liberty Loan bonds and War Savings Stamps, as well as for donations of hospital funds, in concert with the Association's state War Chairman, Miss Matilda Porter. Due to their and their committee's tireless work, "Tennessee women alone contributed one-half of the amount raised throughout the South for hospital work" during World War I.

Lytton, Mrs. Henry of Clarksville — Vice president of Clarksville Equal Suffrage League, 1914.

Marshall, Mary of Franklin — Treasurer of Franklin Equal Suffrage League, 1914.

McCormack, Mrs. Eleanor O'Donnell of Memphis — In 1891, she was named Shelby County's Superintendent of Public Instruction, one of the first women to hold such a post. Active in civic affairs and noted for her organizational skills, she was a founding member of the Tennessee Federation of Women's Clubs. Divisional president of Tennessee Equal Suffrage Association, 1906-1912, she became state president in 1914.

McKinney, Annie B. of Knoxville — Second District Chair of Tennessee Equal Suffrage Association.

McPherson, Marie of Chattanooga — Chattanooga Equal Suffrage League, 1911.

McTeer, Mrs. T. W. of Maryville — President of Tennessee's second Woman Suffrage Society, an active organization formed in 1893 with 25 members. A gathering on Susan B. Anthony's birthday in 1898 at Mrs. McTeer's home was attended by some 100 persons.

Meriwether, Mrs. Davie of Knoxville — First vice chairman of Tennessee Division of Congressional Union, 1916. First vice chairman of Tennessee Chapter of successor, the National Woman's Party, 1918.

Meriwether, Elizabeth Avery of Memphis — One of Tennessee's earliest crusaders for women's rights, she published her own pro-suffrage newspaper, *The Tablet*, in 1872. She went to the polls and cast a vote for Horace Greeley in the 1872 presidential election, but "whether or not it was counted," she later reported, "I cannot say." A delegate to the National Woman Suffrage Convention in 1879, she was an eloquent speaker, and traveled the country with Susan B. Anthony and other suffrage leaders advocating votes for women.

Meriwether, Lide Smith of Memphis — Sister-in-law of Elizabeth Avery Meriwether, she campaigned vigorously for social reform, temperance and woman suffrage. A founder and president of Tennessee's first Equal Suffrage Society in Memphis in 1889. She succeeded Elizabeth Lisle Saxon as president of Tennessee Woman Suffrage Association, and was named "Honorary President for Life" in 1900.

Mills, Helen Wile (Mrs. Reuben) of Nashville —

Member of Nashville Equal Suffrage Association; chaired the 1915 May Day Suffrage Rally. Publicity chairman, 1917, of Nashville Women's Committee of Council of National Defense; compiled October 28, 1917, supplement to *Nash-*

144

ville Tennessean, describing activities of the national, state, and local women's committees. Chairman, 1917, of organization of the Council of Jewish Women for the second Liberty Loan fund-raising campaign; the Council, under her direction, collected half the amount raised in the entire campaign. Later served as president of the Council of Jewish Women (1923).

Milton, Abby Crawford of Chattanooga — She

Tennessee State Library & Archives

spearheaded suffrage movement in Chattanooga. The wife of George Fort Milton, publisher of pro-suffrage *Chattanooga News*, she held a law degree and helped Lookout Mountain Suffrage League secure local enfranchisement for women in 1917. Recruited workers for suffrage from groups as diverse as the Tennessee Woman's Press Club, Tennessee Federation of Garden Clubs, Tennessee Federation of Women's Clubs, Tennessee Daughters of the American Revolution. First president of Tennessee League of Women Voters during ratification campaign, 1920.

Mizell, Georgia Hooper of Nashville — An organizer of the early, but short-lived, Nashville Woman Suffrage Association, 1894. Mother of prominent Nashville suffragist, Bettie Mizell Donelson.

Moorman, Mrs. Maria Y. of Nashville — Member of short-lived Nashville Woman Suffrage Association, 1894.

Morgan, Stella T. of Clarksville — President of Clarksville Equal Suffrage League, 1914.

Morrow, Miss Libbie Luttrell of Nashville — "A founder, an organizer, and president for life" of the Tennessee Woman's Press and Authors Club in 1899; charter member, 1911, of Nashville Equal Suffrage Association; member of press committee for Women's Committee, Council of National Defense and of volunteer Fourth Tennessee Relief Corps during World War I. Editor of the society pages for the suffrage-opposed *Nashville Banner*, she initiated and developed a separate section of the newspaper covering women's civic and professional activities over 30 years. Described as one of the state's "most influential figures....In that frail body there was the soul and spirit of a fighter."

Murfree, Lib of Murfreesboro — Second vice president of Murfreesboro Equal Suffrage League, 1914.

Myer, Annie Lee — Vice president for Middle Tennessee, Tennessee Woman Suffrage Association, 1918.

Napier, Nettie Langston (Mrs. J. C.) of Nashville — Civic leader and activist from the early 1880s to the early 1930s, she was instrumental in bringing the National Association of Colored Women to Nashville in 1897; held national offices of auditor and treasurer. In 1907, founded the Day Homes Club, and was chair of the executive committee of the City Federation of Colored Women's Clubs, founded by J. Frankie Pierce. Chair of the first Colored Woman's Chapter, War Savings Stamps Organization, 1917; charter member of Negro Branch of the Carnegie Library Red Cross Chapter, 1917. Joined J. Frankie Pierce in active campaign for woman suffrage.

O'Daniel, Lillie of Nashville — Defended woman suffrage during a debate on the question in Paris, Tennessee, 1912.

Overall, Frances Holder (Mrs. W. A.) of Nashville

Davidson County Women

— President, Nashville Equal Suffrage Association, 1917. Speaker at rally at suffrage headquarters, 1918, for third Liberty Loan drive; helped organize suffragists' booth for citywide carnival in March, 1918, and active lobbyist for women's rights. Testified before judiciary committee hearing of the Tennessee House of Representatives in favor of a bill granting woman suffrage in presidential and municipal elections, 1919.

Page, Mrs. Elizabeth Frye of Nashville — Writer and journalist; charter member of Tennessee Woman's Press and Authors Club, 1899; charter member, 1911, Nashville Equal Suffrage Association; and feature writer for *Nashville Tennessean*. Speaker, "Why Professional Women Want to Vote," for the 1914 May Day Celebration in Nashville. Founder of Nashville Metaphysical Club and president, 1917-1919.

Pegues, Evelyn of Jackson — Organized mass meetings in and around Jackson for ratification of suffrage amendment, 1920.

Pentacost, Mrs. W. E. of Chattanooga — Well-known W.C.T.U. worker and one of first officers of Chattanooga Suffrage Society, 1911.

Perkins, Mrs. E. M. of Franklin — Vice president of Franklin Equal Suffrage League, 1914.

Phillips, Lillian G. of Tennessee City — When a Nashville newspaper, in 1915, printed a report of a local preacher's argument that giving women the vote would "open the gates of hell," she responded in a letter to the editor: "If such were the case, I could better understand why men, having the ballot, often have such a hell of a time of it."

Pierce, Mrs. J. Frankie of Nashville — Founder of  the City Federation of Colored Women's Clubs in Nashville; a founder of the Tennessee Federation of Colored Women's Clubs; and a founder of the Negro Women's Reconstruction Service League. She organized protests against lack of restroom facilities for blacks in downtown Nashville and was an outspoken advocate of equal suffrage. At the invitation of Catherine Talty Kenny, Mrs. Pierce was a speaker on May 18, 1920, for the first meeting of the Tennessee League of Women Voters, held in the House chambers at the Capitol. "What will the negro [*sic*] woman do with the vote?" she asked. "We are going to make you proud of us and yourselves....We want a state vocational school and a child welfare department of the state, and more room in state schools." Building upon the momentum of women's empowerment after ratification of the 19th Amendment, she intensified her efforts for a state vocational school; the bill creating the Tennessee Vocational School for Colored Girls was passed by the General Assembly on April 7, 1921. Mrs. Pierce became its first superintendent, serving until 1939.

(caption, vertical:) Virginia Edmondson Collection

Pittman, Mrs. A. V. of Memphis — An organizer of the successful May Day Suffrage rally in 1915, she said, "Despite our popularity with the comic papers, our cause is serious. We believe this rally has started people thinking, and will eventually have far-reaching results."

Powell, Mrs. F. of Nashville — Fourth vice chairman of Tennessee Division of the Congressional Union, 1916.

Porter, Miss Matilda of Nashville — State War Chairman of Tennessee Equal Suffrage Association, appointed by Kate Burch Warner after she had sent a telegram to President Woodrow Wilson (upon the country's entrance into World War I, 1917) offering the state Association's services for war work. In addition to organizing fund-raising for four all-female-staffed hospitals overseas, controlled and financed by the American Woman's Equal Suffrage Association, Miss Porter also supervised a weekly class in surgical dressings at the Nashville Association's Tulane Hotel workroom for suffragist volunteers.

Price, Hannah of Morristown — With her sister Anna, she organized a meeting in Morristown in 1900 where several local pastors spoke on equal suffrage. Wrote and published at her own expense a suffrage novel entitled *The Closed Door* in 1913, and sold copies and made speeches throughout Tennessee, North Carolina, and Virginia. Vice-president-at-large of Tennessee Woman Suffrage Association, 1918.

Price, Mrs. Hickman of Nashville — Wrote frequent articles and letters to Tennessee newspapers stating reasons for favoring woman suffrage.

Priest, Mrs. Marshall of Huntingdon — Organized local mass meeting for ratification of suffrage amendment, 1920.

Puryear, Jennie McCarver (Mrs. David) of Memphis — She wrote a suffrage column for *The Commercial Appeal* in 1916. President of Memphis League of Women Voters in 1920, she lobbied (with her husband, Judge David Puryear) for ratification of 19th Amendment during special session in Nashville.

Randolph, Mrs. O. H. of Nashville — Member of Nashville Equal Suffrage League, 1911.

Ransom, Mrs. J. M. of Tullahoma — Vice-president-at-large, Tennessee Equal Suffrage Association, 1915.

Ratterman, Miss Mary of Nashville — Member of Vanderbilt University Equal Suffrage League, 1917; chaired Nashville City Hospital Auxiliary for war work and was delegate to War Fund Campaign in June, 1917. On October 29, 1917, "organized the girls of Nashville into a Godmothers' Auxiliary" for war relief work and was elected chairman; in early 1918, the group's name was changed to the Girls' Auxiliary of the Red Cross.

Reese, Lulu Colyar (Mrs. Isaac) of Memphis — A

socially prominent Clubwoman, she became active in politics as an advocate of free textbooks and anti-child labor laws; was one of the first two women elected to the Memphis City Board of Education. She campaigned for woman suffrage as a member of both the National American Woman Suffrage Association and the National Woman's Party, and was in Nashville in 1920 to lobby for ratification of the suffrage amendment.

Reilly, Grace of Memphis — Corresponding secretary of Memphis Equal Suffrage League; recording secretary of Tennessee Equal Suffrage Association, 1907.

Reno, Mrs. Ettie Kinney of Nashville — In 1908, at the Centennial Club, she delivered one of the earliest pro-suffrage speeches made in middle Tennessee; member of legislative committee of Tennessee Equal Suffrage Association, 1914. Chairman, 1917, of the Noelton Club Auxiliary for Red Cross work. In 1918, she chaired the Speakers Bureau of the Nashville Equal Suffrage Association and was largely responsible for disseminating pro-suffrage information throughout Middle Tennessee.

Roach, Victoria James of Nashville — Third vice president of Nashville Equal Suffrage League, 1914. Member of legislative committee of Tennessee Equal Suffrage Association, 1914.

Robertson, Mrs. G. H. of Jackson — President of Jackson Equal Suffrage League, 1914. Executive committee of Tennessee Equal Suffrage Association, 1914.

Routt, Daisy — An incorporator named in charter of the Tennessee Equal Suffrage Association, 1914.

Rutherford, Sara L. of Knoxville — District vice president, Tennessee Equal Suffrage Association, 1915.

Sanders, Mrs. Newell of Chattanooga — In 1917, she became the first Tennessee woman to vote when local women were enfranchised by a special Lookout Mountain Suffrage bill passed by legislature.

Saxon, Elizabeth Lisle of Memphis — One of the

state's earliest suffrage advocates. In 1885, the National Woman Suffrage Association appointed her president of the yet-to-be-organized Tennessee Suffrage Association, a post she later relinquished to Lide Meriwether. She moved to Washington state where she continued her work for women's rights.

Scott, Mrs. A. Y. of Memphis — President and organizer of a Junior Suffrage League, 1912. Vice chairman of the Tennessee Equal Suffrage Association, 1914. She addressed the Tennessee House of Representatives when a state constitutional amendment to enfranchise women first came to a vote in 1915.

Selden, Mrs. Elise M. of Memphis — Elected presi-

dent of the Tennessee Equal Rights Association in Memphis in 1900, succeeding the founder Lide Meriwether. After reorganization as Tennessee Equal Suffrage Association in 1906, she was corresponding secretary and treasurer.

Sells, Mrs. George of Johnson City — First district chairman of Tennessee Equal Suffrage Association, 1914.

Settle, Mrs. T. G. of Nashville — Secretary of Nashville Equal Suffrage League, 1911.

Skeffington, Mary of Nashville — Information chairman for NAWSA convention in Nashville, 1914.

Smith, Agnes — Vanderbilt University Equal Suffrage League, 1917.

Smith, Anna Carter — Vanderbilt University Equal Suffrage League, 1917.

Smith, Mrs. Blair of Nashville — Nashville Equal Suffrage League, 1911.

Smith, Mrs. Bolton of Memphis — Vice president of Tennessee's first Equal Suffrage Society, organized in Memphis in 1889.

Snow, Mrs. Euclid of Nashville — Vice chairman of finance for NAWSA Convention in Nashville, 1914.

Spencer, Emma of Nashville — Second vice president of Nashville Equal Suffrage League, 1914. Co-chairman (with her mother) of hospitality committee for 1914 NAWSA convention in Nashville.

Spencer, Mrs. W. G. of Nashville — Legislative committee of Tennessee Equal Suffrage Association, 1914. Chairman of hospitality committee for 1914 NAWSA convention in Nashville.

Stahlman, Annie Laurie Wert (Mrs. Frank Carl) of Nashville — Daughter-in-law of publisher E. B. Stahlman, whose *Nashville Banner* opposed woman suffrage. Chaired Fourth, Fifth, and Sixth Wards for second Liberty Loan campaign in October, 1917, and at same time was chairman of the Three-Star Banner Campaign for war-relief funds; she and her committee collected $87,300 from 64 businesses in Nashville, a strong testimonial to her power of persuasion. She used that power to publicly lobby Tennessee legislators for ratification of the suffrage amendment during the special session in 1920.

Staniland, Mrs. Claude Sullivan of Nashville — A leader in Nashville Equal Suffrage League's World War I Liberty Loan fund-raising drive. Member of League of Women Voters Ratification Committee, 1920.

Stegall, Mrs. W. L. of Jackson — Treasurer of Jackson Equal Suffrage League, 1912.

Susong, Mrs. Edith O'Keefe of Greeneville — In 1916, became owner/editor of Greeneville's *The Democrat* newspaper and later absorbed two competing newspapers; publisher of the paper, *The Greeneville Sun*, for 50 years. Ally and friend from 1919 of U.S. Senator Kenneth McKellar of Memphis who supported equal rights for women. Member and youngest president of Tennessee Woman's Press and Authors Club (founded in 1899) and also youngest president of Tennessee Federation of Women's Clubs, 1927.

Tansil, Mamie of Dresden — Treasurer, Tennessee Equal Suffrage Association, 1915.

Teitlebaum, Sarah Lowenstein (Mrs. Henry M.) of

Davidson County Women

Nashville — Charter member of Nashville Equal Suffrage Association. Elected vice chairman, July 20, 1917, of Nashville Division of Women's Committee, Council of National Defense and presided over organizational meeting. Founding chairman in June, 1917, of the Council of Jewish Women's Auxiliary and founding member of the Women's Division of Jewish Welfare of the United War Work Campaign. Tireless worker for women's rights and equal suffrage.

Temple, Miss Mary Boyce of Knoxville — Active suffragist and supporter of many civic causes, including preservation of Knoxville's historic Blount Mansion.

Templeton, Lucy Curtis of Knoxville — Secretary of Tennessee Division of Congressional Union, 1916, and secretary of Tennessee Chapter of National Woman's Party, 1918.

Terrell, Mary Church (Mrs. Robert) of Memphis —

Courtesy of Roberta Church

Member of influential black family in Memphis, she became a nationally prominent human rights campaigner and early suffragist. The founding president of National Association of Colored Women in 1897 and a charter member of National Association for the Advancement of Colored People in 1909, she was also active in National American Woman Suffrage Association, working closely with Susan B. Anthony and Carrie Chapman Catt. In 1919, she joined suffragists of the National Woman's Party in picketing the White House. Known as "mother of the sit-in" for inventing strategies later used in civil rights movement.

Terrett, Miss Amelia of Nashville — First president of earliest, though short-lived, suffrage group in Nashville, founded Feb. 20, 1894. Helped organize Nashville Equal Suffrage League, 1911. Recalling early widespread disapproval of the movement, she later wrote, "Great things were hoped, prayed and planned for, literature was distributed, a petition was circulated, but it took courage even to open one's doors for a suffrage meeting."

Thompson, Mary Penn of Nashville — Fifth vice chairman of Tennessee Division of Congressional Union, 1916.

Townsend, Pauline of Nashville — Initiated speech classes at Ward-Belmont College to "make more effective orators of the suffragists."

Turley, Mary Fite of Nashville — Auditor for Nashville Equal Suffrage League, 1914.

Turnbull, Julia — Vanderbilt University Equal Suffrage League, 1917.

Turney, Mrs. John of Nashville — An attorney and early chairman of Nashville Equal Suffrage League, she wrote that organization's constitution.

Tyson, Mrs. L. D. of Knoxville — Sixth vice chairman of Tennessee Division of Congressional Union, 1916, and of Tennessee Chapter of National Woman's Party, 1918.

Walker, Effie of Memphis — President of both the Memphis Equal Suffrage League and Tennessee Equal Suffrage Association in 1909.

Warner, Katherine ("Kate") Burch (Mrs. Leslie) of  **Nashville** — Member of a socially prominent family, she was one of 19 women who met in Knoxville in the spring of 1897 to organize the Tennessee Federation of Women's Clubs. Although her brother, Dr. Lucius Burch, Dean of Vanderbilt University Medical School, was an influential opponent of woman suffrage, Kate Burch Warner gained greater influence as a suffrage proponent. She was a speaker at the 1916 May Day suffrage rally in Centennial Park and addressed the judiciary committee of the Tennessee House, advocating presidential and municipal votes for women, 1917. President, Tennessee Equal Suffrage Association, 1917-1919, and a confidante of Carrie Chapman Catt. Appointed by Governor Roberts to head a statewide Democratic ratification committee during the special session in 1920.

Davidson County Women

Wells-Barnett, Ida B. of Memphis — Teacher and journalist, she was a fearless crusader against the atrocities of lynching and a passionate advocate of equal rights for all, whose work for human rights was praised by Susan B. Anthony and Frederick Douglass. Forced to leave Memphis when a mob, outraged by her anti-lynching campaign, burned her offices, she eventually settled in Chicago, where she founded the Alpha Suffrage Club, the first of many such groups that brought black women into the suffrage movement.

Wender, Mrs. W. M. of Murfreesboro — President of Murfreesboro Equal Suffrage League, 1914.

Wester, Mrs. C. J. of Chattanooga — Member of Chattanooga Equal Suffrage League, 1911.

Wester, Catherine of Chattanooga — Member of Tennessee Equal Suffrage Association and one of Tennessee's first female architects.

White, Mrs. Hugh L. of Johnson City — State chairman of both the Tennessee Division of the Congressional Union, 1916, and the Tennessee Chapter of its successor, the National Woman's Party, 1918.

White, Sarah of Memphis and Nashville — Member of Tennessee's first Equal Suffrage Society, organized in Memphis in 1889. Later helped organize early Nashville Woman Suffrage Association in 1894.

White, Sue Shelton of Jackson — One of Tennessee's most effective suffragists, she was one of the first women court reporters in the state, 1907. Helped organize Jackson Equal Suffrage League, 1911. Recording secretary of Tennessee Equal Suffrage Association in 1915, she became state chairman of the National Woman's Party in 1918. Arrested for picketing the White House in 1919, she was the only Tennessee woman jailed because of her suffrage work. During 1920 ratification campaign in Nashville, she headed the National Woman's Party campaign, and coordinated their work with Carrie Chapman Catt's NAWSA. In Washington, in the 1920s and 1930s, she held important posts with Democratic National Committee, the Woman's Bureau, and the Social Security Board.

Whiteside, Carrie B. of Gallatin — Secretary of Gallatin Equal Suffrage League, 1914.

Williams, Miss Anita of Nashville — Member of Vanderbilt University Equal Suffrage Association, 1917, and ardent proponent of woman suffrage in speeches and writings. After passage of the 19th Amendment in 1920, served as president of the Nashville League of Women Voters in the early 1920s and president of the Tennessee League, 1926-1930. For the June 15, 1930, sesquicentennial edition of the *Nashville Tennessean*, her comprehensive feature story, "Tennessee's Action Decided Women of Nation Could Vote," offered a comprehensive listing of the state's key suffrage activists.

Williams, Charl Ormond of Memphis — Appointed Superintendent of Shelby County Schools in 1914, she was elected vice chairman of the Democratic National Committee in June of 1920, the first woman to hold so high a post. In Nashville that August, she was chosen to lead the combined suffrage forces as overall chairman of ratification efforts. Later, in a long and distinguished career in Washington, D.C., she served as president of both the National Education Association and the Federation of Business and Professional Women's Clubs, as vice president of Phi Beta Kappa, and was once named one of 12 women "competent to hold the position of President of the United States."

Williams, Mrs. Willoughby of Nashville — Treasurer of Nashville Equal Suffrage League, 1911.

Wilson, Mrs. Benjamin F. of Nashville — Held reception in her home, Wilmor Hall, for officers, delegates, and visitors to the 1914 NAWSA convention in Nashville.

Wilson, Grace — Vanderbilt University Equal Suffrage League, 1917.

Winslow, Mrs. Lucy E. — Vice president for East Tennessee of Tennessee Woman Suffrage Association, 1918.

Winstead, Sue of Franklin — Secretary of the Franklin Equal Suffrage League, 1914.

Wolf, Mary of Memphis — Treasurer of Memphis Equal Suffrage Society in 1894. Second vice president of the Tennessee Equal Suffrage Association, 1908.

Woodruff, Mrs. Frank L. of Jackson — An organizer and second vice president of Jackson Equal Suffrage League, 1911.

Worley, Anna Lee Keys (Mrs. J. Parks) of Bluff City — Elected to fill her deceased husband's unexpired term in the Tennessee Senate in 1921, she became the first woman to serve in the General Assembly. Although she had publicly opposed woman suffrage while a homemaker prior to her husband's death, after her election to the Senate she came under the influence of the state's professional women and sponsored landmark legislation affecting women (Sue Shelton White has been credited as the author of the greater portion of Senator Worley's sponsored legislation). She sponsored the act "removing disabilities from women" and making them eligible to hold any public office in Tennessee, opening the door for the following five women who would be elected to the state legislature by 1927.

LEST WE FORGET

Tennessee State Library & Archives

Suffragists depicted here are:

Inez Milholland

Lillie Deveraux Blake

Elizabeth Cady Stanton

Dr. Anna Howard Shaw

Susan B. Anthony

Elizabeth Tupper Wilkes

Catherine Severance

BIBLIOGRAPHY
Including Videotapes and Internet Uniform Resource Listings

Classification symbols: **E** = *elementary;* **S** = *secondary;* **A** = *adult*

A   Alberti, Johanna. *Beyond Freedom: Feminists in War and Peace.* New York: St. Martin's Press, 1989.

A   Anthony, Katharine. *Susan B. Anthony: Her Personal History and Her Era.* New York: Doubleday, 1954.

E   Ash, Maureen. *The Story of the Women's Movement.* Chicago: Children's Press, 1989.

A   Auster, Albert. *Actresses and Suffragists: Women in the American Theatre, 1890-1920.* New York: Praeger, 1984.

A   Bacon, Margaret Hope. *Valiant Friend: The Life of Lucretia Mott.* New York: Walker Books, 1980.

S,A   Banner, Lois. *Elizabeth Cady Stanton, A Radical for Woman's Rights.* Boston: Little, Brown, 1980.

S,A   Barry, Kathleen. *Susan B. Anthony: A Biography of A Singular Feminist.* New York: New York University Press, 1988.

S,A   Becker, Susan D. *The Origins of the Equal Rights Amendment: American Feminism Between the Wars.* Westport, CT: Greenwood Press, 1981.

A   Beeton, Beverly. *Women Vote in the West: The Woman Suffrage Movement, 1869-1896.* New York: Garland Publishers, 1986.

S,A   Benjamin, Anne M. *A History of the Anti-Suffrage Movement in the United States from 1895 to 1920: Women Against Equality.* Lewiston, NY: Edwin Mellen Press, 1991.

S,A   Blatch, Harriot Stanton. *Challenging Years: The Memoirs of Harriot Stanton Blatch.* New York: Putnam and Sons, 1940.

E   Blumberg, Rhoda. *Bloomers!* New York: Bradbury Press, 1993.

A   Brown, Olympia. *Suffrage and Religious Principle: Speeches and Writings of Olympia Brown.* Metuchen, NJ: Scarecrow Press, 1983.

S,A   Buechler, Steven M. *The Transformation of the Woman Suffrage Movement: The Case of Illinois, 1850-1920.* New Brunswick, NJ: Rutgers University Press, 1986.

S.A   _____. *Women's Movements in the United States: Woman Suffrage, Equal Rights, and Beyond.* New Brunswick, NJ: Rutgers University Press, 1990.

S,A   Buhle, Mary Jo and Paul, editors. *The Concise History of Woman Suffrage: Selections from the Classic Work of Stanton, Anthony, Gage, and Harper.* Urbana, IL: University of Illinois Press, 1979.

S.A   Camhi, Jane Jerome. *Woman Against Woman: American Anti-Suffragism, 1880-1920.* Brooklyn, NY: Carlson Publishing, Inc., 1990.

E,S,A   Casey, Paula F. *Generations.* Memphis: Vote 70, Inc., 1989; reissued 1995. 12-1/2-minute video about the struggle for woman suffrage, climaxing in the August 18, 1920, vote in the Tennessee House of Representatives, Nashville, which ratified the 19th Amendment of the U. S. Constitution.

S,A   _____. " The Final Battle: Tennessee's Vote for Women Decided the Nation," *Tennessee Bar Journal,* Vol. 31, No. 5, Sept./Oct., 1995; Nashville: Tennessee Bar Association, 1995.

S,A   Catt, Carrie Chapman, and Nettie Rogers Shuler. *Woman Suffrage and Politics: The Inner Story of the Suffrage Movement.* Seattle, WA: University of Washington Press, 1970; reprint of original 1923 Scribner imprint.

E   Connell, Kate. *They Shall Be Heard: Susan B. Anthony and Elizabeth Cady Stanton.* n.p., n.d.

E   Corbin, Carole Lynn. *The Right to Vote.* New York: Franklin Watts Publishing Co., 1985.

S,A   Cornwell, Ilene J. "Notable Women in Tennessee History," *Tennessee Blue Book, 1975-1976.* Nashville: Office of the Secretary of State, 1975.

S,A   _____, compiler and editor. Profiles of Harry Burn, Joseph Hanover, Anne M. Davis, Sarah R. Frazier, Marion S. Griffin, Elizabeth L. Miller, and Anna Keys Worley in *Biographical Directory of the Tennessee General Assembly, Vol. III, 1901-1931.* Nashville: Tennessee Historical Commission, 1988.

S,A   _____. "Votes for Women!" *The Tennessee Conservationist* Magazine, Vol. LVI, No.4, July/August 1990. Nashville: Tennessee Department of Conservation, 1990.

S,A   _____ . Profiles of Josephine Pearson, J. Frankie Pierce, Anne Dallas Dudley, Sue Shelton White, Lizzie Crozier French, and other suffragists. *She Hath Done What She Could: A Tribute to Tennessee's Remarkable Women* (work-in-progress). Note: Profiles of various Tennessee women are posted on Ilene Jones-Cornwell's Internet homepage under "Tennessee Women's Network." **http://www.nashville.com/~ilene.jones-cornwell**

S,A   Cullen-DuPont, Kathryn. *Elizabeth Cady Stanton and Women's Liberty*. New York: Facts on File, 1992.

A   Daley, Caroline, and Melanie Nolan. *Suffrage and Beyond: International Feminist Perspectives*. New York: New York University Press, 1994.

E,S,A   Davis, Louise. "Wilted Roses v. Woman's Vote," *Nashville Tales*. Gretna, LA: Pelican Publishing Co., 1981.

S,A   Davis, Paulina Wright. *A History of the National Woman's Rights Movement*. New York: Source Book Press, 1970; reprint of original 1871 imprint.

A   Dorr, Rheta Childe. *Susan B. Anthony: The Woman Who Changed the Mind of a Nation*. New York: Stokes Publishing, 1928.

S,A   DuBois, Ellen Carol. *Elizabeth Cady Stanton — Susan B. Anthony: Correspondence, Writings, Speeches*. New York: Schocken Books, 1981; second, revised edition by Boston's Northeastern University Press, 1992.

S,A   _____. *Feminism and Suffrage: The Emergence of an Independent Women's Movement in America, 1848-1869*. Ithaca, NY: Cornell University Press, 1978.

A   _____. *Harriot Stanton Blatch and the Winning of Woman Suffrage*. New Haven, CT: Yale University Press, 1997.

S,A   Dudley, William, editor. *The Women's Rights Movement: Opposing Viewpoints*. San Diego, CA: Greenhaven Press, Inc., 1996.

E   Duffy, James. *Radical Red*. New York: Schribner [Children's Press], 1993.

S,A   Edwards, G. Thomas. *Sowing Good Seeds: The Northwest Suffrage Campaigns of Susan B. Anthony*. Portland, OR: Oregon Historical Society Press, 1990.

A   Englander, Susan. *Class Conflict and Class Coalition in the California Woman Suffrage Movement, 1907-1912*. San Francisco, CA: Mellen Research University Press, 1992.

S,A   Flexner, Eleanor. *Century of Struggle: The Women's Rights Movement in the United States*. Cambridge, MA: Belknap Press of Harvard University Press, 1975.

S,A   Foner, Philip S. *Frederick Douglass on Women's Rights*. Westport, CT: Greenwood Press, 1976.

S,A   Ford, Linda G. *Iron-Jawed Angels: The Suffrage Militancy of the National Woman's Party, 1912-1920*. Lanham, MD: University Press of America, Inc., 1991.

S,A   Fowler, Robert B. *Carrie Catt: Feminist Politician*. Boston, MA: Northeastern University Press, 1986.

A   Friedl, Betty, editor. *On to Victory: Propaganda Plays of the Woman Suffrage Movement*. Boston, MA: Northeastern University Press, 1987.

S,A   Frost, Elizabeth, and Kathryn Cullen-DuPont. *Women's Suffrage in America: An Eyewitness History*. New York: Facts on File, 1992.

A   Garner, Les. *Stepping Stones to Women's Liberty: Feminist Ideas in the Women's Suffrage Movement, 1900-1918*. Rutherford, NJ: Fairleigh Dickinson University Press, 1984.

A   Gilmore, Rose Long. *Davidson County Women in the World War, 1914-1919*. Nashville, Tennessee: Foster and Parkes Company, 1923.

E,S   Gehret, Jeanne. *Susan B. Anthony and Justice for All*. Fairport, NY: Verbal Images Press, 1994. **E, S**

E   Gleiter, Jan, and Kathleen Thompson. *Elizabeth Cady Stanton*. Austin, TX: Raintree Publishers, 1988.

S,A   Goodstein, Anita S. Profiles from work-in-progress, "Southern Feminists, 1870-1930: A Generational Study." Dr. Goodstein is a member of the advisory board for *She Hath Done What She Could* and a contributor of women's profiles; see previous Cornwell listing.

S,A   Griffith, Elisabeth. *In Her Own Right: The Life of Elizabeth Cady Stanton*. New York: Oxford University Press, 1984.

A   Grimes, Alan. *The Puritan Ethic and Woman Suffrage.* New York: Oxford University Press, 1967.

S,A   Gurko, Miriam. *The Ladies of Seneca Falls: The Birth of the Woman's Rights Movement.* New York: Macmillan, 1974.

A   Hall, Florence Howe. *Julia Ward Howe and the Woman Suffrage Movement.* New York: Arno Books, 1969; reprint of original 1913 imprint.

A   Harper, Ida Husted. *The Life and Work of Susan B. Anthony.* Three volumes. Indianapolis, IN: Bowen-Merrill, 1899, 1908.

A   Hartry, Bert. Unpublished 1988 biography and accession chronology of Sue Shelton White's papers, Arthur and Elizabeth Schlesinger Library on the History of Women in America, Radcliffe College, Cambridge, MA.

S,A   Hays, Elinor. *Morning Star: A Biography of Lucy Stone, 1818- 1893.* New York: Harcourt, Brace and World, 1961.

A   Hecker, Eugene A. *Short History of Women's Rights from the Days of Augustus to the Present Time.* New York: G. P. Putnam's Sons, 1910.

S,A   Irwin, Inez H. *The Story of Alice Paul and the National Woman's Party.* Fairfax, VA: Donlinger's Publishers, Ltd., 1977; reprint of 1921 imprint.

S,A   Jablonsky, Thomas J. *The Home, Heaven, and Mother Party: Female Anti-Suffragists in the United States, 1868-1920.* Brooklyn, NY: Carlson Publishing, Inc., 1994.

S,A   James, Edward T., and Janet Wilson, editors. *Notable American Women, 1607-1950.* Three volumes. Cambridge, MA: Belknap Press of Harvard University Press, 1971.

S,A   Jones, Beverly Washington. *Quest for Equality: The Life and Writings of Mary Eliza Church Terrell, 1863-1954.* Brooklyn, NY: Carlson Publishing, Inc., 1990.

S,A   Kimmel, Michael, and Thomas Mosmiller, editors. *Against the Tide: Pro-Feminist Men in the United States, 1776-1990.* Boston, MA: Beacon Press, 1992.

S,A   Kraditor, Aileen S. *The Ideas of the Woman Suffrage Movement, 1890-1920.* New York: Norton Publishing Co., 1981.

A   Kugler, Israel. *From Ladies to Women: The Organized Struggle for Woman's Rights in the Reconstruction Era.* Westport, CT: Greenwood Press, 1987.

E   Levin, Pamela. *Susan B. Anthony.* New York: Chelsea Junior World Biographies, 1993.

S,A   Linkugel, Wil A., and Martha Solomon. *Anna Howard Shaw: Suffrage Orator and Social Reformer.* Westport, CT: Greenwood Press, 1991.

S,A   Louis, James P. "Sue Shelton White," *Notable American Women, 1607-1950,* Vol. III. Cambridge, MA: Belknap Press of Harvard University Press, 1971.

S,A   Lunardini, Christine A. *From Equal Suffrage to Equal Rights: Alice Paul and the National Woman's Party, 1910-1928.* New York: New York University Press, 1986.

S,A   Lutz, Alma. *Created Equal: A Biography of Elizabeth Cady Stanton, 1815-1902.* New York: Day Publishers, 1940.

S,A   _____. *Susan B. Anthony: Rebel, Crusader, Humanitarian.* Washington, D.C.: Zenger Publishing Co., 1970; reprint of 1959 Beacon imprint.

S,A   McHenry, Robert, editor. *Famous American Women: A Biographical Dictionary from Colonial Times to the Present.* New York: Peter Smith Publications, 1984.

E   McKissack, Pat and Fredrick. *Mary Church Terrell: Leader for Equality.* Hillside, NJ: Enslow Publishers, 1991.

A   Melder, Keith E. *Beginnings of Sisterhood: The American Woman's Rights Movement, 1800-1850.* New York: Schocken, 1977.

S,A   Meriwether, Elizabeth Avery. *Recollections of 92 Years, 1824-1916.* Nashville: Tennessee Historical Commission, 1964; reprint by EPM Publishers, McLean, VA, 1995.

E   Monsell, Helen. *Susan B. Anthony: Champion of Women's Rights.* New York: Aladdin Books, 1960.

A   Morgan, David. *Suffragists and Democrats: The Politics of Woman Suffrage in America.* East Lansing, MI: Michigan State University Press, 1972.

E   Morin, Isobel V. *Women of the U. S. Congress.* Minneapolis, MN: Oliver Press, 1994.

E O'Neal, Zibby. *A Long Way to Go*. New York: Puffin Books, 1990.

A O'Neill, William. *Everyone Was Brave: A History of Feminism in America*. Chicago, IL: Quadrangle Books, 1971.

S,A Pankhurst, E. Sylvia. *Suffragette: The History of the Women's Militant Suffrage Movement, 1905-1910*. New York: Sturgis Walton, 1911.

S,A Peck, Mary Gray. *Carrie Chapman Catt: A Biography*. Westport, CT: Hyperion Press, 1976; reprint of 1944 imprint.

S,A Perkins, Alice, and Teresa Wolfson. *Frances Wright: Free Enquirer*. New York: Harper & Brothers, 1939.

S,A Prescott, Grace Elizabeth. "The Woman Suffrage Movement in Memphis: Its Place in the State, Sectional, and National Movements," *West Tennessee Historical Society Papers*. Memphis: West Tennessee Historical Society, 1964.

A *Proceedings of the Woman's Rights Conventions, Held at Seneca Falls and Rochester, New York, July and August, 1848*. New York: R. J. Johnson, printer, 1870.

A Rembaugh, Bertha, compiler. *Political Status of Women in the United States; a Digest of the Laws concerning Women in the Various States and Territories*. New York: G. P. Putnam's Sons, 1911.

S,A Scott, Anne Firor, and Andrew M. Scott. *One-Half the People: The Fight for Women's Suffrage*. Philadelphia, PA: J. B. Lippincott and Co., 1975; reprint by University of Chicago Press, 1982.

S,A Shaw, Anna Howard. *Anna Howard Shaw: The Story of a Pioneer*. Cleveland, OH: Pilgrim Press, 1994; reprint of original 1915 Harper imprint.

S,A Sherr, Lynn, and Jurate Kazickas. *Susan B. Anthony Slept Here: A Guide to American Women's Landmarks*. New York: Random House-Times Books, 1994.

S,A Sherr, Lynn, editor. *Failure Is Impossible: Susan B. Anthony in Her Own Words*. New York: Random House-Times Books, 1995.

S,A Sims, Anastasia. "'Powers that Pray' and 'Powers that Prey': Tennessee and the Fight for Woman Suffrage," *Tennessee Historical Quarterly*, Winter, 1991. Nashville: Tennessee Historical Society, 1991.

A Sinclair, Andrew. *The Emancipation of the American Woman*. New York: Harper and Row, 1966.

E Smith, Betsy C. *Women Win the Vote*. Englewood Cliffs, NJ: Silver Burdett Press, 1989.

A Solomon, Martha M., editor. *A Voice of Their Own: The Woman Suffrage Press, 1840-1910*. Tuscaloosa, AL: University of Alabama Press, 1991.

A Squire, Belle. *Woman Movement in America*. Chicago, IL: A. C. McClurg Co., 1911.

A Stanton, Elizabeth Cady, et al. *The History of Woman Suffrage*. Six volumes. New York: Ayer Publishing, 1969; reprint of separate volumes published in 1887, 1902, and 1922.

S,A Stanton, Elizabeth Cady. *Eighty Years and More: Reminiscences 1815-1897*. New York: Schocken Books, 1971; reprint of 1898 imprint.

E Stein, R. Conrad. *The Story of the Nineteenth Amendment*. Chicago, IL: Children's Press, 1982.

S,A Stevens, Doris. Edited by Carol O'Hare. *Jailed for Freedom: American Women Win the Vote*. Troutdale, OR: NewSage Press, 1995.

E Sullivan, George. *The Day the Women Got the Vote— A Photo History of the Women's Rights Movement*. New York: Scholastic Press, Inc., 1994.

S,A Taylor, A. Elizabeth. *The Woman Suffrage Movement in Tennessee*. New York: 1957; reprint by Hippocrene Books, 1978.

E Tedrow, T. L. *The Great Debate*. Nashville: Thomas Nelson Publishing Co., 1992.

A Terborg-Penn, Rosalyn. "Discontented Black Feminists: Prelude and Postscript to the Passage of the Nineteenth Amendment," *Decades of Discontent: The Woman's Movement, 1920-1940*. Lois Scharf and Joan M. Jensen, editors. Boston, MA: Northeastern University Press, 1987.

S,A Terrell, Mary Church. *A Colored Woman in a White World*. Salem, NH: Ayer Publishing, 1980; reprint of 1957 imprint.

A United States Senate, *Hearings before a Joint Committee of the Committee of the Judiciary and the Committee on Woman Suffrage, March 13, 1912*. Washington, DC: Government Printing Office, 1912.

E   Van Steenwyk, Elizabeth. *Ida B. Wells-Barnett: Woman of Courage.* New York: F. Watts, 1992.

S,A   Van Voris, Jacqueline. *Carrie Chapman Catt: A Public Life.* New York: Feminist Press, 1987.

A   Waggenspack, Beth M. *The Search for Self-Sovereignty: The Oratory of Elizabeth Cady Stanton.* Westport, CT: Greenwood Press, 1989.

S,A   Wedell, Marsha. *Elite Women and the Reform Impulse in Memphis, 1875-1915.* Knoxville: University of Tennessee Press, 1993.

E   Weisberg, Barbara. *Susan B. Anthony.* New York: Chelsea House Publishers, 1988.

S,A   Wheeler, Leslie, editor. *Loving Warriors: Selected Letters of Lucy Stone and Henry B. Blackwell, 1853 to 1893.* New York: Dial Press, 1981.

S,A   Wheeler, Marjorie Spruill, editor. *New Women of the New South: The Leaders of the Woman Suffrage Movement in the Southern States.* New York: Oxford University Press, 1993.

S,A   _____. *One Woman, One Vote: Rediscovering The Woman Suffrage Movement.* Troutdale, OR: NewSage Press, 1995.

S,A   _____. *Votes for Women! The Woman Suffrage Movement in Tennessee, the South, and the Nation.* Knoxville: University of Tennessee Press, 1995.

S,A   Yellin, Carol Lynn. "Countdown in Tennessee," *American Heritage* Magazine, Dec. 1978.

S,A   _____, editor. *Tennessee Women: Past and Present.* Memphis: International Women's Year Coordinating Committee and Tennessee Committee for the Humanities, 1977.

S,A   Zibart, Carl. *Yesterday's Nashville.* (Seemann's Historic Cities Series No. 16). Miami, FL: E.A. Seemann Publishing Company, 1976.

Videotapes

E,S,A   *Dreams of Equality.* New York: Seneca Falls National Women's Hall of Fame, circa 1990. VHS videotape, 28 minutes, providing overview of first Women's Rights Convention in 1848 in Seneca Falls and the birth of the women's equal rights movement. Available from National Women's Hall of Fame, Seneca Falls, NY, 13148.

E,S,A   *Generations.* Memphis: VOTE 70, Inc., 1989; reissued 1995. VHS videotape, 12-1/2 minutes about the struggle for woman suffrage, climaxing in the August 18, 1920, vote in the Tennessee House of Representatives, Nashville, which ratified the 19th Amendment. Available from VOTE 70, Inc., 109 N. Main Street, #812, Memphis, TN 38103-5019 $29.95 (plus $3.00 S & H)

E,S,A   *How We Got the Vote — The Exciting Story of the Struggle for Female Equality.* Windsor, CA: National Women's History Project and Republic Pictures Home Video, circa 1995. VHS videotape, 52 minutes offering overview of suffrage movement. Available from National Women's History Project, 7738 Bell Road, Windsor, CA 95492-8518. The NWHP Internet homepage offers colorful graphics, profiles, suggestions for women's studies, kits for classroom activities, etc. **http://www.nwhp.org/**

E,S,A   *One Woman, One Vote.* Annandale, VA: Public Broadcasting System video originally produced for PBS's *The American Experience* series, 1995. VHS videotape, 109 minutes providing synopsis of the suffrage movement in America. Available from Educational Films, 5101-F Backlick Road, Annandale, VA 22003. For price, call 800-344-3337. PBS also offers a colorful, interactive homepage on the Internet. **http://www.pbs.org/**

E,S,A   *There's No Such Thing as Woman's Work.* Washington, D.C.: U.S. Department of Labor, Women's Bureau, 1987. VHS videotape, 30 minutes of women's history.

E,S,A   *The Women Get the Vote.* New York: CRM McGraw-Hill Films, circa 1990. VHS black and white videotape, 25 minutes offering historical footage of events and persons prominent in the woman suffrage movement.

Internet Uniform Resource Listings

"Stand Among Great Women" is the theme of the National Women's Hall of Fame homepage on the Internet, which offers a visual tour of the Hall, profiles of prominent suffragists, and nomination forms.
http://www. women.com/news/hall/

"Foregrounding Women in History in Children's and Young Adult Books." On-line emphasis to document the contributions of women, posted by Rutgers University.
http://www.scils.rutgers.edu/special/kay/femchild.html

"History of the Suffrage Movement." On-line historical section marking the 75th anniversary in 1995 of passage of the 19th Amendment; text covers Seneca Falls Convention in 1848, profiles of Susan B. Anthony, Elizabeth Cady Stanton, and other suffrage leaders, as well as an in-depth bibliography of the U.S. Suffrage Movement compiled by Mary M. Huth. Posted by University of Rochester, NY.
http://www.rochester.edu/SBA/hisindx.html

"National American Woman Suffrage Collection" and "Woman Suffrage Association Collection, 1848-1921." A feature of the American Memory on-line homepage of the Library of Congress in Washington. Links lead to a bibliography, images, holdings in the NAWSA Collection, on-line exhibit hall, and a scanned image of U.S. House Joint Resolution One proposing the 19th Amendment to the states.
http://lcweb2.loc.gov/ammem/amdtd.html

"Tennessee Women's Network." Profiles of Tennessee women posted on homepage of Ilene Jones-Cornwell through The Nashville Exchange.
http://www.nashville.com/~ilene.jones-cornwell

"Women in Tennessee History: An Online Bibliography & Research Guide." Homepage posted by Todd Library of Middle Tennessee State University in Murfreesboro. Links to other sources for Tennessee history and women's history.
http://www.mtsu.edu/%7Elibrary/wtn/wtn-home.html

Women's International Center homepage offers women's profiles, Living Legacy Awards, details on Sistership Fund, links to other women's resources on the Internet, books, articles, etc.
http://www.wic.org/

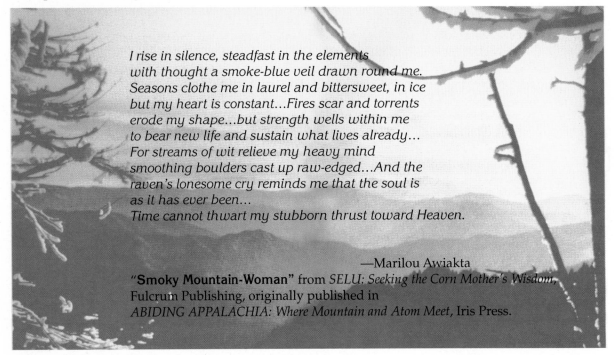

I rise in silence, steadfast in the elements
with thought a smoke-blue veil drawn round me.
Seasons clothe me in laurel and bittersweet, in ice
but my heart is constant...Fires scar and torrents
erode my shape...but strength wells within me
to bear new life and sustain what lives already...
For streams of wit relieve my heavy mind
smoothing boulders cast up raw-edged...And the
raven's lonesome cry reminds me that the soul is
as it has ever been...
Time cannot thwart my stubborn thrust toward Heaven.

—Marilou Awiakta
"Smoky Mountain-Woman" from *SELU: Seeking the Corn Mother's Wisdom*,
Fulcrum Publishing, originally published in
ABIDING APPALACHIA: Where Mountain and Atom Meet, Iris Press.

ENFRANCHISEMENT NOW MEANS THE SKY'S THE LIMIT, IN WOMAN'S SPHERE

Acknowledgments

This book was made possible through the generosity and support of the following:

Patrons

Mertie Buckman

Happy Snowden Jones

Katherine Hinds Smythe

Brig and Ellen C. Klyce

Jim and Ellida S. Fri (in honor of David and Carol Lynn Yellin)

Woman Suffrage 75, Inc. (Paula F. Casey, President, Carole Kennedy, Treasurer)

AAUW Educational Foundation

Sponsors

NETWORK of Memphis, Inc.

Jeanne and Henry Varnell

Shelby County Assessor Rita C. Clark

Shelby County Mayor Jim Rout

Baker, Donelson, Bearman, Caldwell law firm (in honor of suffragist Bettie Donelson)

Dorothy O. Kirsch

The Hon. Julia S. Gibbons and Shelby County Atty. Gen. Bill Gibbons

Dick Lightman

Dottie Jones

Mary Rose McCormick

The Goldsmith Foundation, Inc.

Tennessee League of Women Voters Educational Fund

University of Memphis

Hanover, Walsh, Jalenak & Blair law firm (in honor of Rep. Joe Hanover)

Margaret Louise Askew & Patrick Foley

Barbara Hyde

Tandy Gilliland

Dr. Roger and Sheila Jordan Cunningham

Ira and Barbara Lipman

YWCA of Greater Memphis

Flournoy S. Rogers (in honor of suffragist Elise Massey Selden)

Contributors

The Little Tea Shop (Suhair A. Lauck)
Donna Sue and Wayne Shannon
Paul J. and Frances F. Casey
M. K. Gandhi Institute for Nonviolence
Young & Perl, PLC
Barbara Ann Locke Ballard
Summer L. Bicknell
Motamedi Glassart (Peri Motamedi)
Bill and Claudia S. Haltom
Memphis City Councilman John and Ellen Vergos
Dr. Tony Jimenez
Karen B. Shea
Jim Jamieson
Dabney Roberts
Pat Gates
Dr. Glenda H. Willingham
Karla Houston
Mary W. Robinson
Gail S. Murray
Lois A. Freeman
Kathi Matthews
Cyd Mosteller
Unity Christ Church (Rev. Thelma Hembroff)
Pat Spence
Jocelyn Dan Wurzburg
Ginger Ralston
U.S. Attorney Veronica Coleman (Western District)
Sally Blood
Sigrid B. Catanzaro
Debbie Norton
Mr. and Mrs. Gordon Brent
Babs Feibelman
Jed and Jeanne Dreifus
Dick and Marge Routon
The Hon. Kay S. Robilio
The Hon. Janice Holder
The Hon. Bernice Donald
Silver DeWitt
Dee Nollner
Joe and Flo Worden
Nancy Sowell
Aurelia K. Kyles
Trisha Horton
Dr. Beverly Bond
Alvin and Rosalva King
John Burton Tigrett
Elizabeth Toles
Mimi Dann
Edith Burch Caywood

Other Assistance Provided by:

Tom Jones (Mayor Jim Rout's Office)
Beth Fortune (Gov. Don Sundquist's Press Secretary)
Marilyn Dillihay and Carolyn Tomlin (Sen. Steve Cohen's Office)
Jackie Floyd and Vanessa Cooper (Rep. Ulysses Jones' Office)
Charles Burch, Chester Irby, Jennifer Manore, and Maggie
    McDonald (Wilson Graphics)
Dr. Jim Crook (Director, UT School of Journalism, Knoxville)
Rob Heller (UT School of Journalism, Knoxville)
Dr. Kelly Leiter (Dean Emeritus, UT College of Communications)
Wanda Sobieski (Sobieski, Messer & Associates, Knoxville, TN)
Bennett Tarleton (Tennessee Arts Commission, Nashville)
Alan LeQuire (Nashville sculptor)
Beth Dixon, Mack McCaul, Vicki Grimes, Sherry Tucker and
    Madeleine Landrum-Noe (Community Foundation of
    Greater Memphis)
Mac Pirkle and Sherry Ridlon (Tennessee Repertory Theatre)
Patricia LaPointe and John Dougan
    (Memphis Room, Memphis & Shelby County Library)
Sherry Little (U.S. Senate Rules Committee, Washington, DC)
Ethel Casey Harlow (Norfolk, VA)
Thea Rozetta Lapham (Kalamazoo, Michigan)
Edith P. Mayo (Curator Emeritus, Smithsonian Institution)
Ann Stone, Karen Staser, and June Springer
    (National Museum of Women's History, Washington, DC)
Bob Cooney (Cooney Graphic Design, Point Reyes Station, CA)
Kassie Hassler, Karina McDaniel, and Jacci Herrick
    (Tennessee State Library & Archives)
McClung Historical Collection, Knoxville Public Library
Sherry Campbell, Great River Publishing
Memphis Pink Palace Museum
The University of Memphis, Mississippi Valley Collection
Special Collections Library, UT-Knoxville
Tennessee State Museum
Lydia McKnight and Ethel Ward Collection
Additional photography and art by Dugan/Foster Productions
Marilou Awiakta
Shirley Zollotuchen
Lisa Houston Montgomery (Publisher, Women's News of the
    Mid-South)
and all the fine folks at Oden Marketing and Design - Memphis
    (www.odenvision.com)

Paper for the book covers donated by

INTERNATIONAL ⒶPAPER

Thanks to Rose Flenorl and Pat King

"EQUAL PARTNERS NOW, MA"